Implementation of Non-Strict
Functional Programming Languages

RESEARCH MONOGRAPHS IN PARALLEL AND DISTRIBUTED COMPUTING

Kenneth R. Traub
MIT Laboratory for Computer Science

Implementation of Non-Strict Functional Programming Languages

Pitman, London

The MIT Press, Cambridge, Massachusetts

PITMAN PUBLISHING
128 Long Acre, London WC2E 9AN

© Kenneth R. Traub 1991

First published 1991

Available in the Western Hemisphere and Israel from
The MIT Press
Cambridge, Massachusetts (and London, England)

ISSN 0953-7767

British Library Cataloguing in Publication Data
Traub, Kenneth R.
 Functional implementation of non-strict functional programming languages.
 —(Research monographs in parallel and distributed
 computing : ISSN 0953-7767)
 1. Computer systems. Programming languages
 I. Title   II. Series
 005.13

 ISBN 0-273-08827-0

Library of Congress Cataloging-in-Publication Data
Traub, Kenneth R.
  Implementation of non-strict functional programming languages /
 Kenneth R. Traub.—1st MIT Press ed.
   p.   cm.—(Research monographs in parallel and distributed
 computing)
   ISBN 0-262-70042-5 (pb)
   1. Functional programming (Computer science)   2. Functional
 programming languages.   I. Title.   II. Series.
 QA76.62.T73   1990
 005.13—dc20

Reproduced and printed by photolithography
in Great Britain by Biddles Ltd, Guildford

Contents

Preface to the Book

This book is the second major revision of my doctoral thesis: first from thesis to technical report, and now from technical report to monograph in the *Research Monographs in Parallel and Distributed Computing* series. In going from thesis to technical report, the chapter on code generation (Chapter 5 in the present volume) was completely rewritten; in going from technical report to book, all of the remaining technical material save Chapter 4 was completely rewritten. In addition, the order of the chapters is different in the book than in the technical report.

While the presentation of the material has changed dramatically in the 27 months since I finished the original thesis, the spirit of the work is the same. The overall framework of partitioning a program based on constraint graphs, derived from dependence graphs that have potential and certain edges, has not changed. The main improvement in the present volume is that the mathematics has been greatly simplified, and at the same time the results are demonstrated with greater rigor.

One type of revision that has *not* been made is any attempt to incorporate other researchers' results that have appeared between the time the thesis was completed and the present. The frame of reference for this book is still mid-1988, as it was for the thesis.

Many thanks are due to people who have helped make the book form of this work possible. John Cushion of Pitman Publishing deserves a very warm thank-you for being understanding of the many delays I incurred while revising the manuscript. I also thank Jim Richey, my supervisor at Motorola, Inc., for his encouragement. For my work being accepted into the *Research Monographs in Parallel and Distributed Computing* series, I thank Chris Jesshope, head of the editorial board, Arvind, who initially recommended my thesis in his capacity as editorial board member, and Simon Peyton Jones, who was kind enough to review the technical report for the board. Finally, I am indebted to many people who helped proofread yet another version of the manuscript. I owe particular thanks to Shail Gupta, who very carefully read all the mathematical sections and gave me detailed comments and corrections. I also thank Maria Carlon, Andrea Carnevali, Peter DeWolf, Niamh Doherty, Kattamuri Ekanadham, and Jeff Sutherland for their proofreading assistance.

Preface to the Thesis

This thesis is the culmination of four years spent at the MIT Laboratory for Computer Science. It is uniquely a product of that working environment, and I am grateful for the support and friendship of my colleagues there.

I wish especially to thank Arvind, my thesis advisor, who first suggested the topic to me as a potential master's thesis in 1985. His intuition and conviction about the importance of this work led to its "promotion" to the doctoral level, and he has continually cajoled me to view the work in an ever-broader context and approach it from more and more relevant points of view. Without his influence, this work would not have been nearly as significant a contribution to the field as I feel it is now. I also am grateful to him for helping me to finish on schedule.

I also wish to thank my readers, Rishiyur S. Nikhil and Stephen Ward, for their time and patience in reading drafts of my work. Nikhil provided many thoughtful technical comments with an occasional welcome interjection of his inimitable wit, while Steve's perspective was a great help in overcoming some of the inbred preconceptions of my research group.

Several other people have helped in the preparation of this thesis. David Culler, Steve Heller, and Natalie Tarbet were very kind in offering to proofread various drafts. I had many enjoyable discussions with Bob Iannucci about the material as it was being developed. It is a pleasure to acknowledge my officemate of three years, Vinod Kathail, who was always willing to educate me about lambda calculus and related mathematical methods; his influence is clearly visible in Chapter 4. Serge Plotkin provided the construction used in the proof of Section 8.8.

I have felt privileged in my four years here to work with the members of the Computation Structures Group, without a doubt the most talented group of individuals I have ever encountered. In addition to those already mentioned, I wish to thank Greg Papadopoulos, Richard Soley and Suresh Jagannathan for their interest in and enthusiasm for my work. Steve Heller, Andrew Chien, and Kalyn Culler provided much-needed moral support.

Finally, I wish to thank my parents, the value of whose love and support is beyond measure.

The author has been supported in part by a National Science Foundation Fellowship and an A. T. & T. PhD Scholarship.

To my parents,
Pat and Carol Traub

Key to Mathematical Symbols

Symbol	Description	Section
$x^{(n)}$	Identifier of arity n	4.1
$\diamondsuit$	The answer (an identifier)	4.1
$newid(x,y)$	New identifier formed from x and y	4.2,4.9
$\vdash$	One step reduction	4.2
$\vdash_\alpha$	Reduction of redex α	4.2
ρ	Rewrite rule (R1a, R2, ...)	4.2
σ	Substitution	4.8
σ_C	Substitution associated with context C	4.8
$\mathcal{NV}[\![\ldots]\!]$	Non-free variables	4.8
$A^{S_0 \vdash^* S_1}$	Set of redexes reduced in $S_0 \vdash^+ S_1$	6.1
$reduced(S)$	Set of identifiers reduced in S	6.2
$\vec{R}^{S_0}$	Requirement graph for program S_0	6.2
Υ	Dependence set	6.3
$\vec{D}^{S_0}$	Dependence graph for program S_0	6.3
$\Upsilon_{C,x}^{f}$	Certain dependence set for x in f	6.4
$\Upsilon_{F,x}^{f}$	Full dependence set for x in f	6.4
$\mathcal{LV}[\![\ldots]\!]$	Local variables	6.4
(V, D_C, D_F)	Function dependence graph	6.4
$\vec{D}_C$	Certain dependence graph	6.4
$\vec{D}_F$	Full dependence graph	6.4
$\vec{D}_P$	Potential dependence graph	6.4
$Strict(\hat{f})$	Arguments of $\hat{f}$ inferred strict	7.4
$Ignored(\hat{f})$	Arguments of $\hat{f}$ inferred ignored	7.4
Θ	Partitioning (set of threads)	8.1
θ	Thread	8.1
D_Θ	Imputed dependences of partition Θ	8.1
$\vec{S}$	Separation graph	8.2
$\vec{A}$	*A priori* ordering constraint	8.2

1 Introduction

In *non-strict* functional languages, a data structure may be read before all its components are written, and a function may return a value before finishing all its computation or even before all its arguments have been evaluated. Such flexibility gives expressive power to the programmer, but makes life difficult for the compiler because it may not be possible to totally order instructions at compile time; the correct order can vary dramatically with the input data. Many compilers for non-strict languages rely on *lazy evaluation*, in which a subexpression is not evaluated until known (at run time) to contribute to the final answer. By scheduling each subexpression separately, lazy evaluation automatically deals with the varying orderings required by non-strictness, but at the same time incurs a great deal of overhead. Recent research has employed strictness analysis and/or annotations to make more scheduling decisions at compile time, and thereby reduce the overhead, but because these techniques seek to retain laziness, they are limited in effectiveness.

We present an alternative compilation strategy which deals with non-strictness independent of laziness, through the analysis of data dependence. Our analysis determines which instructions can be ordered at compile time and which must be scheduled at run time in order to implement non-strictness properly. We then have the option of imposing laziness or ignoring it—and we find that choosing the latter path can lead to significantly reduced overhead. Abandoning laziness means certain programs (those which use "infinite objects") may fail to terminate properly. We suspect, however, that non-strictness and not the ability to handle infinite objects is the more important feature for the programmer. Preserving non-strictness but not laziness leads to a new evaluation order, which we term "lenient" evaluation.

We discuss our strategy in the context of both sequential implementations and parallel implementations where the object code is partially sequentialized. We also show how lazy code can be generated from our framework.

The guiding principle behind our compilation method is simply that compilation is a process of choosing the order in which subexpressions will be evaluated. Unlike imperative programs, functional programs do not give any explicit indication of subexpression ordering; this is why they are termed "declarative." But sequential code is by definition ordered, so if sequential code is to be produced from functional programs, the compiler must take ordering decisions. A compiler must perform considerable analysis to make these decisions correctly, because this ordering information is not explicit in the source code—this sort of analysis is the heart of any compiler for a non-strict functional language. Existing functional language compilers perform this analysis indirectly, by attempting to emulate an evaluator for the language (typically, a lazy evaluator) which executes subexpressions in proper sequence. In contrast, we attack the ordering issue head on, and consequently we are able to achieve a much cleaner separation between describing the behavior object code must exhibit to faithfully implement the semantics and developing techniques to achieve that behavior on the target architecture. We find that non-strict object code can be described abstractly as a set of sequential threads, each internally ordered but whose relative order with respect to other threads is determined at run time. We then formulate the conversion of a source program into these sequential threads as first determining the constraints on thread construction imposed by the language semantics, and then partitioning the original program into threads based on these constraints. From there, the abstract threads may be converted into concrete object code for a particular target architecture, given the execution mechanisms it provides.

The technical material in this book may be divided in three large parts. The first part, Chapter 4, presents an operational semantics for functional programs, based on a rewrite system called *functional quads*. This system allows us to define precisely the meaning of lazy and lenient evaluation, and it also provides the mathematical underpinning of dependence analysis. The second part, Chapter 5, shows how to generate sequential code from a functional quads program. This chapter assumes that the program has already been partitioned into threads, and concentrates on optimization and implementation. At the end of this chapter is a method for partitioning suitable for both lazy and lenient evaluation, by coalescing small threads to form larger ones. Chapters 6, 7, and 8 comprise the third part of the book, describing how data dependence graphs may be used to partition a program for lenient evaluation. Chapter 6 formalizes the notion of data dependence, and shows how data dependence relates to the order of subexpression evaluation in the rewrite system. Chapter 7 presents practical techniques for computing data dependence graphs, along with proofs of correctness. Chapter 8 shows how to use the data dependence graph to partition a program into threads. As for the other chapters of this book, the remainder of this chapter describes some notational conventions used in this book, Chapter 2 sets the stage by reviewing the current state of the art in functional language compiling, including strict and lazy evaluation, Chapter 3 illustrates the kind of code generated by conventional techniques and by our techniques, comparing the overhead, and Chapter 9 concludes.

1.1 Notation: Functional Programs

Modern functional programming languages have a number of advanced features, including pattern matching, powerful iteration facilities, algebraic and abstract data types, and type inference systems. Functional programming examples in this book will be presented in a minimal kernel language, which we describe here. This language is sort of the "least common denominator" of such common non-strict functional languages as Miranda [71], LML [9], and the forthcoming Haskell [73]; it includes numbers, simple data structures, arithmetic expressions, conditional expressions, curried function application, and lexical scoping through "letrec" blocks. All of the advanced features mentioned above can be expressed in the kernel language through source-to-source transformations. The issues related to type systems, too, are absent in the kernel language, for we can assume that type-checking is done before conversion to the kernel language. The concrete syntax of the kernel language is patterned after Id Nouveau [48], but this is not meant to imply that Id syntax has any particular advantages over the syntax of other languages. The kernel used here simply has an uncluttered, easy-to-read appearance in Id syntax.

The grammar of our language is given below.

$$\begin{array}{lll}
\textit{Expression} & ::= & \textit{Number} \mid \textit{Boolean} \mid \textit{Identifier} \mid \textit{Expression Op Expression} \mid \\
& & \text{if } \textit{Expression } \mathbf{then} \textit{ Expression } \mathbf{else} \textit{ Expression} \mid \\
& & \textit{Expression Expression} \mid \textit{Block} \mid (\textit{Expression}) \\
\textit{Op} & ::= & \texttt{+} \mid \texttt{-} \mid \texttt{*} \mid \texttt{/} \mid \texttt{==} \mid \texttt{<} \mid \ldots \\
\textit{Block} & ::= & \{ \textit{ Binding } ; \textit{ Binding } ; \ldots \text{ in } \textit{Expression } \} \\
\textit{Binding} & ::= & \textit{Identifier} = \textit{Expression} \mid \textit{Identifier Identifier} \ldots = \textit{Expression}
\end{array}$$

A brief description of these features:

Application Function application is written by juxtaposition, so if f is a function of three arguments, and g a function of two, a legal expression is:

```
f 5 (g x 3) y
```

where the second argument of f is the result of applying g to x and 3. Functions in Id are *curried*, so that a partial application like (g 5) is simply a function of one argument which calls g on 5 and that argument. Application, therefore, associates to the left.

Infix Expressions To improve the readability of arithmetic expressions, infix notation is provided as a syntactic sugar for the application of arithmetic, relational, and logical primitives. Thus, we have

```
x + y   ≡   (+) x y
```

where (+) represents the primitive addition function. The usual precedence and associativity rules apply to the infix operators, with application having highest precedence.

Conditionals An expression of the form if E_1 then E_2 else E_3 evaluates to the value of E_2 or E_3, depending on whether E_1 evaluates to true or false, respectively.

Blocks Blocks allow names to be given to expressions; each binding introduces a new name whose scope is the entire block. This "letrec" scoping rule allows bindings to be recursive or mutually recursive. A binding either gives a name to the value of an expression, as in:

```
{...
x = y * 5;
...}
```

or defines a new function, as in:

```
{...
dist x y = sqrt(x * x + y * y);
...}
```

In a function definition binding, the scope of the function name (the leftmost identifier) is the whole block, while the scope of the formals (the other identifiers on the left hand side) is only the body of the function (the right hand side). The number of formals is the *arity* of the function. Functions of zero arity are not supported.

The value of a block expression is the value of the expression following the `in` keyword.

Primitives We assume a basic repertoire of primitive functions for manipulating the primitive data types. We have already mentioned the arithmetic, relational, and logical operators, for which infix syntax is provided. We also assume primitives for data structures. In general we provide tagged n-tuples, with associated constructor functions, selector functions, and tag predicates. Specifically, for each n-ary type t we provide:

$$\texttt{make\_t } v_1 \ldots v_n \quad \longrightarrow \quad \langle t, v_1, \ldots, v_n \rangle$$

$$\texttt{sel\_t\_i } \langle t, v_1, \ldots, v_i, \ldots, v_n \rangle \quad \longrightarrow \quad v_i$$

$$\texttt{is\_t? } v \quad \longrightarrow \quad \begin{cases} \texttt{true} & \text{if } v = \langle t, v_1, \ldots, v_n \rangle \\ \texttt{false} & \text{otherwise} \end{cases}$$

0-ary types are supported; they have no selectors, and instead of a constructor function there is just a constant.

For convenience, we will often make use of the 2-ary "cons" type, with constructor `cons`, selectors `hd` and `tl`, and predicate `cons?`, along with the 0-ary `nil` and its predicate `nil?`.

1.2 Notation: Sets, Relations, and Graphs

Given a set A, a binary relation $\vdash$ on A is a subset of $A \times A$; we write $a_0 \vdash a_1$ if $(a_0, a_1) \in \vdash$. We also write $a_0 \vdash^0 a_0$, and $a_0 \vdash^{i+1} a_{i+1}$ if $a_0 \vdash^i a_i$ and $a_i \vdash a_{i+1}$. We write $a_0 \vdash^\epsilon a_1$ if $a_0 \vdash^0 a_1$ or $a_0 \vdash a_1$, $a_0 \vdash^+ a_1$ if $a_0 \vdash^i a_1$ for some $i > 0$, and $a_0 \vdash^* a_1$ if $a_0 \vdash^i a_1$ for some $i \geq 0$; $\vdash^\epsilon$, $\vdash^+$, and $\vdash^*$ are called the *reflexive closure*, the *transitive closure*, and the *reflexive transitive closure* of $\vdash$, respectively. A relation is reflexive (transitive) if it is equal to its own reflexive (transitive) closure. Given a subset $A' \subseteq A$, the *restriction* of a relation to this subset, notation $(\vdash \mid A')$, is the set $\vdash \cap (A' \times A')$.

A directed graph $\vec{E}$ is an ordered pair (V, E) where $E \subseteq V \times V$; V is the set of *vertices*, and E the set of *edges*. Because we will have many graphs with the same vertex set, we use a non-standard convention whereby the graph is represented by the edge set symbol with an arrow on top. Since the edge set is a binary relation on the vertices, all of the terminology in the preceding paragraph applies. We use the notation $u \xrightarrow{E} v$ to indicate that $(u, v) \in E$, and so $u \xrightarrow{E}^i v$, $u \xrightarrow{E}^\epsilon v$, $u \xrightarrow{E}^+ v$, and $u \xrightarrow{E}^* v$ indicate that between u and v there is a path of length i, a path of length zero or one, a path of length at least one, and a path of length at least zero, respectively. A graph is *cyclic* if there exists $u \in V$ such that $u \xrightarrow{E}^+ u$, and *acyclic* otherwise. If $V' \subseteq V$, then $(V', (E \mid V'))$ is the *induced subgraph* of $\vec{E}$ on V'.

An undirected graph is a graph such that for any $u, v \in V$, if $(u, v) \in E$, then $(v, u) \in E$ also. We use the slightly informal notation $\{u, v\} \in E$ to indicate that $(u, v), (v, u) \in E$ for an undirected graph.

2 Background—Functional Language Compilers

To produce sequential object code, whether for a von Neumann architecture or a parallel architecture which executes sequential code segments in parallel, many decisions about the relative order of subexpression evaluation must be taken at compile time. In an imperative programming language such as Fortran, Pascal, C, *etc.*, all of these decisions are made by the programmer and communicated to the compiler through the textual ordering of the program. Imperative compilers, therefore, need only worry about ordering if they wish to change the programmer's ordering, say to perform code motion optimizations. In declarative programming languages, however, the programmer makes no assertions about the ordering of subexpressions; instead, the programmer describes how the results of one computation are used by another. It is up to the compiler to choose an order which satisfies the data dependences specified by the programmer.

For functional languages, the standard practice is to define an interpreter, and generate compiled code for a program which mimics the order of evaluation steps performed by the interpreter on that program. There are two standard functional language interpreters, each having a simple rule for deciding what expression to evaluate next:

The Strict Interpreter To evaluate (f e_1 ... e_n), where f has arity n, first evaluate each of the argument expressions e_1 through e_n, and then evaluate the body of f, passing the evaluated arguments.

The Lazy Interpreter To evaluate (f e_1 ... e_n), where f has arity n, evaluate the body of f, passing the arguments unevaluated.

Data constructors are treated like procedure calls, with the strict interpreter evaluating the component expressions before building the structure, and the lazy interpreter leaving the components unevaluated. The rules for letrec blocks are analogous: the strict interpreter evaluates the right-hand sides of the bindings before binding the variables and evaluating the final expression, while the lazy interpreter evaluates the final expression with the right-hand sides of the bindings unevaluated (in both cases this is a little trickier than it sounds because the bindings can refer to one another; we defer the details until the next chapter). Strict and lazy evaluation are identical for the remaining language constructs: constants, identifiers, conditionals, and arithmetic. It should be noted, however, that in lazy evaluation an identifier might be bound to an unevaluated expression. Simply referring to such an identifier does not evaluate the expression, but if the argument to an arithmetic operation or the predicate of a conditional is unevaluated, it must be evaluated before further progress can be made.[1] The net effect in lazy evaluation is that an expression is

---

[1]In some sense, it is an implementation choice *how much* an argument to a primitive need be evaluated.

not evaluated before it is known to contribute to the final answer. In place of *strict* and *lazy* are sometimes found the terms *applicative-order* and *normal-order*, or *call-by-value* and *call-by-need*.[2]

We illustrate the difference between strict and lazy evaluation with a small example:

```
examp a b =
  {f x y z = if x < 0 then y * y else z * z;
   in
      f a (b+4) (b-17)};
```

Suppose we call `examp` with arguments of 10 and 20. Under strict evaluation, we have a call to internal procedure `f`, so we first have to evaluate its arguments, yielding 10, 24, and 3. We then call `f`, which compares 10 to 0, selects the "else" clause, multiplies 3 times 3, and returns 9 as the answer. Notice that we performed the addition (b+4) even though its value was ultimately ignored. Under lazy evaluation, neither (b+4) nor (b-17) would be evaluated before calling `f`. But once inside `f`, when the "else" clause has been selected, we need the value of z, so we then perform the subtraction (b-17). The answer is the same, but we have avoided the addition (b+4).

In some sense, the difference between strict and lazy evaluation is one of efficiency, as lazy evaluation seeks to avoid the computation of useless intermediate results. But in fact, lazy evaluation gives more expressive power to the programmer than does strict evaluation, because there are programs which produce answers under lazy evaluation but not under strict evaluation. The most obvious subclass of these programs are ones in which the useless intermediate results avoided by lazy evaluation require an infinite amount of computation under strict evaluation. An example:

```
{ints_from n = cons n (ints_from (n+1));
 in
    nth 10 (ints_from 1)}
```

((nth i l) returns the *i*th element of list *l*.) Under strict evaluation, the call to `ints_from` results in an infinite recursion, but under lazy evaluation the calls to `ints_from` for *n* larger than 10 are not made, since they do not contribute to the final result. The utility of programs like this which manipulate "infinite lists" was one of the earliest reasons for interest in lazy evaluation [22]. We will have a lot more to say about the relative expressive power of various evaluation methods in Chapter 3.

The above exposition of strict and lazy evaluation was intentionally informal, to avoid burdening the reader with a lot of detail and notation. The reader can rest assured that

---

For example, to evaluate (x > 0) we need only evaluate x enough to determine its sign. For pragmatic reasons, of course, expressions denoting scalar types are generally evaluated completely when any information about their values is needed. On the other hand, a data structure selector function will evaluate its argument only enough to get the desired component.

[2]A note on usage: *strict* and *lazy* are most often used when distinguishing between evaluation rules applied consistently in an implementation. On the other hand, *call-by-value* and *call-by-need* tend to be used when both mechanisms are available in the same implementation, at the discretion of the programmer [16]. *Applicative-order* and *normal-order* are most correct when applied to lambda calculus, where they are also called *leftmost-innermost* and *leftmost* (or *leftmost-outermost*).

we will define them very precisely in Chapter 4; it may be worth rereading this chapter and the next after the formal definition has been presented.

In the remainder of this chapter we focus only on how today's compilers produce object code which mimics strict or lazy evaluation. Strict compilers draw mainly on Lisp compiler technology, the most important aspects coming from Steele's pioneering Rabbit compiler [62] and the later Orbit compiler [44] from Yale. The lazy approach has three substrands: force-and-delay style compilers [26, 30], combinator and supercombinator graph reduction [69, 34], and abstract machine based compilers [37, 39]. We discuss all of these techniques below. We are mainly concerned with strategy in this chapter; in the next we examine in detail the object code produced from these compilers.

2.1   Strict Compilers

Most imperative programming languages have strict procedure calls, so strict functional compilers have a lot in common with imperative compilers. But in functional languages, procedures are first-class objects and may be created and manipulated more freely than in most imperative languages. Not surprisingly, then, strict functional compilers are based on compilers developed for Lisp and its variants, as procedures are also first-class in Lisp. Lisp-like languages have a well-defined functional subset, and so Lisp compiler technology carries over directly into the functional regime. The first compiler to concentrate on efficient implementation of first-class procedures was the Rabbit compiler [62], developed for the Scheme dialect of Lisp [54]. Rabbit technology was subsequently refined and put into operation by the Orbit compiler [44].

The two main innovations in these compilers were the use of the continuation passing style (CPS) transformation [63, 61] and efficient procedure construction and invocation. The CPS transformation is used to express a variety of complex imperative control constructs in terms of procedure calling; since these imperative constructs are absent in functional languages, CPS is not of great interest here. In a functional context, all CPS accomplishes is fixing the relative ordering in which arguments to the same procedure are evaluated.

Efficient handling of procedures, on the other hand, is critically important to functional compilation, because first-class procedures are heavily used in the functional programming style. The overhead associated with procedures and procedure calls stems from parameter (and result) passing and from the use of free variables bound in enclosing lexical scopes (the "environment"). The environment problem has two sides: the values of free variables must be recorded at the time the procedure is created, and they must be accessed when the procedure is called. The main insight in Rabbit/Orbit is that there need not be a uniform convention for parameter passing, nor for environment representation; instead, these can be customized for efficiency on a procedure by procedure basis. Among the customizations:

- If all callers of a procedure can be identified and are in the same activation as where the procedure is created, then parameters, results, and the environment can be passed in registers rather than on the stack. (Figure 2.1a)

- If a procedure can only be accessed by its creating activation and that activation's descendants (*i.e.*, if the procedure does not "escape upward"), then the procedure

example_a x y =	example_b x l =	example_c x y =
{f a = a * x;	{f a = a * x;	{f a = (a+x)/y;
in	in	g b = x/(b-y);
f (y-5)+	map f l};	in
f (y+8) };		cons f g};
Arguments, results, and environment in registers.	Downward-only function: environment on stack.	Procedures share environment for **x** and **y** on heap.
(a)	(b)	(c)

Figure 2.1: Procedure Linkage Optimization by Orbit

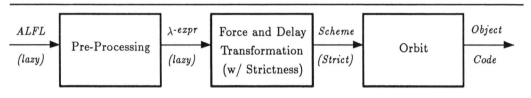

Figure 2.2: Force-and-Delay Lazy Compilation: the ALFL Compiler

can be compiled to fetch its environment variables from the stack, as in Algol. This saves the overhead of constructing the environment, since the stack is already there. (Figure 2.1b)

- If a procedure escapes upward, then the environment must be allocated on the heap. If several procedures are created in the same activation, however, it may be possible to share their environments or a portion thereof, or share them with their parent. (Figure 2.1c)

With these and other procedure-calling optimizations, Orbit is able to achieve superior performance compared with other compilers, especially for programs which make heavy use of procedures [44].

Lisp and strict functional language compilers also face the problems of register allocation, optimization, *etc.*, faced by compilers for languages such as Fortran, C, and Pascal. We will not delve into these issues, as they are adequately described elsewhere [2], and are not significantly different in the functional context.

2.2   Lazy Compilers: Force-and-Delay

As we discussed earlier, lazy evaluation requires that argument expressions be passed to procedures unevaluated, and that primitives like arithmetic must cause such unevaluated expressions to be evaluated. By introducing unevaluated expressions as first-class objects into the language, Henderson [26] developed a source-to-source transformation which makes explicit where expressions are delayed and where the delayed expressions are to be evaluated. The transformed code can be executed using strict evaluation, but will behave as if executed under lazy evaluation. The ALFL compiler [30] uses this transformation to convert programs written in a lazy functional language, ALFL, into Scheme, which is then compiled into object code by Orbit (see Figure 2.2).[3]

Henderson's transformation is summarized in Figure 2.3. (delay e) is not a procedure application, but is instead a special form which evaluates to an unevaluated representation of e called a *thunk*.[4] As we mentioned before, thunks are first-class objects and may be passed freely between procedures, stored in data structures, *etc.* The force procedure takes an object, and if it is a thunk, evaluates the unevaluated expression recorded in the thunk, repeating the process as necessary to obtain a non-thunk value. To achieve anything approaching efficiency, force must also *memoize* the value of the thunk so that later forces of the same thunk will simply fetch the memoized value. Without being any more specific about the representation of a thunk, we note that a thunk must carry a proper environment for evaluating e, if e has any free variables.

The overhead of performing lazy evaluation compared to strict evaluation is directly reflected by the appearance of force and delay in the transformed code. Wherever a delay appears, the compiled program must include code to allocate storage for the thunk (enough to hold a pointer to the code for e, a pointer to its environment, and later, its evaluated value) and code to construct the thunk's environment. Wherever a force appears, there must be code to check whether the value being forced is a non-thunk value, previously evaluated thunk, or unevaluated thunk. In the latter case, there may also be overhead in setting up the environment for the thunk's expression, usually in the guise of saving registers or pushing stack.

Efficiency is improved, therefore, by eliminating as many forces and delays as possible. The derived rules in Figure 2.3 are examples of this. For example, since + forces both its arguments, there is no need to delay arguments when we can recognize a call to the + operator. A procedure that always forces a particular argument is said to be *strict* in that argument. *Strictness analysis* [18, 32, 15] is commonly employed to determine the strictness of user-defined procedures; strictness information allows delays to be eliminated as illustrated by the last derived rule in Figure 2.3. We will discuss strictness analysis and its applications in detail in Section 2.5.

The ALFL compiler from Yale [30] is one example of a lazy compiler based directly on the force-and-delay transformation. To implement force and delay, the ALFL compiler uses Henderson's observation that a delayed expression may be represented as a procedure of no arguments, so that forcing the expression is just calling that procedure. The resulting translation of delay and definition of force are shown in Figure 2.4. The output of the ALFL compiler is actually Scheme code, which is then fed to the Orbit compiler to produce object code for a sequential machine. Notice that all of the efficient procedure

---

[3]In [30], the ALFL compiler is described as a combinator-based compiler. In fact, it only uses combinators as an intermediate form for doing optimizations like common subexpression elimination, constant folding, and inline substitution. After these optimizations the combinator code is translated back into lambda-expressions; this whole process is shown as "pre-processing" in Figure 2.2. In effect, the pre-processing phase is just source-to-source optimization, which happens to use combinators internally.

[4]Also called a *promise*, *recipe*, or a *closure*. We will use the term *closure* in a broader sense, referring to the code/environment pair compiled from any lexically nested procedure definition, whether part of a thunk or not. The term *promise* will be given a special meaning in Chapter 5 as a placeholder for an unevaluated value.

10

<u>*Basic Transformation Rules*</u>

e_1 e_2	$\rightarrow$	(force e_1) (delay e_2)
if e_1 then e_2 else e_3	$\rightarrow$	if (force e_1) then e_2 else e_3
{x1 = e_1;		{x1 = (delay e_1);
$\cdots$		$\cdots$
xn = e_n;	$\rightarrow$	xn = (delay e_n);
in		in
e_{in}}		e_{in}}

<u>*Implementation of Primitive Functions*</u>

cons x y	=	cons^S x y	
hd x	=	hd^S (force x)	similarly for tl
x + y	=	(force x) +^{S} (force y)	similarly for -, *, >, *etc.*

<u>*Derived Transformation Rules*</u>

cons e_1 e_2	$\rightarrow$	cons^S (delay e_1) (delay e_2)	
hd e_1	$\rightarrow$	hd^S (force e_1)	similarly for tl
e_1 + e_2	$\rightarrow$	(force e_1) +^{S} (force e_2)	similarly for -, *, >, *etc.*
f $e_1 \cdots e_n$	$\rightarrow$	f (delay e_1) $\cdots$ (delay e_n)	if f's arity is n
f $e_1 \cdots e_{i-1} e_i e_{i+1} \cdots e_n$	$\rightarrow$	f (delay e_1) $\cdots$	
		(delay e_{i-1}) e_i (delay e_{i+1})	if f is strict in
		$\cdots$ (delay e_n)	its ith argument

Note: The S superscript indicates a strict primitive.

Figure 2.3: Conversion of Lazy Programs to Strict Programs

call machinery in Orbit carries over directly to the implementation of thunks in the ALFL compiler, since they are translated into procedures before processing by Orbit. Thus, the ALFL compiler achieves excellent performance relative to other lazy compilers, because Orbit is able to optimize the management of environments for thunks.

2.3   Lazy Compilers: Graph Reduction

Graph reduction was among the earliest lazy implementations of functional languages [69], and provided much of the impetus for research in the field. The idea in graph reduction is to translate the original program into a *combinator graph*, which is "executed" by successive application of rewrite rules which transform the graph into the final answer. The object code from a graph reduction compiler, therefore, is not object code for conventional hardware, but code which must be executed by a software interpreter (see Figure 2.5). Graph reduction is of interest here only because it forms the basis for the abstract machine compilers, to be discussed in the next section. It should be pointed out, however, that much research effort has been devoted to hardware architectures which directly execute combinator graphs, both uniprocessor [58, 65] and multiprocessor [51].

Here is an example showing the reduction of the program (1 + (2 * 3)) in two steps:

```
(delay e)  →
  {thunkfn () =
    %% Sequential code follows.
    {val = e;
     ⟨code to update thunk with val⟩;
     return val};
   thunk = mk_thunk thunkfn;
   in
     thunk}
```

```
force x =
  if isthunk(x) then
    if thunk_evaluated(x) then
      fetch_memoized_value(x)
    else
      (thunk_closure x) ()   [apply to no args]
  else
    x
```

Figure 2.4: Implementation of force and delay

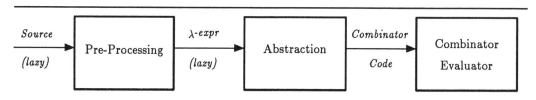

Figure 2.5: Graph Reduction Lazy Compilation

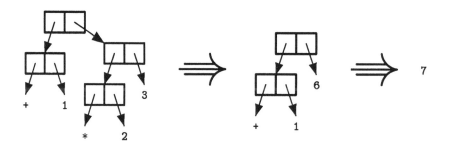

The nodes of a combinator graph represent application, and since all functions are curried in graph reduction, the first graph is just the graphical representation of ((+ 1) ((+ 2) 3)). The leaves of the graph are constants, which include *combinators* such as +. Associated with each combinator is a reduction rule, and the reduction rule for + says that an instance of + applied to two integers is reduced to the integer which is their sum. When a subgraph is reduced, the reduced version replaces the original in the graph, as shown in the second graph above. Performing the first reduction exposes another opportunity for reduction, and this second reduction reduces the graph to the answer. In general, there may be many reducible subgraphs ("redexes"), and a proper choice of which to reduce at each step is necessary to achieve lazy evaluation. The rule which corresponds directly to the rule for lazy evaluation given on page 6 always selects the leftmost redex, which in terms of the graph is the subgraph located closest to the bottom of the graph's "spine," which extends to the left from the root node. More elaborate strategies are also possible [11].

In addition to primitive reduction rules such as those for +, user-defined functions can be treated as reduction rules in their own right. Suppose we had the following program:

```
{f x y = x - (g y (x + x*y));
 g a b = if a < 0 then b else 7;
 in
    f (/ 6 2) 4}
```

This program's graph before and after the first step of reduction is shown below:

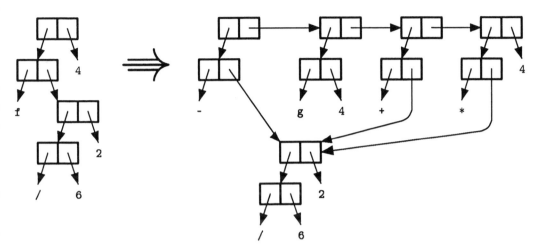

Notice that the argument (/ 6 2) to f is effectively delayed, since it remains unevaluated after the call to f is reduced. Furthermore, when it is eventually evaluated, its value will replace the top node of the subgraph which represents it. Since the reduction of f caused the unevaluated subgraph to be shared, so will the result. Hence, the values of delayed expressions are memoized when evaluated, just as they were in the force-and-delay implementation discussed earlier.

In graph reduction, all of the subexpression delaying mechanism needed to support lazy evaluation is embedded in the graph interpreter. All the compiler must do is produce a set of combinator reduction rules and a graph representing the query expression. Producing combinator definitions is slightly more difficult than our example above implies, for a function definition can only be used as a reduction rule if it has no free variables. One technique for removing free variables from a function is simply to include them in the formal parameter list and in every reference to that function. This method is called *lambda lifting* [38], and is illustrated below:

```
f x y l =                            f x y l =
  {g a = a + y;                        {g yy a = a + yy;
   in                                   in
      (map g l), g x};                     (map (g y) l), g y x};
```

(arrow between the two code blocks: →)

Another technique is Hughes' *mfe*-abstraction [34]. Any technique which adds new combinators to the set of primitives is called a *supercombinator* technique; it is also possible to

13

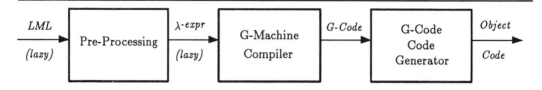

Figure 2.6: Abstract Machine Lazy Compilation: the LML/G-Machine Compiler

compile a program into a fixed set of primitive combinators [69]. The fixed set approach is not of much practical use on conventional hardware, but has been used in specialized machines where the set of combinators can be viewed as an instruction set [55, 65].

The main difficulty with combinator approaches is that they are basically interpretive, since they do not result in code directly executable by conventional hardware. In fact, the only difference between graph reduction and what is normally called an interpreter is the sharing of computation made possible by the graph representation. The desire to implement graph reduction efficiently led to the development of abstract machine approaches, discussed next.

2.4 Lazy Compilers: Abstract Machines

Abstract machine compilation produces object code for conventional hardware which mimics the behavior of a graph reduction interpreter, and therefore of a lazy evaluator. In graph reduction, each combinator is a reduction rule which controls the behavior of a graph interpreter. In the abstract machine approach, a combinator is compiled into conventional object code which performs graph manipulations simulating an application of that combinator's reduction rule. In effect, the graph interpreter has been compiled into the combinator definitions. The term "abstract machine" refers to an intermediate step in the compilation process: the program is first compiled into code for an abstract machine whose instructions include primitives for manipulating combinator graphs, and then from abstract instructions into conventional object code. One well-known abstract machine compiler is the compiler for Lazy ML [9], outlined in Figure 2.6, based on the G-machine [37] abstract machine. Another recently proposed abstract machine is the Three Instruction Machine (TIM) [21]. In our discussion here we ignore the intermediate code and just describe in general terms the target code produced from it.

Suppose we had this combinator definition:

```
f x = g x x
```

where g is the name of another combinator. In graph reduction, reducing a call to f would first rewrite the graph:

and then proceed to reduce the newly rewritten graph. The LML compiler imitates this with the following code for f (expressed in an informal "quads" notation):

```
function f (x, Top)
Temp1   := mkap(g, x)
Temp2   := mkap(Temp1, x)
Ans     := eval(Temp2)
Top[*]  := Ans
return Ans
```

Eval evaluates a graph by traveling down the spine of its argument until a the name of a combinator is found. If its arity is satisfied, pointers to its argument graphs (found in cells along the spine) are passed to the code for that combinator as arguments. Also passed as argument is a pointer to the top node of the combinator call, so that it can be updated with the answer. So the x in the code above is really a pointer to the subgraph for x, and Top points to the original application node.

   The interesting aspect of the G-machine approach is that the code for a combinator can perform computation instead of just building graphs. Suppose that instead of (g x x), the right hand side of f were (+ x x). With the translation given above, the code for f would build the graph for (+ x x) and then evaluate it, ultimately causing x to be evaluated and added to itself. The actual LML compiler would instead generate the following code:

```
function f (x, Top)
Temp1   := eval(x)
Ans     := Temp1 + Temp1
Top[*]  := Ans
return Ans
```

which just evaluates the graph for x, adds it to itself, and updates the graph.

   The LML compiler was able to avoid building the graph for (+ x x) because the graph was to be evaluated immediately after construction. Of course, graphs still need to be built when arguments must be delayed according to the principles of lazy evaluation. Consider again the example from page 13:

```
{f x y = x - (g y (x + x*y));
 g a b = if a < 0 then b else 7;
 in
   f (/ 6 2) 4}
```

In compiling f, the LML compiler would not build a graph for the subtraction, nor for the application of g. On the other hand, a graph *would* be built for (x + x*y), since that expression might be ignored by g. Early G-machine compilation schemes would actually build a graph containing + and * combinators. On the other hand, it has been pointed out [39, 50] that more efficient code is possible by defining a combinator h for this subexpression:

```
{f x y = x - (g y (h x y));
 h x y = (x + x*y);
 g a b = if a < 0 then b else 7;
 in
    f (/ 6 2) 4}
```

Now, the delayed expression (x + x*y) appears in the graph as (h x y), and h is compiled into efficient code which just performs an addition and multiplication of values on the stack. If this transformation is applied consistently, we get a new combinator like h for each delayed subexpression, and the only graph nodes built are applications of these combinators to the delayed expressions' free variables (which may themselves be delayed expressions).

A moment's reflection reveals that we have come full circle and arrived at nothing more or less than a force-and-delay implementation. A delayed expression appears in the graph as a pointer to code (the combinator) along with an environment for its free variables (the arguments to which it is applied). So the graphs built are really just thunks. When such a graph is reduced it is overwritten with its value, but this is equivalent to the memoization of a thunk's value when forced. Given the high quality of target code that can be generated from G-code, it seems that the G-Machine LML compiler can be very competitive with the force-and-delay ALFL compiler. The same is probably true for other abstract machine based compilers.

From a pedagogical point of view, force-and-delay style lazy compilation is a bit easier to deal with, since the force-and-delay notation is succinct and avoids extraneous notions like combinator graphs. In the remainder of this book, therefore, we will take force-and-delay compilers as representative of the state of the art in lazy compilation, knowing that the abstract machine approach yields essentially equivalent results. In fact, the abstract machine formalism can impose limitations on object code quality not present in the force-and-delay style. For example, we saw in Section 2.2 how Orbit can avoid building thunk environments in the heap when it can show that the thunk does not escape upward—it compiles the thunk to fetch its free variables directly from its parent stack frames. There seems to be no way to accomplish a similar optimization in the G-machine framework, because activations do not have pointers to their parent frames. Of course, there is every reason to believe that a suitably modified G-machine or some other abstract machine could form the basis of a compiler as good as a force-and-delay compiler. For our purposes, the important fact is that the approaches are essentially equivalent despite their very different appearance.

2.5 Strictness Analysis

Delayed expressions are the principal source of overhead in lazy implementations, and so good lazy compilers expend a lot of effort in eliminating as much delaying as possible without disturbing the termination properties of the program. To discover opportunities for this optimization, current lazy compilers rely on various forms of *strictness analysis*.

Strictness analysis is based on the notion of a strict function:

Definition 2.1 *A function f of n arguments is* strict *in its ith argument if*

$$f(x_1, \ldots, x_{i-1}, \bot, x_{i+1}, \ldots, x_n) = \bot$$

for all $x_1, \ldots, x_{i-1}, x_{i+1}, \ldots, x_n$.

As Mycroft points out [47], if a function f is strict in its ith argument it is always safe to evaluate that argument before calling f. Why? Assume that $f(e_1, \ldots, e_n)$ terminates; its value is therefore greater than $\bot$. Since f is strict in its ith argument, e_i must also be greater than $\bot$. But if e_i were never evaluated by f, it would carry no more information than $\bot$. So we conclude that e_i is always evaluated by f whenever f terminates, and so it is safe to evaluate e_i before calling f.[5] On the other hand, if f does not terminate, nothing is changed by evaluating e_i early, even if e_i also does not terminate.

Strictness analysis attempts to determine in which arguments, if any, the functions of a program are strict. When compiling a call to a function, delays are eliminated from strict argument positions as determined by the analysis (see the last derived rule in Figure 2.3). Of course, strictness is an undecidable property [47], so any method of strictness analysis will be to some degree an approximation; a great deal of research has been devoted to finding strictness analysis methods that are more precise and/or more efficient. Mycroft's original work as well as a number of other efforts [18, 32, 15] are based on *abstract interpretation* [20] of the source program. Another approach is *backwards analysis* (also called *context analysis*), which appears to have some practical advantages over abstract interpretation [35, 74].

If higher-order functions are allowed, strictness analysis becomes more complex. Calls where the name of a function is syntactically applied to all arguments (*i.e.*, a first-order call) can be optimized as before, but a more complex analysis is needed to optimize a general application of one expression to another. In such a situation, the delay of the argument can be removed if it can be shown that all possible values for the function expression are strict in that argument. Abstract interpretation methods can be extended to handle higher-order functions [32, 15], but more work seems to be needed to make these techniques practical. It should be noted, however, that first-order strictness analysis can be used with higher-order languages, as long as pessimistic decisions are taken when general applications are encountered.

---

[5]Actually, we can only conclude that e_i can be evaluated sometime before the call to f *returns*. To also conclude that e_i can be evaluated before anything inside of f is computed, we must note that since f is free from side effects, no computation within f can possibly affect e_i before f returns. Evaluation of e_i before f begins is therefore indistinguishable from evaluation of e_i just before f returns. Note that this is not true for non-strict languages with side-effects like Id [48] (with unrestricted use of I-structures) or Josephs' language [40], and so strictness is not a valid criterion for early evaluation of arguments in those languages.

A more serious shortcoming of present-day strictness analysis is its ineffectiveness on non-flat domains (*i.e.*, data structures). Suppose a unary function f is strict in its argument according to the definition above, and that the argument expression e in some call to f returns a tuple. From our previous discussion, we know that we have to get more information from e than $\perp$ if f is to terminate. Unfortunately, we do not know *how much* information: we could evaluate e to $\langle \perp, \perp \rangle$, $\langle v_1, \perp \rangle$, $\langle \perp, v_2 \rangle$, or $\langle v_1, v_2 \rangle$ (and of course this continues recursively if v_1 or v_2 are themselves data structures). We are forced to take the most conservative position and only perform the minimum evaluation possible on e; in the force-and-delay framework, this means we can force e before the call, but not any of its components. Putting it another way, we can never remove delays from the arguments to a data constructor. This is a very serious defect considering the frequency with which calls to data structures are made in typical functional programs. Extending strictness analysis to eliminate delays from data structure creation is an active area of research [74].

Finally, we should note that some researchers [16, 31] have proposed the use of strictness *annotations*, which allow the programmer to direct the compiler to remove a particular delay regardless of the consequences.

3 Lenient Evaluation

At the beginning of Chapter 2 we noted that lazy evaluation gives more expressive power to the programmer than does strict evaluation, because there are programs which produce answers under lazy evaluation but not under strict evaluation. As we have seen, though, this expressive power comes at the expense of run-time overhead, in the form of delayed computation. Given that there is a trade-off between expressiveness and efficiency, it is reasonable to ask whether there is some other evaluation strategy which is more expressive than strict evaluation yet more efficient than lazy evaluation.

To answer this question, we examine the ways in which lazy evaluation is more expressive than strict evaluation. We focus first on *non-strictness* in lazy evaluation—the property that arguments are passed unevaluated to procedures. We show how non-strictness allows fuller use of recursion than is possible under strict evaluation, and therefore gives the programmer the ability to specify more complicated patterns of data dependence. From there we see that lazy evaluation imposes stronger constraints on evaluation than needed simply to achieve non-strict behavior. These constraints stem from *laziness*, which seeks to prevent evaluation that does not contribute to the final answer. Laziness is responsible for yet a different kind of expressive power: the ability to manipulate "infinite" data structures. The next logical step is to imagine implementing non-strictness but not necessarily achieving laziness. We call this *lenient evaluation*, and examine how it is achieved and how it allows for reduced overhead compared to lazy evaluation.

3.1 Expressive Power from Non-Strictness

To illustrate how non-strictness allows a more unrestricted use of recursion, we present this small example:

```
{a = cons 2 (hd a);
 in
    a}
```

We would like this program to return $\langle 2, 2 \rangle$, but this requires that (hd a) be passed to cons unevaluated—we cannot evaluate (hd a) before calling cons, as a has no value until cons returns. The need for non-strictness extends to the calling of procedures, as a slight modification of this program shows:

```
{f x y = cons x y;
 a = f 2 (hd a);
 in
    a}
```

Neither of these programs is correctly executed by a strict interpreter, because the strict interpreter tries to evaluate (hd a) before a has a value. Depending on the implementation, the strict interpreter will either complain about a being undefined, or simply deadlock.

The reader unfamiliar with strict functional languages may wonder at this point how letrec is implemented in those languages. We quote from the Scheme manual [54]:

> The [variables on the left hand sides] are bound to fresh locations holding undefined values; the [expressions on the right hand sides] are evaluated in the resulting environment (in some unspecified order); each variable is assigned to the result of the corresponding [right hand side]; the [final expression] is evaluated in the resulting environment; and the value of the [final expression] is returned. Each binding of a variable has the entire letrec expression as its region, making it possible to define mutually recursive procedures.
>
> One restriction on letrec is very important: it must be possible to evaluate each [right hand side] without referring to the value of any variable. If this restriction is violated, then the effect is undefined, and an error may be signaled during evaluation of the [right hand sides]. ... In the most common uses of letrec, all the [right hand sides] are lambda expressions and the restriction is satisfied automatically.

Lambda expressions on the right hand sides satisfy the restriction automatically because evaluating them only means constructing a closure for them, requiring the *locations* of the left hand side variables but not their values.

In the rest of this section, we present some more examples of programs which exploit the free use of recursion allowed by non-strictness; all of them make use of non-lambda right hand sides in letrec expressions.

Before proceeding to the examples, however, we should clarify what we mean by the term *non-strictness*, a term frequently used in the literature but not defined very precisely. We will use the term to describe a particular semantic property of a functional programming language, and by extension to describe a functional language implementation which achieves that property. By non-strict we do not simply mean anything that is different from strict semantics; that would not be a very useful definition. Instead, we note that the distinguishing feature of strict semantics is that arguments to procedures and data constructors are completely evaluated before the procedure body or data constructor is invoked. By non-strict, then, we mean that arguments are not necessarily evaluated before a procedure or data constructor is invoked. But more than this, we *require* that an implementation invoke the procedure or data constructor before the arguments are evaluated if this is the only way progress can be made. In the example above, progress could not be made unless cons was called before evaluating the argument (hd a). The semantic property that thus becomes available to the programmer is the assurance that computation will be delayed whenever necessary to allow the continued execution of the program.

3.1.1 Cyclic Data Structures

Cyclic data structures are often useful, but are impossible to construct in a functional language without non-strictness. Here is a simple example of constructing a circular list:

```
{a = cons 1 (cons 2 (cons 3 a)));
 in
    a}
```

Non-strictness is required because of the reference to a on the right hand side of a's binding.

A less trivial example constructs a doubly-linked list. An ordinary list is a collection of cells, where each cell is a two-tuple containing that cell's element and the next cell: $c_i = \langle v_i, c_{i+1} \rangle$. The cells of a doubly linked list are three-tuples which contain the next cell and also the previous cell: $c_i = \langle v_i, c_{i-1}, c_{i+1} \rangle$. The following program constructs a doubly-linked list from an ordinary list:

```
doubly_link l prev =     % Initial call: (doubly_link l nil)
  if nil? l then
    nil
  else
    {this = 3_tuple (hd l) prev next;
     next = doubly_link (tl l) this;
     in
        this};
```

Again, non-strictness allows the mutual recursion between the definitions of this and next.

3.1.2 Dynamic Programming

In dynamic programming, a table of some sort is constructed where most elements are defined in terms of other elements already computed. Here is a program which generates a list of factorials from 1 to n using dynamic programming:

```
make_fact_list n =
  {fact_list = cons 1 (gen_fact_list 2 n);
   gen_fact_list i n =
     if i > n then
       nil
     else
       cons (i * (nth (i - 1) fact_list))
            (gen_fact_list (i + 1) n);
   in
      fact_list}
```

Here, each element of the list is defined in terms of the previous element; this is done by using the nth function to read the $(i-1)$th element when computing the ith element. As a result, make_fact_list only does $O(n)$ multiplications, compared to the $O(n^2)$ that would be required if it simply computed $i!$ for each value of i.

In this example, the data structure is not cyclic, but the data dependences in the program are: fact_list's definition calls gen_fact_list, but gen_fact_list examines the value of fact_list. The circular dependences are necessary in functional programming, because the programmer cannot take the imperative approach of allocating an empty structure and filling in the components one at a time. The nearest functional equivalent of the imperative approach would *copy* the entire data structure at each step, at a prohibitive cost in time and space.[1] Non-strictness allows the data structure to be constructed only once even though its definition "reads itself." This dynamic programming technique shows up in such well-known examples of functional programming as Turner's "paraffins" program [70] and the "wavefront" program for matrices [7], and can even be used to solve the "backpatching" program cited by advocates of logic programming [53].

The factorial example is somewhat artificial in that dynamic programming is not necessary to generate a list of factorials efficiently:

```
non_dynamic_fact_list n =
  {fact_list = (gen_fact_list 1 1 n);
   gen_fact_list i prod n =
     if i > n then
       nil
     else
       cons (i * prod)
            (gen_fact_list (i + 1) (i * prod) n);
   in
     fact_list}
```

On the other hand, this kind of table generation is often programmed using bulk data constructors, as in the following program which uses a general purpose `make_list` primitive:

```
yet_another_fact_list n =
  {fact_list = make_list f 1 n;
   f i =
     if i == 1 then
       1
     else
       i * (nth (i-1) fact_list);
   in
     fact_list}
```

(`make_list` f 1 n) constructs a list each of whose elements is $f(i)$, for i from 1 to n. Primitives like this are more commonly used to construct arrays—indeed, they may be the only option available to the functional programmer [7]—but to use these primitives efficiently, non-strictness is once again essential.

The point of all this, of course, is not to compute factorials more efficiently, but to illustrate how non-strictness allows more efficient programs than are possible under strict evaluation.

---

[1] In some instances, the compiler could optimize the copying program into one which updates a structure in place; see [28, 27] for details.

3.1.3 Conditional Dependence

This program is a bit contrived, but illustrates that the applications of non-strict recursion are not limited to data structures:

```
conditional_example x =
  {a = if x > 0 then bb else 3;
   b = if x < 0 then aa else 4;
   aa = a + 5;
   bb = b + 6;
   in
     aa+bb};
```

The order in which this program's subexpressions are evaluated depends on the value of x. If x is positive, we first evaluate b (4), then bb (10), then a (10), then aa (15), and finally the answer (25). If x is negative, however, we first evaluate a (3), then aa (8), then b (8), then bb (14), and the answer (22).

This program has the surprising behavior that the order in which the two additions are performed depends on the value of x, even though those two additions lie outside the conditionals.

3.2 Expressive Power from Laziness

In the last section, we saw that non-strictness allows more complicated patterns of data dependences than are allowed under strict evaluation: we could make cyclic data structures, define structures in terms of themselves, even have apparent cyclic data dependences that "untangle" themselves at run time. In all of these programs, evaluation of some expressions needed to be delayed until their evaluation was possible—strict evaluation would always try to evaluate them too early, when some of their free variables were still undefined. Lazy evaluation delays *every* expression, and delays each one until the last possible moment, when execution cannot proceed further without it. So it should come as no surprise that all of the programs in the last section execute correctly under lazy evaluation, since lazy evaluation will certainly introduce sufficient delays to insure that the delayed expressions are executable. In fact, if there is any evaluation order which will produce an answer from a program, lazy evaluation will also produce an answer from that program [72]. So lazy evaluation enjoys all the expressive power that comes with non-strictness.

But lazy evaluation provides some additional expressive power beyond that discussed in the previous section: the power to manipulate "infinite" objects. The most famous example of this is the functional sieve of Erastothenes for finding prime numbers. We quote the description of the sieve given by Henderson [26]:

> Make a list of the integers, commencing at 2. Repeat the following process of marking the numbers in the list:
>
> 1. The first unmarked number of the list is prime, call it p.
>
> 2. Mark the first unmarked number in the list and each pth number thereafter whether previously marked or not (here you are marking all multiples of p).

23

3. Repeat from 1.

Typically, the sieve is used to find all primes less than some number n, so the initial list is a list from 2 to n. An imperative algorithm might start with an array, and at Step 2 scan through the array marking off array elements (say by setting them to zero). Of course, this approach does not carry over into the functional framework, so the usual solution uses a list of numbers, and "marking" multiples is accomplished by making a new list with the multiples removed:

```
sieve l =
  if nil? l then
    nil
  else
    cons (hd l)
         (sieve (remove_multiples (hd l) (tl l)));
```

Here (remove_multiples i l) returns a list containing those elements of input list l which are not multiples of i. If we want a list of all primes less than 100, then, we need only call sieve on a list of the integers from 2 to 100.

Now suppose that instead of all primes less than n, we want the first n primes. This is a bit harder to do with the sieve, since we do not know how big to make the original list of integers. Here is where lazy evaluation enters the picture: we simply start with a list of *all* the integers.

```
{ints_from x = cons x (ints_from (x+1));
 all_primes = sieve (ints_from 2);
 in
    first_n_elements n all_primes}
```

(ints_from 2) is a list of all integers starting with 2, and so all_primes is the list of all the primes, from which we simply extract the first n elements. Now if we tried executing this program under strict evaluation, we would go into an infinite loop as we actually tried to build the entire list of integers. But lazy evaluation does no computation not required for the final answer, so no more than the first n elements of all_primes are evaluated, and no more iterations of ints_from are performed than the value of the nth prime (541, if $n = 100$).

This is a very different sort of expressive power than we saw in the previous section. In that section, we saw how non-strictness allowed complicated patterns of data dependence. In the sieve, the data dependences are straightforward, but the *control flow* is not. Ints_from appears to be an infinite loop, because there is no conditional to break the recursion. Sieve, too, is apparently infinite: the nil? predicate in its conditional never returns true because the input list is infinite, and so the conditional there is superfluous (and is omitted in [26]). The control over these recursions comes not from code within the procedures themselves, but from the procedure that reads the all_primes list, namely, first_n_elements. Lazy evaluation has effectively induced the control structure of first_n_elements onto sieve and ints_from.

24

3.3 Lenience: Non-strictness Without Laziness

We have seen that there are two distinct kinds of expressive power available in lazy evaluation not found in strict evaluation. One is the ability to specify complicated patterns of data dependence, specifically, data dependences which have the syntactic appearance of cycles but which are resolved because they go through different components of the same data structure, or because the cycles are broken by conditionals. The other is the ability to express complicated control structure, where the execution of procedures which produce a data structure is controlled by the procedures which use that data structure. Both require some delaying of evaluation: the former (*non-strictness*) requires that expressions be delayed until all of their input data are available (already computed or obtainable by forcing some other delayed expressions), while the latter (*laziness*) requires that they be delayed until no further progress can be made without them. Since laziness delays expressions until the last possible moment, it automatically introduces enough delay to achieve non-strictness.[2]

We define *lenient* evaluation to be an evaluation strategy which achieves non-strictness but not necessarily laziness. For the implementation, this implies that expressions must be delayed until their input data are available, but not necessarily any longer. For the programmer, it means unrestricted use of letrec and the attendant flexibility in data dependences, but not the consumer-directed control structure required for the finite use of infinite data structures. More operationally, it means that conditionals are the only means of controlling whether or not expressions are evaluated, and should be included whenever there is the possibility of infinite loops. The control structure available under lenient evaluation, therefore, is exactly what is available under strict evaluation.

We should point out that strict languages like Scheme provide explicit force and delay operators to the programmer, so that infinite object algorithms can be implemented. The same option is available to lenient implementations. A variation is to provide explicit delays but *implicit* forces, making it transparent to the consumer of a data structure whether it is infinite or not. Programming style and methodology for lenient languages with explicit delay constructs is a topic of current research [25].

3.3.1 An Example of Lenient Object Code

Lenient evaluation does not delay expressions as long as does lazy evaluation, so we expect it to have less delay-related overhead. Specifically, lenient evaluation allows more delays to be eliminated at compile time, and in other cases allows separate delayed expressions to be combined. To illustrate, let us return to the `fact_list` example from Section 3.1.2.

---

[2]We wish to reiterate a rather subtle point alluded to in Section 2.5. Lazy evaluation delays expressions until the last possible moment, but with strictness analysis some arguments to some procedures may be evaluated early, before the call is made. It is tempting to think that this works because strictness analysis shows that an argument is always forced, *i.e.*, known to contribute to the answer before the call is made. While this is true, a stronger condition is required to eliminate the delay: the argument must be evaluable (have all its input data available) before the call. As we pointed out in the footnote on page 17, if an argument is always forced it must be evaluable before the call since no information can propagate to the argument from the call until it returns. The same implication does not hold for the delayed expressions of a letrec; all of the right-hand sides of the program in Section 3.1.3 are forced, but they still must be delayed for the dependences to be unraveled.

```
make_fact_list n =
  {fact_list = cons 1 (gen_fact_list 2 n);
   gen_fact_list i n =
     if i > n then
       nil
     else
       cons (i * (nth (i - 1) fact_list))
            (gen_fact_list (i + 1) n);
   in
     fact_list}
```

Consider how a lazy compiler would compile the internal procedure gen_fact_list. The
best lazy compiler would introduce forces and delays as follows:

```
gen_fact_list i n =
  if i > n then
    nil
  else
    cons (delay (i * (nth (i - 1) fact_list)))
         (delay (gen_fact_list (i + 1) n));
```

Strictness analysis reveals nth strict in all its arguments, and gen_fact_list strict in
i and n. Thus, no delays appear in the calls to these procedures, nor is there need to force
i or n (since all calls to gen_fact_list will evaluate them before the call). The object
code generated would be as follows (in informal "quads" notation):

```
          function gen_fact_list (i, n, fact_list)
          Temp1    := i > n
          if Temp1 goto L1
          Ans      := allocate 2
          Temp2    := ⟨Thunk for Th1 closed over i, fact_list, Ans⟩
          Temp3    := ⟨Thunk for Th2 closed over i, n, Ans⟩
          Ans[1]   := Temp2
          Ans[2]   := Temp3
          return Ans
    L1:    return nil

          function Th1 (i, fact_list, cell)
          Temp1    := i - 1
          Temp2    := call nth(Temp1, fact_list)
          Ans      := i * Temp2
          cell[1] := Ans
          return Ans

          function Th2 (i, n, cell)
          Temp1    := i + 1
          Ans      := call gen_fact_list(Temp1, n)
          cell[2] := Ans
          return Ans
```

This notation omits the details of procedure linkage and thunk representation. We assume that the compiler chooses the best linkage and thunk representation possible (see Section 2.1), but it should be noted that both thunks in this example escape upward, and so require expensive heap-allocated environments.

Now consider generating lenient code for `gen_fact_list`. When we reach the "else" arm of the conditional we know that the values of i and n are available, since they were needed by the predicate. On the other hand, `fact_list` is not available, since its value is computed by `gen_fact_list` and will only be available after it returns. The expression `(i * (nth (i - 1) fact_list))` must be delayed, therefore, but `(gen_fact_list (i + 1) n)` need not.

```
gen_fact_list i n =
  if i > n then
    nil
  else
    cons (delay (i * (nth (i - 1) fact_list)))
         (gen_fact_list (i + 1) n);
```

The object code is as follows:

```
        function gen_fact_list (i, n, fact_list)
        Temp1    := i > n
        if Temp1 goto L1
        Temp2    := i + 1
        Temp3    := call gen_fact_list(Temp2, n)
        Ans      := allocate 2
        Temp4    := ⟨Thunk for Th1 closed over i, fact_list, Ans⟩
        Ans[1]   := Temp4
        Ans[2]   := Temp2
        return Ans
  L1:   return nil

        function Th1 (i, fact_list, cell)
        Temp1    := i - 1
        Temp2    := call nth(Temp1, fact_list)
        Ans      := i * Temp2
        cell[1]  := Ans
        return Ans
```

We see that for this example, lenient evaluation has removed half the overhead needed for lazy evaluation.

3.4   Semantics or Implementation Technique?

We have discussed at length the relative expressive power of strict, lenient, and lazy implementations of functional languages. Our concern with expressive power is mainly for expository reasons. By examining functional programs from which we expect a certain kind of behavior, we can see what an implementation must do to achieve that behavior. We can then capture the behavioral differences in succinct operational terms: lenient implementations add non-strictness to strict implementations, lazy implementations add laziness. The operational notions correspond directly to kinds of expressive power: non-strictness allows more complex data dependences, laziness allows more complex control structure. This view has allowed us to emphasize the distinction between non-strictness and laziness, which heretofore have been considered synonymous in the literature.

But even though strict, lenient, and lazy implementations differ in expressive power, it is not entirely accurate to think of them as having three distinct semantics. More to the point is that there is one semantics for functional languages, which strict, lenient, and lazy implementations implement with varying degrees of faithfulness.[3] So strict, lenient, and lazy evaluation can be thought of as compilation techniques rather than as separate classes of languages, which differ in their approach to subexpression scheduling. Strict compilation bases scheduling on the syntactic call graph, lenient compilation employs an analysis of data dependence to schedule based on availability of data, while lazy compilation schedules

---

[3]Of course, it is always possible to devise a formal semantics which exactly models a given implementation. For example, Stoy [64] gives a semantics for strict lambda calculus through a modification to the standard semantics which artificially "strictifies" all lambda expressions.

based on whether an expression is needed for the final answer. As we have remarked earlier, strict, lenient, and lazy compilation are respectively more faithful to the standard semantics, but also respectively introduce more run-time overhead.

3.5   Compilation as Ordering: Sequential Threads

As we discussed in Chapter 2, existing lazy compilers are based on one of two approaches. Force-and-delay compilers view compilation as introducing force and delay primitives into the program to convert it to strict semantics. Abstract machine compilers try to generate code which emulates the behavior of an abstract graph reduction architecture. As we have seen, both yield approximately equivalent code, but the way in which they go about it is heavily influenced by the basic view they take.

The starting point for the compilation method presented in this book is simply that compilation is a process of choosing the order in which subexpressions will be evaluated. Unlike imperative programs, functional programs do not give any explicit indication of subexpression ordering; this is why they are termed "declarative." But sequential code is by definition ordered, so if sequential code is to be produced from functional programs, the compiler must take ordering decisions. Because this ordering information is not explicit in the source code, the compiler must perform considerable analysis to make these decisions correctly, and in fact most of the compiler technology that is unique to non-strict functional languages is connected with making ordering decisions.

While sequential code demands that ordering decisions be taken at compile time, non-strictness can require that some be deferred until run time. The program in Section 3.1.3 is a good example: the relative ordering of the two statements aa = a + 5 and bb = b + 6 depends on input data, and so the compiler cannot sequentialize them even though they lie outside the conditionals which create the variation according to input. The product of compiling a non-strict program, therefore, will not be a single piece of sequential code but a collection of sequential *threads*.

How can we characterize a sequential thread? Certainly a sequential thread is a segment of sequential code, where the instructions are ordered at compile time. Furthermore, the relative order in which different threads execute is *not* fixed at compile time, but allowed to vary according to input data. Of course, this description could apply as well to code segments between conditional branch instructions in ordinary imperative code, or to code generated for individual procedures and subroutines. The key feature is that sequential threads are generated from program portions that do not have any explicit control transfers between them; the run-time switching between threads is directed only by the communication of values between threads. That is, when an executing thread needs a value that is to be computed by another thread, it must suspend its own execution and allow that other thread to proceed. The hallmark of sequential threads, therefore, is scheduling controlled by *tests to determine whether another subexpression has been evaluated*. Code which consists of sequential threads will always make use of *presence bits* of one sort or another. We will use the term "multi-threaded" to describe object code in which a compiled procedure consists of a collection of sequential threads.

With this definition of threads in mind, the force-and-delay code produced by lazy compilers is easily seen to be a type of multi-threaded code. Each *delay* results in a small piece of sequential code, invoked when some other piece of code needs the value it computes. So thunks are just sequential threads, and removing a *delay* from a subexpression amounts to embedding one thread in another. (These comments apply equally well to abstract machine based compilers.) Seen in this light, strictness analysis and all of the other compilation techniques unique to lazy evaluation are methods of producing as large threads as possible, minimizing the overhead of switching between them.

3.6 Code Generation Options

By taking a view of non-strict compilation as choosing a set of sequential threads for a program, we immediately separate two classes of concern. The first is deciding what set of threads will be produced from a given program. This is primarily a semantic issue, as the threads must give an ordering among subexpressions which correctly implements the meaning of the program according to the semantics. The second concern is how the multi-threaded mechanism is to be implemented on the target architecture. These issues are mostly pragmatic; they include such details as whether presence bits are implemented in hardware or software, whether threads may execute concurrently, how threads are scheduled, *etc.* This separation is not present in existing lazy compilers, because those compilers take as their starting point a particular implementation of multiple threads (either as forces and delays or as abstract machine code) which fixes both the semantics and most of the run-time mechanisms.

In contrast, the bulk of our compilation method deals with sequential threads very abstractly, so that it addresses the semantic issues independent of the implementation mechanisms. As we have suggested in our extensive discussion of lenient evaluation, we will describe how to produce an appropriate set of threads for lenient semantics. Because lenient evaluation captures the notion of non-strictness in isolation from laziness, the exposition of our compilation method will reveal how non-strictness is responsible for most of the difficulty in taking ordering decisions at compile time. In fact, we will show how lazy code may also be produced in our framework, and it will simply turn out to be a further refinement of the threads produced for lenient evaluation. In this sense, our compilation method is neutral toward the issue of lenient vs. lazy evaluation: either option is supported.

Many options also exist in the mechanisms chosen to implement multi-threaded code. We will discuss a number of these, including whether presence bits are in hardware or software, whether concurrency is supported, and whether threads are scheduled eagerly or on demand. All of these choices turn out to be more or less orthogonal, and all may be chosen independently of whether the threads generated implement lenient or lazy semantics (although demand-driven scheduling is required for lazy evaluation).

So we see that lenient evaluation provides not only an alternative semantics to lazy evaluation, but also a completely new perspective on compiling non-strict programming languages. With the motivation and goals of lenient evaluation firmly in mind, we proceed to the theory and practice of lenient compilation.

3.7   A Footnote: Non-Sequentiality

Before proceeding, we should say a word or two about *non-sequential* programming languages and how they relate to our discussion of multi-threaded code. "Sequentiality" has several different meanings, but the most relevant meaning here is Huet-Lévy sequentiality [11], which for our purposes says that when a thread suspends for lack of some value, it can always identify the thread which will produce that value. Without this guarantee, an implementation might have to evaluate many threads simultaneously in order to be sure of evaluating the one which produces the needed value; if it arbitrarily chose one to which to devote its full attention, it might happen to choose a thread which diverges. Of course, actual parallel hardware is not needed, but to implement a non-sequential language there must be at least a *simulation* of parallelism. A well-known example of a non-sequential construct is "parallel OR," a binary function which returns true if one of its arguments is true, even if the other argument fails to terminate. In this book, however, we will only consider functional languages which are sequential in the sense of Huet and Lévy, and so we need not worry about simulating parallelism.

One is tempted to consider the kind of multi-threaded code we have discussed as somehow "non-sequential," since it does not consist of a single sequential thread as is found in most programming language implementations. But, as we have seen, the use of multi-threaded code does not imply non-sequentiality in the sense described above. It is worth noting, however, that compiled code from a non-sequential language *would* likely be multi-threaded.

4   Functional Quads

In Section 1.1 we introduced a small kernel functional language, and in Chapters 2 and 3 we described in general terms how programs are evaluated under strict, lenient, and lazy evaluation. We will now formalize all of this, and describe syntax and semantics very precisely.

The centerpiece of our study is a very minimal functional language which we call "functional quads." Functional quads was designed to meet the following goals:

- It should serve as a model of both lenient and lazy evaluation; hence, it must be non-strict.

- It should have primitive constructs for each of the functional language features normally treated as primitive by functional language implementations. Specifically, its primitive constructs should include scalar types (numbers, booleans, *etc.*), arithmetic and other scalar primitives, conditionals, data structures, first-class functions, and "letrec" recursion. It should also reflect the fact that many implementations can treat "first-order" function calls (a known function applied to all arguments simultaneously) more efficiently than higher-order calls.

- It should be minimal, in the sense that it does not include features which can *and ordinarily would* be implemented in terms of more primitive features.

- It should have a well-defined operational semantics which accurately models the behavior of realistic functional language implementations. Specifically, there must be a natural correspondence between operations in the operational semantics and in a functional language implementation, and the operational semantics should accurately model sharing of computation which takes place in an implementation.

- The language and its operational semantics should have a formal structure which makes it easy to study the relationships between the individual computations which comprise the execution of a program.

We should point out that when we speak of functional language implementations we are of course referring to *compiled* implementations, not interpreters.

The mathematical basis of functional quads is an *abstract reduction system* [33, 43]. In this respect, it is similar to the lambda calculus, and the reader may wonder why we need to introduce a new model of functional computation when the lambda calculus is so well known. The reason is that the lambda calculus fails rather miserably in meeting the second and fourth goals above: in lambda calculus, the *only* primitive constructs are functions and function application, and so the other primitive features mentioned above must be simulated in lambda calculus through the use of functions. Numbers, for example, may be simulated with Church numerals, and recursion through the **Y** combinator [10]. Such simulations are far removed from their typical implementation as machine arithmetic and cyclic references, and furthermore do not have the same sharing properties as in an implementation. There are, of course, many examples in the literature of extensions to lambda calculus to include primitive data types and functions [10, 42], as well as graphical representations which model certain kinds of sharing [69, 75], but these are still somewhat removed from real implementations, and do not share the wide acceptance and plentiful theory of lambda calculus. The fifth goal above would require still another set of extensions to lambda calculus (*e.g.*, Lévy's labeled lambda calculus [45]). In short, since lambda calculus itself does not meet our needs, we are better off constructing a system that meets them exactly. Since we are modeling functional computation, of course, our system will not be very different in spirit from lambda calculus.

Our preoccupation with operational semantics comes about because the questions raised by sequential implementation—namely, in what order machine instructions will execute—are fundamentally operational in nature. Working with an abstract system instead of actual machine code, however, allows us to abstract away unimportant details, including details of how and where memory is allocated, how presence bits are maintained, procedure linkage and environment representation, *etc.* The term "functional quads" is derived by analogy to the quads notation [2] commonly used as an abstraction of imperative code for von Neumann machines, which hides similar details. Our intuition is that functional quads can play as universal a role as sequential quads, serving as the basis for all kinds of functional language compilers, whether for sequential or parallel architectures, with lenient or lazy semantics, for von Neumann, dataflow, or reduction machines.

In the first part of this chapter, we present the syntax and operational semantics of functional quads along with a discussion of how functional languages relate to functional quads and how functional quads relate to sequential code. In the second part, we investigate the theoretical properties of functional quads as an abstract reduction system. Among our results are some very strong assertions about the relationships between computations performed in different executions of the same program, and about the equivalence of intermediate results obtained in different executions. These results in turn expose the parallelism inherent in functional quads and the relationship between lenient and lazy evaluation.

Functional quads and its reduction system was inspired in large part by the rewrite rule operational semantics for Id given by Arvind, Nikhil, and Pingali [7].

4.1   Syntax

The syntax of functional quads is given in Figure 4.1. Some important details:

- The syntactic category *Identifier* is partitioned into an infinite number of sets, each corresponding to a different *arity*. A parenthesized superscript indicates the arity of an identifier; *e.g.*, *Identifier*$^{(2)}$ is an identifier in the arity 2 set. As the grammar for bindings indicates, the arity indicates how many formal parameters are present in an identifier's definition; the arity will affect how identifiers will be rewritten by

Scalar	::=	*Number* | `true` | `false`	
Struct	::=	< *StructTag*$^{(n)}$, $\underbrace{\textit{Identifier}^{(0)} \ldots , \textit{Identifier}^{(0)}}_{n}$ >	$n \geq 0$
Partial	::=	(*Identifier*$^{(n)}$ $\underbrace{\textit{Identifier}^{(0)} \ldots \textit{Identifier}^{(0)}}_{i}$)	$0 \leq i < n$
Value	::=	*Scalar* | *Struct* | *Partial*	
Primary	::=	*Identifier*$^{(0)}$ | *Value*	
Simple	::=	*Primary* | `const` *Value* | *Primary Op Primary* |	
		`if` *Primary* `then` *Block* `else` *Block* |	
		`sel_t_i` *Primary* | `is_t?` *Primary* |	
		Primary Identifier$^{(0)}$	
Op	::=	`+` | `-` | `*` | `/` | `==` | `<` | ...	
Block	::=	{ *Binding* ; *Binding* ; ... `in` *Identifier*$^{(0)}$ }	
Binding	::=	*Identifier*$^{(0)}$ `=` *Simple* |	
		Identifier$^{(n)}$ $\underbrace{\textit{Identifier}^{(0)} \ldots \textit{Identifier}^{(0)}}_{n}$ `=` *Block*	$n \geq 1$
State	::=	*Binding* ; *Binding* ; ...	

- A *State* must also be name-consistent, as defined in the text.

Figure 4.1: Syntax of Functional Quads

the abstract reduction semantics. Arity should not be confused with *type*, which is a semantic property, not a syntactic one.

- Structure tags are also partitioned into sets according to arity, where the arity of a tag indicates the number of components a structure with that tag has. For each n-ary structure tag t there are keywords `sel_t_1`, ..., `sel_t_n`, and `is_t?` which correspond to selectors and a predicate. No special syntax for constructors is needed as the syntax for *Struct* serves this purpose. Structure tags have no connection with identifiers, and are not first class.

- A *State* is a complete program; by convention it should contain a binding for the special identifier $\diamond^{(0)}$, whose value is considered to be the result of the program. Typically, a program will consist of a number of bindings defining functions along with a binding for $\diamond^{(0)}$ which applies one of these functions to some arguments.

Beyond being partitioned according to arity, the syntactic set *Identifier* has a dyadic function *newid* defined over it, which allows the generation of new identifiers from old ones. Specifically, if $A^{(0)}$ and $B^{(i)}$ are identifiers of arity zero and $i \geq 0$, respectively, then $newid(A, B)$ is an identifier of arity i uniquely determined by A and B. There is nothing mathematically unorthodox about this; we are merely asserting that the set *Identifier* has a structure wherein certain members are related to others through the *newid* relation. We will use *newid* when we give the semantics of function application, in which we need new identifiers to construct a copy of the called function, distinguishable from all other calls; through *newid*, each new identifier will be uniquely determined by the caller and the old identifier. Readers interested in the mathematical details of *Identifier* and *newid* may consult the appendix to this chapter (Section 4.9).

The actual syntactic set *State* is a subset of that generated by the grammar in Figure 4.1, for we also require that a state be *name-consistent*. The semantics given in the next section give a "letrec" interpretation to the syntactic sets *Block* and *State*; name-consistency is simply a group of restrictions on identifiers to make sure that scoping rules are properly obeyed and preserved by the semantics. A state is name-consistent if it satisfies these three conditions:

1. All identifiers are defined in scope, that is, any identifier appearing on the right hand side of a binding must also appear on the left hand side of some binding in an enclosing block or in the state.

2. All identifiers appearing on left hand sides are pairwise distinct. We really mean *all* left hand side identifiers: a left hand side identifier, no matter how deeply nested in blocks it appears, must be distinct from every other left hand side identifier, whether in the same block, an enclosing block, an enclosed block, or a non-overlapping block. For the purposes of this rule, "left hand side identifier" also includes formal parameters.

3. If a state or block contains a binding of the form

$$x = Primary\ Identifier;$$

   then no other left hand side anywhere in the state, no matter how deeply nested, contains an identifier that is $newid(newid(\ldots newid(x, y_n) \ldots, y_2), y_1)$ for any $y_1, \ldots, y_n$ and $n > 0$.

Condition (1) above requires that any identifier used in an expression have an associated definition, while conditions (2) and (3) make sure that there are no multiple definitions. (The motive for condition (3) will become apparent when we discuss the semantics of function calls in the next section.) For the sake of simplicity, the latter two conditions are actually a bit more stringent than is necessary to make everything work out; this is inconsequential since the conditions only affect the choice of identifiers, which in any event is arbitrary as far as the meaning of the program is concerned.

To illustrate functional quads, here is a definition for factorial, expressed in Section 1.1's kernel language and in functional quads:

Kernel Language	Functional Quads

```
        Kernel Language                          Functional Quads

fact x =                                fact⁽¹⁾ x⁽⁰⁾ =
  if x <= 0 then                          {p⁽⁰⁾ = x⁽⁰⁾ <= 0;
    1                                      res⁽⁰⁾ =
  else                                       if p⁽⁰⁾ then
    x * (fact (x - 1));                         {in 1}
                                             else
                                               {xx⁽⁰⁾ = x⁽⁰⁾ - 1;
                                                fxx⁽⁰⁾ = (fact⁽¹⁾) xx⁽⁰⁾;
                                                xfxx⁽⁰⁾ = x⁽⁰⁾ * fxx⁽⁰⁾;
                                                in
                                                   xfxx⁽⁰⁾};
                                           in
                                             res⁽⁰⁾};
```

The functional quads program translates the kernel as:

$$\text{fact}^{(1)}\ x^{(0)} =$$
$$\{p^{(0)} = x^{(0)} \leq 0;$$
$$\text{res}^{(0)} =$$
$$\quad \text{if } p^{(0)} \text{ then}$$
$$\quad\quad \{\text{in } 1\}$$
$$\quad \text{else}$$
$$\quad\quad \{xx^{(0)} = x^{(0)} - 1;$$
$$\quad\quad fxx^{(0)} = (\text{fact}^{(1)})\ xx^{(0)};$$
$$\quad\quad xfxx^{(0)} = x^{(0)} * fxx^{(0)};$$
$$\quad\quad \text{in}$$
$$\quad\quad\quad xfxx^{(0)}\};$$
$$\text{in}$$
$$\quad \text{res}^{(0)}\};$$

A functional quads program to compute the factorial of five, therefore, would be:

$$\Diamond^{(0)} = \text{fact}^{(1)}\ 5;\ \text{fact}^{(1)}\ x^{(0)} = \{\ldots\};$$

In general, we can easily translate a kernel program into functional quads by flattening blocks where they do not belong, introducing new ones where they are required, and introducing new identifiers for unnamed subexpressions; we discuss this in more detail in Section 4.4.

Since the arity of an identifier can be inferred by looking at the binding which defines it, we will henceforth omit most arity superscripts. The origin of the name "functional quads" should be clear: the restricted syntax for expressions gives programs an appearance akin to the sequential quads notation used to describe sequential object code, where each line describes a single computation. It should be emphasized, however, that unlike sequential quads there is no significance to the *order* of bindings in functional quads; we discuss this further in Section 4.5.

4.2   Semantics

We give the semantics of functional quads operationally, as an abstract reduction system [33, 43].

Definition 4.1 *An* abstract reduction system (ARS) *is a structure* $\langle \Sigma, \vdash \rangle$ *consisting of a set* Σ *and a binary relation* $\vdash$ *on* Σ.

For our purposes, Σ is the set of all name-consistent states and $\vdash$ is the *one-step reduction* relation, to be defined below. The idea is that $a \vdash b$ if b is the state obtained from performing one step of evaluation on a. We will define $\vdash$ in such a way that "one step" of evaluation will be the application of a primitive, or the selection of a conditional, or the application of a function, or the substitution of a value.

We define $\vdash$ through *rewrite rules*, which concisely describe the pairs of states such that $a \vdash b$. For example, there is the following rewrite rule:

$$x = y; \ y = V \implies x = V; \ y = V$$

Each binding on the left hand side of the rule is to be matched against a separate binding of a state a. If such a match is found, then $a \vdash b$ where b is the state constructed by replacing the matched bindings of a with the bindings given by the right hand side of the rule. The bindings which match the left hand side need not appear in the same order as in the rule, nor need they be consecutive, and the bindings which replace them may be added to the state in any order and at any position. For example, the rule above implies that among other pairs, $\vdash$ holds for the following pairs of states:

$$\Diamond = i; \ j = i + 5; \ i = 3; \ \vdash \ \Diamond = 3; \ i = 3; \ j = i + 5;$$

Here we have matched $\Diamond$ with x, i with y, and 3 with V.

Below we present the complete set of rewrite rules, with explanations. Throughout, V denotes any value, $x^{(0)}$, $y^{(0)}$, and $z^{(0)}$ any identifier of arity 0 (omitting the superscript when apparent from context), $f^{(n)}$ any identifier of arity $n > 0$, P any primary, and B any binding.

$$x = y; \ y = V; \implies x = V; \ y = V; \tag{R1a}$$

$$x = y \ Op \ P; \ y = V; \implies x = V \ Op \ P; \ y = V; \tag{R1b}$$

$$x = P \ Op \ y; \ y = V; \implies x = P \ Op \ V; \ y = V; \tag{R1c}$$

$$x = \text{if } y \text{ then } \{\ldots\} \text{ else } \{\ldots\}; \implies x = \text{if } V \text{ then } \{\ldots\} \text{ else } \{\ldots\}; \atop y = V; \tag{R1d}$$

$$x = \text{sel\_t\_i } y; \ y = V; \implies x = \text{sel\_t\_i } V; \ y = V; \tag{R1e}$$

$$x = \text{is\_t? } y; \ y = V; \implies x = \text{is\_t? } V; \ y = V; \tag{R1f}$$

$$x = y \ z; \ y = V \implies x = V \ z; \ y = V \tag{R1g}$$

Collectively, these rules allow an identifier to be substituted by the value to which it is bound, for all contexts in which the grammar allows a *Primary* in an expression. Because only values are substituted, the computation which reduces an identifier to a value is shared among all references to that identifier. The choice of when *Primary* appears in the grammar as opposed to *Identifier*$^{(0)}$, and therefore the choice of substitution rules, is carefully based on semantic grounds, as we discuss in Section 4.5.

$$x = \text{const } V \implies x = V \tag{R2}$$

The const statement and this rewrite rule do not give functional quads any additional expressive or computational power, but are included as a technical convenience. It allows initial states to be restricted from having bindings of the form $x = V$.

$$x = \text{if true then } \{B_{t,1}; \ldots; B_{t,n} \text{ in } y_t\} \text{ else } \{\ldots\}; \quad \Longrightarrow \quad \begin{array}{l} x = y_t; \\ B_{t,1}; \ldots; B_{t,n}; \end{array} \tag{R3}$$

There is also an analogous rule for if false .... After execution of this rule, the selected arm becomes part of the state, and so its bindings become subject to execution. The identifiers bound in the new bindings added to the state cannot conflict with bindings already there, because of the pairwise distinctness aspect of name-consistency.

$$x = V_1 + V_2; \quad \Longrightarrow \quad x = V_3; \tag{R4}$$

where $V_3 = V_1 + V_2$. There are similar rules for -, *, >=, *etc.*

$$x = \text{sel}\_t\_i \ <t, y_1, \ldots, y_i, \ldots, y_n>; \quad \Longrightarrow \quad x = y_i; \tag{R5}$$

$$x = \text{is}\_t? \ <t, y_1, \ldots, y_n>; \quad \Longrightarrow \quad x = \text{true}; \tag{R6a}$$

$$x = \text{is}\_t? \ V; \quad \Longrightarrow \quad x = \text{false}; \tag{R6b}$$

for any V which is not a *Struct* with tag t.

$$x = (f^{(n)} \ y_1 \ \ldots \ y_{i-1}) \ y_i; \quad \Longrightarrow \quad x = (f^{(n)} \ y_1 \ \ldots \ y_{i-1} \ y_i); \tag{R7}$$

where $1 \le i < n$.

$$\begin{array}{l} x = (f^{(n)} \ z_1 \ \ldots \ z_{n-1}) \ z_n; \\ f^{(n)} \ y_1 \ \ldots \ y_n = \{B_{f1}; \ldots; B_{fm} \text{ in } z_f\}; \end{array} \quad \Longrightarrow \quad \begin{array}{l} x = z'_f; \\ f^{(n)} \ y_1 \ \ldots \ y_n = \{\ldots\}; \\ B'_{f1}; \ldots B'_{fm}; \\ y'_1 = z_1; \ldots; y'_n = z_n; \end{array} \tag{R8}$$

where the primes indicate consistent α-renaming of all identifiers appearing on left hand sides within the body of $f^{(n)}$, together with the formals, such that they are given unique names not appearing anywhere else in the state. (By "all identifiers appearing on left hand sides" we are including formals of internal definitions and the binding lists of all enclosed blocks, so that the only identifiers unaffected by the renaming are free variables of the function f.) The choice of α-renaming is not arbitrary: for each identifier $y^{(i)}$ that is to be renamed, it is renamed to $newid(x, y^{(i)})$ (where x is the same x as in the statement of the rule). In this way, we preserve a connection between the caller and the new computation added to the state. (We point out that condition (3) of name-consistency (page 35) insures that the new bindings added to the state by this rule do not conflict with any already present.)

As an exercise, we invite the reader to verify that name-consistency is preserved by all of the rules above.

All of these rules have the effect of replacing all or part of an expression which occurs on the right hand side of a binding. In this way, this abstract reduction system bears a strong resemblance to a term rewriting system, except that while the replacements in a term rewriting system are context-free, in this system a replacement depends upon other components of the state. In a term rewriting system, the subexpression that is replaced is called a *redex*, and we will adopt that terminology to refer to the portion of the state which changes; in Rules R1a through R1g, the redex is the occurrence of y on the right hand side of the binding for x, while in Rules R2 through R8 the redex is the entire right hand side of the binding for x. We will sometimes use the notation $x \vdash_\alpha y$ to indicate that a particular redex α within x is rewritten to arrive at state y (a notion we will formalize in Section 4.6).

Executing a program is modeled by the abstract reduction system as successive application of rewrite rules to an initial state until no more rewriting is possible. Here is an example, in which the selected redex is underlined at each step (note that this is just one of many possible reduction sequences from this initial state):

```
◊ = sel_cons_1 b; b = (f) a; a = 3 + 4; f x = {y = <cons,x,y>; in y};
⊢
◊ = sel_cons_1 b; b = yy; a = 3 + 4; f x = {...}; yy = <cons,xx,yy>; xx = a;
⊢
◊ = sel_cons_1 b; b = <cons,xx,yy>; a = 3 + 4; f x = {...}; yy = ...; ...
⊢
◊ = sel_cons_1 <cons,xx,yy>; b = <cons,xx,yy>; a = 3 + 4; f x = {...}; ...
⊢
◊ = xx; b = <cons,xx,yy>; a = 3 + 4; f x = {...}; yy = <cons,xx,yy>; xx = a;
⊢
◊ = xx; b = <cons,xx,yy>; a = 7; f x = {...}; yy = <cons,xx,yy>; xx = a;
⊢
◊ = xx; b = <cons,xx,yy>; a = 7; f x = {...}; yy = <cons,xx,yy>; xx = 7;
⊢
◊ = 7; b = <cons,xx,yy>; a = 7; f x = {...}; yy = <cons,xx,yy>; xx = 7;
```

Here we have implicitly assumed that $newid(\mathtt{b}, \mathtt{x}) = \mathtt{xx}$ and $newid(\mathtt{b}, \mathtt{y}) = \mathtt{yy}$. Notice that the call to procedure f is executed before the argument a is reduced to a value, illustrating how the use of identifiers in functional quads models non-strictness. Data structures are non-strict because they are considered values even though they contain identifiers whose values have not yet been computed. Similarly, rules R7 and R8 make functions non-strict because they apply even when the arguments to functions are non-value identifiers.

By saying that the elements of Σ in the ARS $\langle \Sigma, \vdash \rangle$ are states, we are actually glossing over a minor technical point. In our description of rewrite rules, we noted that the order in which bindings appeared in the state is immaterial, and similarly there was complete freedom in how new bindings were added to the state. If a state a has a different ordering of its bindings but is otherwise syntactically equal to another state b, then a and b are indistinguishable as far as the reduction relation $\vdash$ is concerned, and we should really consider them to be identically the same. To be extremely precise, then, we should say that each element of Σ is not a state but an equivalence class of states which are syntactically equal but for permutation of the state bindings, and when we write something like

$$\Diamond = \mathtt{i}; \mathtt{j} = \mathtt{i} + 5; \mathtt{i} = 3; \quad \vdash \quad \Diamond = 3; \mathtt{i} = 3; \mathtt{j} = \mathtt{i} + 5;$$

it is tacitly understood that the states on either side of the $\vdash$ symbol are just representatives from their respective equivalence classes. This said, we shall henceforth disregard it entirely, and simply ignore the order in which state bindings happen to be written.[1] Many readers will recognize that a similar equivalence class argument crops up in lambda calculus, where $\lambda a.a$ and $\lambda b.b$ are considered the *same* lambda expression even though they are syntactically different (see [10], Appendix C). On the other hand, in functional quads we shall *not* use this sort of equivalence class argument to deal with the issue of α-renaming, hence the states $\Diamond$ = a; a = 5; and $\Diamond$ = b; b = 5; are *different* states. Our use of *newid* obviates the need for such equivalence.

4.3 Additional Functional Quads Examples

A firm understanding of the functional quads reduction system is necessary to understand the remaining technical material in this book. To assist the reader, we highlight some subtle aspects of the system with more examples.

4.3.1 Name Consistency

The name-consistency rules given on page 35 constrain the choice of identifiers in functional quads programs, so that the semantics are sound.

The first name-consistency condition is that all identifiers are defined in scope. For example, the following state is *not* name-consistent, because a and b are not bound in the scope of their use as operands to + in the first binding:

```
◇ = a + b;
p = 2 < 3;
c = if p then {a = 5 + 6; in a} else {...};
f x = {b = x * 5; d = b + b; in d};
```

On the other hand, the following state *is* name-consistent; the use of a and b are in scope.

```
◇ = c + d;
a = 2 * 3;
b = 5 * 6;
p = a < b;
c = if p then {u = a * b; in u} else {...};
f x = {v = a / b; w = v - x; in w};
```

The second name-consistency condition says that all identifiers on left hand sides of bindings must be pairwise distinct, no matter how deeply nested each appears. This is stronger than merely requiring that identifiers defined in the same scope must be distinct. For example, the following state is *not* name-consistent, because a is defined twice:

```
◇ = i + j;
p = 2 < 3;
i = if p then {a = 2 * 3; in a} else {...};
j = if p then {a = 4 * 5; in a} else {...};
```

---

[1] We could, if we liked, extend this equivalence over permutation to the bindings of other blocks contained within a state, but there is no reason to for the purposes of our theory.

and the following state is *not* name-consistent, because i, a, b, and f are all defined twice:

```
◇ = i + j;
p = 2 < 3;
i = if p then
        {a = (f⁽¹⁾) 3;
         b = if p then {a = 5 * 6 in a} else {...};
         f⁽¹⁾ b = {i = b * 5; in b};
         in b}
      else {...};
f⁽¹⁾ e = i * e;
j = f + 6;
```

The third name-consistency condition insures that function application (reduction via the R8 rule) does not introduce multiple definitions. For example, assuming $newid(x, a) = xa$, the following state is *not* name consistent:

```
◇ = x + xa;
xa = 2 * 3;
x = (f) 5;
f z = {a = z * 8; in a};
```

If the R8 rule were applied to the state above, the following state would result (also assuming $newid(x, z) = xz$):

```
◇ = x + xa;
xa = 2 * 3;
x = xa;
xz = 5;
xa = xz * 8;
f z = {a = z * 8; in a};
```

which has a multiple definition of xa.

4.3.2   Only the State Contains Redexes

The meaning of the rewrite rule notation is that the left hand side of each rule must match a binding in the state. Inner blocks may contain bindings that look like redexes, but in fact they are not. For example, in the following state:

```
◇ = (f) i;
p = 2 < 3;
i = if p then {a = 3 * 4; in a} else {...};
f x = {b = 5 * 6; c = x + b; in c};
```

there are only two redexes: an R8 redex in the binding for ◇, and an R4 redex in the binding for p. The bindings for a and b do not contain redexes, because they are not in the state. On the other hand, after a few steps of reduction the conditional will have been reduced via the R3 rule:

```
◇ = (f) i;
p = true;
i = a;
a = 3 * 4;
f x = {b = 5 * 6; c = x + b; in c};
```

at which point the binding for a *does* contain a redex. Similarly, the function will be applied after the R8 rule is applied to the binding for ◇:

```
◇ = cc;
bb = 5 * 6;
cc = xx + bb;
xx = i;
p = true;
i = a;
a = 3 * 4;
f x = {b = 5 * 6; c = x + b; in c};
```

(Here we assume $newid(◇, \mathbf{x}) = \mathbf{xx}$, $newid(◇, \mathbf{b}) = \mathbf{bb}$, and $newid(◇, \mathbf{c}) = \mathbf{cc}$.) Now the binding for bb contains a redex, although the binding for b still does not.

The previous example also demonstrates how *newid* is used only in reducing function applications, not conditionals.

4.3.3 Nested Functions

The rewrite rules have been constructed so that nested functions (functions defined in the bodies of other functions) are properly modeled, even if such functions refer to identifiers in enclosing scopes. The following example illustrates how free variables are handled, as well as "upward" functions.

```
f x = {z = x + 10;
       g⁽¹⁾ y = {u = y + z; in u};
       r = const (g⁽¹⁾);
       in r};
a = (f) 4;
b = (f) 5;
c = a 6;
d = b 7;
◇ = c + d;
```

Notice that the inner function g refers to z, defined in the enclosing scope. Notice, too, that the function g is returned "upward" from f, even though it refers to f's formal parameter (indirectly, through z).

Reduction of the R8 redex in the binding for a yields the following state (in the remainder of this example, the results of *newid* are indicated by concatenation; *e.g.*, $newid(\mathbf{a}, \mathbf{r}) = \mathbf{ar}$):

```
f x = {...};
a = ar;
ax = 4;
az = ax + 10;
```
$ag^{(1)}$ `ay = {au = ay + az; in au};`
```
ar = const (ag⁽¹⁾);
b = (f) 5;
c = a 6;
d = b 7;
◇ = c + d;
```

Next, reduction of the R8 redex in the binding for b yields:

```
f x = {...};
a = ar;
ax = 4;
az = ax + 10;
ag⁽¹⁾ ay = {au = ay + az; in au};
ar = const (ag⁽¹⁾);
b = br;
bx = 4;
bz = bx + 10;
bg⁽¹⁾ by = {bu = by + bz; in bu};
br = const (bg⁽¹⁾);
c = a 6;
d = b 7;
◇ = c + d;
```

Notice how there are two new, distinct, copies of g in the state, ag and bg.

After applying the R2 rule to the bindings for ar and br, the R1a rule to the bindings for a and b, and the R1g substitution rule to the bindings for c and d, the state looks like this:

```
f x = {...};
a = (ag⁽¹⁾);
ax = 4;
az = ax + 10;
ag⁽¹⁾ ay = {au = ay + az; in au};
ar = (ag⁽¹⁾);
b = (bg⁽¹⁾);
bx = 4;
bz = bx + 10;
bg⁽¹⁾ by = {bu = by + bz; in bu};
br = (bg⁽¹⁾);
c = (ag⁽¹⁾) 6;
d = (bg⁽¹⁾) 7;
◇ = c + d;
```

Now the R8 rule can be applied to the binding for c. Recall that the R8 rule states that only formals and identifiers defined within the function body are to be renamed. After applying the rule:

```
f x = {...};
a = (ag⁽¹⁾);
ax = 4;
az = ax + 10;
ag⁽¹⁾ ay = {au = ay + az; in au};
ar = (ag⁽¹⁾);
b = (bg⁽¹⁾);
bx = 4;
bz = bx + 10;
bg⁽¹⁾ by = {bu = by + bz; in bu};
br = (bg⁽¹⁾);
c = cau;
cay = 6;
cau = cay + az;
d = (bg⁽¹⁾) 7;
◇ = c + d;
```

Notice that az did *not* get renamed, as it was a free variable of ag. All calls to ag (*i.e.*, all calls to a's value in the original state) would share the computation of az. On the other hand, az is distinct from bz, which is the version of z resulting from the other call to f.

This example shows how functional quads properly models sharing in the presence of nested function definitions, without the need for lambda lifting or a similar transformation.

4.4   From a Functional Language to Functional Quads

We have given functional quads a syntax similar to that of the kernel language we introduced in Section 1.1, and so it may appear that the relationship between the two is no more deep than concrete syntax. In fact, the conversion from a functional language to functional quads should be considered a process of compilation: a functional language and functional quads each have their own well-defined semantics, and so the translation from one to the other is a matter of achieving in the functional quads semantics the meaning of the original functional language program. This translation may be straightforward or not, depending on how closely the two semantics match.

In describing the kernel language in Section 1.1 and in using it in examples (Chapter 3), we intentionally assumed a semantics that mirrors the semantics of functional quads. Translating from that particular kernel language to functional quads, therefore, is mostly a matter of introducing identifiers and blocks to conform to the restricted syntax of functional quads. The following translation schema $\mathcal{Q}$ translates a kernel language definition into a functional quads definition by adding identifiers. We assume that the kernel program has already been α-renamed so that each identifier is uniquely defined, and we use T to denote a new unique identifier and the symbol § to denote concatenation of bindings:

$$\mathcal{Q}[\![f \; y_1 \; \cdots \; y_n = E]\!] \; = \; f \; y_1 \; \cdots \; y_n = \{\mathcal{Q}[\![T_1 = E]\!] \; \text{in} \; T_1\}$$

$$\mathcal{Q}[\![x = C]\!] = x = C$$
$$\mathcal{Q}[\![x = f]\!] = x = (f^{(n)})$$
$$\mathcal{Q}[\![x = y]\!] = x = y^{(0)}$$
$$\mathcal{Q}[\![x = E_1 \; Op \; E_2]\!] = \mathcal{Q}[\![T_1 = E_1]\!] \, \S \, \mathcal{Q}[\![T_2 = E_2]\!] \, \S \, x = T_1 \; Op \; T_2$$
$$\mathcal{Q}[\![x = \texttt{if} \; E_1 \; \texttt{then} \; E_2 \; \texttt{else} \; E_3]\!] = \mathcal{Q}[\![T_1 = E_1]\!] \, \S$$
$$x = \texttt{if} \; T_1 \; \texttt{then} \; \{\mathcal{Q}[\![T_2 = E_2]\!] \; \texttt{in} \; T_2\}$$
$$\texttt{else} \; \{\mathcal{Q}[\![T_3 = E_3]\!] \; \texttt{in} \; T_3\}$$
$$\mathcal{Q}[\![x = \texttt{make}\_t \; E_1 \; \ldots \; E_n]\!] = \mathcal{Q}[\![T_1 = E_1]\!] \, \S \cdots \S \, \mathcal{Q}[\![T_n = E_n]\!] \, \S$$
$$x = \langle t, T_1, \ldots, T_n \rangle$$
$$\mathcal{Q}[\![x = \texttt{sel}\_t\_i \; E]\!] = \mathcal{Q}[\![T_1 = E]\!] \, \S \, x = \texttt{sel}\_t\_i \; T_1$$
$$\mathcal{Q}[\![x = \texttt{is}\_t? \; E]\!] = \mathcal{Q}[\![T_1 = E]\!] \, \S \, x = \texttt{is}\_t? \; T_1$$
$$\mathcal{Q}[\![x = E_1 \; E_2]\!] = \mathcal{Q}[\![T_1 = E_1]\!] \, \S \, \mathcal{Q}[\![T_2 = E_2]\!] \, \S \, x = T_1 \; T_2$$
$$\mathcal{Q}[\![x = \{B_1; \ldots; B_n \; \texttt{in} \; E\}]\!] = \mathcal{Q}[\![B_1]\!] \, \S \cdots \S \, \mathcal{Q}[\![B_n]\!] \, \S \, \mathcal{Q}[\![x = E]\!]$$

This is by no means the best translation possible. For example, extra identifiers are introduced if the original program contains a binding like a = b + c; this is easily corrected by adding some more rules to the translation. There are, however, some other choices facing the designer of a translation that are much less trivial in nature.

Some choices amount to source-to-source optimizations. A good example is common subexpression elimination: if two identifiers in the same block are bound to the same expression, one can be eliminated (and the references to it suitably renamed). Another important optimization is "fetch elimination" [67], which bypasses a fetch from a data structure when the value stored there can be identified. An example:

```
   ...                                ...
   a = <tuple,x,y>;                   a = <tuple,x,y>;
   b = sel_tuple_1 a;      ⟶          b = x;
   ...                                ...
```

This optimization is particularly important when tuples are used as a substitute for multiple values. For a discussion of other traditional compiler optimizations in a functional setting, see [67] and [60].

Other choices in the translation to functional quads try to match the functional quads program to the capabilities and/or requirements of the compilation phases which follow. For example, an implementation may be able to compile better procedure calls when a known function is applied to all arguments. Thus, we would want to add a statement:

$$\mathcal{Q}[\![x = f \; E_1 \; \ldots \; E_n]\!] = \mathcal{Q}[\![T_1 = E_1]\!] \, \S \cdots \S \, \mathcal{Q}[\![T_n = E_n]\!] \, \S$$
$$x = (f^{(n)} \; T_1 \; \ldots T_{n-1}) \; T_n$$

so that a single first-order application statement is generated instead of n partial application statements. Another implementation-dependent transformation is the promotion of

45

internal definitions to top-level via *lambda lifting* [38]; this may be required if an implementation has no primitive way of dealing with internal definitions.

Still other choices affect the sharing and/or scheduling of computation. It is possible, for instance, to achieve greater sharing in some situations by performing *mfe abstraction* [34]. Another option involves the scheduling of computation in conditionals. The translation schema above enforces the property that code within an arm of a conditional is not evaluated until the predicate becomes a value. If "eager" conditionals are desired, however, an alternate translation of conditionals can be used:

$$\mathcal{Q}[\![x \text{ = if } E_1 \text{ then } E_2 \text{ else } E_3]\!] = \mathcal{Q}[\![T_1 \text{ = } E_1]\!] \S \mathcal{Q}[\![T_2 \text{ = } E_2]\!] \S \mathcal{Q}[\![T_3 \text{ = } E_3]\!] \S$$
$$x \text{ = if } T_1 \text{ then } \{\text{in } T_2\} \text{ else } \{\text{in } T_3\}$$

To summarize, functional quads has a particular semantics, which the translation from the functional source language must take into account. All of the decisions related to assigning meaning to source language constructs are encoded into the functional quads for a program, and so our task in describing the generation of sequential code is limited to faithfully implementing the operational semantics given for functional quads.

4.5   Functional Quads vs. Sequential Quads

Functional quads has been carefully designed so that its computation steps correspond closely with computation steps in the familiar sequential quads which model sequential object code. In the previous section we saw how functional languages can be translated into functional quads, and that this is fairly straightforward if the original language's semantics are similar to that of functional quads (most importantly, if the original language is non-strict). The translation from sequential quads into target code is well-known von Neumann compiler technology, involving register allocation, procedure linkage optimization, *etc.* The only difference between functional and sequential quads is that in functional quads the ordering of subexpressions and delaying of computation is implicit, but in sequential quads it is explicit. As we discussed in Chapter 3, the heart of functional language compilation lies precisely in determining the ordering of subexpression evaluation and in deciding what to delay, so the meat of a functional language compiler is concentrated into the translation from functional quads to sequential quads.

For example, here is a functional quads fragment:

```
...; x = 2 * 3; z = x + y; y = 4 * 5; ...
```

Each binding can be directly translated into a sequential quads statement, but in addition we must choose their relative ordering. One possible translation is this fragment:

```
...
y := 4 * 5
x := 2 * 3
z := x + y
...
```

Another possible translation would interchange the first two statements. Correctness of a functional quads to sequential quads translation requires the statement ordering chosen to be consistent with a possible reduction sequence of the original functional quads program. The sequence above, for example, is consistent with the following reduction sequence:

$$\ldots;\ x = 2 * 3;\ z = x + y;\ y = \underline{4 * 5};\ \ldots$$

$\vdash$

$$\ldots;\ x = \underline{2 * 3};\ z = x + y;\ y = 20;\ \ldots$$

$\vdash$

$$\ldots;\ x = 6;\ z = \underline{x} + y;\ y \doteq 20;\ \ldots$$

$\vdash$

$$\ldots;\ x = 6;\ z = 6 + \underline{y};\ y = 20;\ \ldots$$

$\vdash$

$$\ldots;\ x = 6;\ z = \underline{6 + 20};\ y = 20;\ \ldots$$

$\vdash$

$$\ldots;\ x = 6;\ z = 26;\ y = 20;\ \ldots$$

There is a one-to-one correspondence between expressions in a functional quads program and its sequential quads counterpart, and also between variables. Furthermore, executing a sequential quads statement is modeled in functional quads as the reduction of some substitution rules (R1a through R1g) followed by a computational rule (R2 through R8). Above, for example, the sequential quads statement z := x + y was modeled by the third, fourth, and fifth reductions in the functional quads sequence. We can examine the sequential quads statement at a finer level, however, and note that it is really composed of two operand fetches and an addition—and each of these has an exact counterpart in functional quads. This explains why substitution was limited to the seven cases covered by rules R1a through R1g: they cover the cases where the corresponding sequential quads must fetch from the corresponding variable. If other substitution rules were added to functional quads, they would not correspond to any movement of data in the corresponding sequential quads program, and could lead to infinite sequences of such vacuous reductions. For example, if a substitution rule were added which allowed substitution for a variable appearing within a data structure, a cyclic structure could lead to the following infinite reduction sequence:

$$a = \text{<cons,a,b>} \overset{?}{\vdash} a = \text{<cons,<cons,a,b>,b>} \overset{?}{\vdash}$$
$$a = \text{<cons,<cons,<cons,a,b>,b>,b>} \overset{?}{\vdash} \ldots$$

This reduction sequence does not correspond to any sequence of computations that would take place in an actual implementation.

The technique of translating functional quads into sequential quads is taken up in the four chapters that follow. In the remainder of this chapter, we establish some mathematical properties of the functional quads reduction system, which form the foundation of our compilation method.

4.6 Mathematical Properties of Reduction

We now formalize some of the concepts we introduced in Section 4.2. The following two definitions are standard [43]:

Definition 4.2 *A normal form of an abstract reduction system $\langle \Sigma, \vdash \rangle$ is an $a \in \Sigma$ such that there is no $b \in \Sigma$ for which $a \vdash b$.*

Definition 4.3 *A reduction sequence in an ARS $\langle \Sigma, \vdash \rangle$ is a sequence of elements from Σ $a_0, a_1, \ldots$ such that $a_i \vdash a_{i+1}$, $i \geq 0$. A terminating reduction sequence of length n is a finite reduction sequence $a_0, \ldots, a_n$ such that a_n is a normal form.*

We also wish to formalize the notion of identifying a particular redex within a state.

Definition 4.4 *A redex specifier for functional quads is a pair $\alpha = \langle x, \rho \rangle$ where x is an identifier of arity zero and ρ is the name of a rewrite rule (an element of the set $\{R1a, R1b, \ldots, R8\}$). A redex $\alpha = \langle x, \rho \rangle$ exists in a state S_0 if S_0 contains a binding of the form $x = E$ which matches rewrite rule ρ (perhaps together with other bindings from S_0, depending on the rule). If a redex α exists in a state S_0, then $S_0 \vdash_\alpha S_1$ where S_1 is the state obtained from applying the specified rule to the specified redex.*

A redex specifier can denote at most one redex in a given state because name-consistency guarantees the uniqueness of identifiers bound in a state.

All of the theory we will develop in the framework of functional quads depends on the following three properties of the functional quads reduction system (the names of these properties are not standard):

Property 4.5 (Commutivity) *Let α and β be distinct redexes in a, and let b and c be such that $a \vdash_\alpha b$ and $a \vdash_\beta c$. Then there exists d such that $b \vdash_\beta d$ and $c \vdash_\alpha d$.*

This property says that given two redexes, rewriting them consecutively yields equivalent results regardless of order. This very strong property implies, among other things, confluence (the Church-Rosser property) and that all reduction sequences to normal form are of equal length.[2]

Property 4.6 (Redex Uniqueness) *Let α be a redex in a. If $a \vdash_\alpha b$, then there is no c such that $b \vdash^* c$ and α exists in c.*

In other words, the same redex (where "same" means having the same reduction specifier α) cannot be reduced twice. This implies that the redex specifiers defined above are adequate to identify a particular step in a reduction sequence.

Property 4.7 (Strong Dependence) *For all a, b, c, d such that $a \vdash^* b \vdash_\alpha c \vdash_\beta d$, if β does not exist in b then α is reduced before β in every reduction sequence that begins with a and includes β.*

---

[2] A weaker version of this property which does not identify the redexes α and β is called the *Diamond Property* [10], or WCR^1 [43].

48

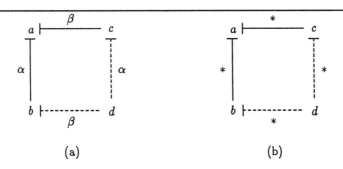

This says that if the reduction of a redex α introduces a new redex β in some reduction sequence, then reduction of α is a necessary precondition for the creation of β in any reduction sequence.

As we mentioned, the commutivity property implies confluence, which in turn implies that normal forms are unique, an important property indeed if functional quads is to be a model of computation. Adding the redex uniqueness property will allow us to show that in every reduction sequence of a given program to normal form (indeed, to any arbitrary derivable form) the same set of redexes are reduced. We will not make use of the strong dependence property until Chapter 6, where it will allow us to infer sufficient constraints upon the order in which redexes are reduced from a consideration of all possible orderings.

In the remainder of this section we prove that functional quads has each of the three properties above, and also prove some results that follow from the properties.

Theorem 4.8 (Figure 4.2a) *Functional quads has the Commutivity property.*

Proof. Let $\alpha = \langle x_\alpha, \rho_\alpha \rangle$ and $\beta = \langle x_\beta, \rho_\beta \rangle$. We consider two cases depending on whether $x_\alpha = x_\beta$:

Case 1 ($x_\alpha \neq x_\beta$). If $a \vdash_\alpha b$, the only way b differs from a is that new bindings may have been added and that the right hand side of x_α's binding will have changed. Now the redex β is completely unaffected by this, since the binding for x_β is unchanged, as are any other bindings involved in reducing β (such as $y = V$; or $f\ y_1\ \ldots\ y_n = \{\ldots\}$;, which cannot contain redexes and are therefore not affected by α). So β exists in b, and reducing it in b makes the same changes to the state as reducing it in a. By symmetry, α exists in c (where $a \vdash_\beta c$), and reducing it in c makes the same changes as reducing it in a. The net changes made to the state by reducing both α and β are independent of the order in which they are performed, and so $b \vdash_\beta d$ and $c \vdash_\alpha d$.

Case 2 ($x_\alpha = x_\beta$) In this case, it must be that $\rho_\alpha = $ R1b and $\rho_\beta = $ R1c (or vice versa), and the same argument about non-interference in Case 1 applies. ∎

Another way of looking at it is that reducing a redex never duplicates an existing redex, nor does it remove any redex other than the one reduced. We are also depending on the way new identifiers are introduced by Rule R8; the use of *newid* insures that they are created in a way which does not depend on the relative order in which various R8 redexes are reduced.

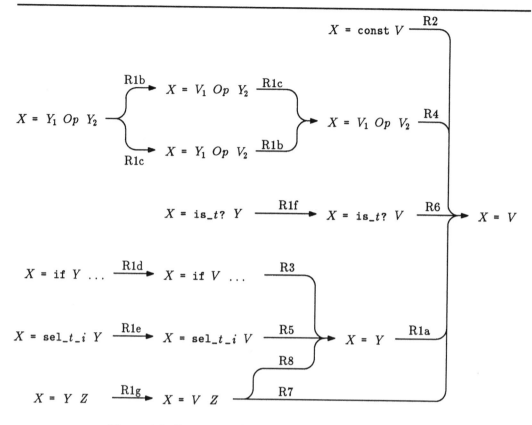

Figure 4.3: Summary of Possible Rewritings of Bindings

Corollary 4.9 (Confluence (Figure 4.2b))

$$\forall a, b, c \quad a \vdash^* b \land a \vdash^* c \Rightarrow \exists d\, b \vdash^* d \land c \vdash^* d$$

Proof. Standard [43] (see also the proof of Lemma 4.12). ∎

Corollary 4.10 *Normal forms in functional quads are unique.*

Theorem 4.11 *Functional quads has the Redex Uniqueness property.*

Proof. Figure 4.3 enumerates all the syntactic possibilities for a binding of the form $x = E$;, and shows which rules can transform one into the other. On no path in this diagram does the same rule appear twice, so if $\alpha_1 = \langle x, \rho_1 \rangle$ and $\alpha_2 = \langle x, \rho_2 \rangle$ are two redexes reduced in some reduction sequence, $\rho_1 \neq \rho_2$. ∎

The following lemma strengthens Corollary 4.9 (confluence) by identifying the redexes needed to unite two states.

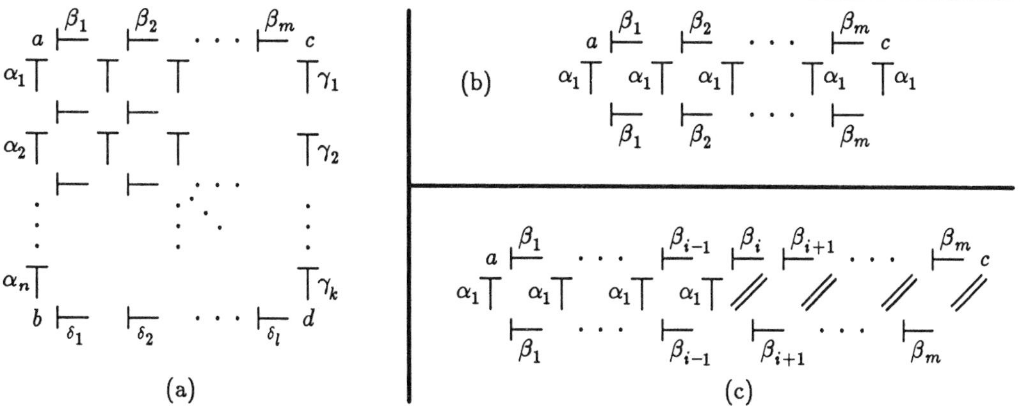

Figure 4.4: Proof of Lemma 4.12

Lemma 4.12 *Let* $a \vdash_{\alpha_1} \cdots \vdash_{\alpha_n} b$ *and* $a \vdash_{\beta_1} \cdots \vdash_{\beta_m} c$ *be two finite reduction sequences. Then there exists* d *such that* $b \vdash_{\delta_1} \cdots \vdash_{\delta_l} d$ *and* $c \vdash_{\gamma_1} \cdots \vdash_{\gamma_k} d$, *and furthermore the following hold:*

$$(\gamma_1, \ldots, \gamma_k) = (\alpha_1, \ldots, \alpha_n) - \{\beta_1, \ldots, \beta_m\}$$
$$(\delta_1, \ldots, \delta_l) = (\beta_1, \ldots, \beta_m) - \{\alpha_1, \ldots, \alpha_n\}$$

where the notation $(x_1, \ldots, x_n) - \{y_1, \ldots, y_m\}$ *indicates the sequence obtained by removing elements of the set* $\{y_1, \ldots, y_m\}$ *from the sequence* $(x_1, \ldots, x_n)$, *maintaining the same order between the* x*'s that remain.*

Proof. We construct d by using Theorem 4.8 (commutivity) to "tile" the reduction diagram, as shown in Figure 4.4a. Consider the uppermost row of tiles. There are two cases depending on whether $\alpha_1 = \beta_i$ for some i. If not, then $\gamma_1 = \alpha_1$ (Figure 4.4b). If so, then there is no γ reduction in the first row (Figure 4.4c). Continuing this argument for the remaining $n-1$ rows gives the γ-sequence result (note that the bottom edge of each row will contain all β's which are not the same as any α already executed; Theorem 4.11 guarantees that none of the α's which follow will be the same as a β that is missing from the bottom edge). A symmetric argument gives the δ-sequence result. ∎

Theorem 4.13 *Let* $a \vdash_{\alpha_1} \cdots \vdash_{\alpha_n} b$ *be a finite reduction sequence. Then all reduction sequences from* a *to* b *are permutations of* $(\alpha_1, \ldots, \alpha_n)$.

Proof. Suppose the theorem were false; then there is a reduction sequence $a \vdash_{\beta_1} \cdots \vdash_{\beta_m} c$ where $b = c$ and either $\{\alpha_1, \ldots, \alpha_n\} - \{\beta_1, \ldots, \beta_m\} \neq \emptyset$ or $\{\beta_1, \ldots, \beta_m\} - \{\alpha_1, \ldots, \alpha_n\} \neq \emptyset$. Consider the former; there is some α_i which is not equal to any β. We can use the tiling argument from Lemma 4.12 to construct the diagram in Figure 4.5a. Since α_i is absent from the paths $a \vdash^* c$ and $a \vdash^* a'$, by the lemma it is absent from the paths $a' \vdash^* c'$ and $c \vdash^* c'$. Hence the reduction from c' to c'' must be of α_i, and so we have $c \vdash^* \vdash_{\alpha_i} \vdash^* d$. But $b = c$, so we also have $a \vdash^* \vdash_{\alpha_i} \vdash^* b \vdash^* \vdash_{\alpha_i} \vdash^* d$, violating the redex uniqueness theorem.

51

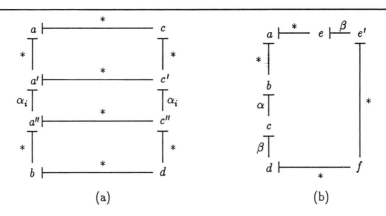

Figure 4.5: Proof of Theorems 4.13 and 4.15

Contradiction. A symmetric argument handles the case where there is some β_i not equal to any α. ∎

One of the consequences of this theorem is that all reduction sequences from a given state to normal form are of the same length, and so whether normal form is reached is independent of reduction strategy. We discuss this further in the next section.

We will also find the converse of the previous theorem useful:

Theorem 4.14 *Let* $a \vdash_{\alpha_1} \cdots \vdash_{\alpha_n} b$ *be a finite reduction sequence and let* $a \vdash_{\beta_1} \cdots \vdash_{\beta_n} c$ *be another reduction sequence where* $(\beta_1, \ldots, \beta_n)$ *is a permutation of* $(\alpha_1, \ldots, \alpha_n)$. *Then* $b = c$.

Proof. By Lemma 4.12 there exists d such that $b \vdash^* d$ and $c \vdash^* d$, but by the lemma both of these sequences must be empty. ∎

These two theorems allow us to sensibly speak of the set of redexes reduced in reducing a state S_0 to another state S_1; we will denote this set by $A^{S_0 \vdash^* S_1}$.

Theorem 4.15 *Functional quads has the Strong Dependence property.*

Proof. We are given $a \vdash^* b \vdash_\alpha c \vdash_\beta d$ where β does not exist in b; so performing the reduction $b \vdash_\alpha c$ *creates* the redex β. There are a limited number of possible combinations for α and β; for example, if α is an R1b redex, then β must be an R4 redex. Suppose the strong dependence property does not hold; then there is a sequence $a \vdash^* e \vdash_\beta e'$ where the reduction from a to e does not include α. We can apply Lemma 4.12 to unite d and e', so that we have $d \vdash^* f$ and $e' \vdash^* f$, where α is reduced somewhere along $e' \vdash^* f$ (see Figure 4.5b). But in fact, since β was reduced in arriving at e', α cannot possibly exist in any successor of e'; continuing the example above, if β is an R4 redex then after reducing β the right hand side of β's binding is a value, and will never contain an R1b redex. Contradiction. (We leave the details of the other cases as an exercise for the reader.) ∎

This theorem does not say that α will always create β; for example, if β is an R4 redex then in general there is an R1b redex and an R1c redex that must precede it, and only the second of these will create β. What the theorem *does* say is that there are no disjunctive preconditions for a redex—a redex cannot be created by the reduction of *either* of two other redexes, for example. We will not make any use of the strong dependence property until chapter 6.

4.7   Termination, Weak Normal Forms, and Lazy Evaluation

We have seen that normal forms produced from a given program are always the same, regardless of the evaluation order used in their derivations. We now examine the question of whether the choice of evaluation order affects whether a normal form is reached at all. Answering this question will allow us to contrast lenient and lazy evaluation within the functional quads framework.

In fact, Theorem 4.13 showed that in functional quads, all derivations to a normal form are of equal length, and so evaluation order has no effect on whether normal form is reached. This property seems a bit surprising at first; we know that lazy evaluation of functional programs terminates on programs where other evaluation orders fail, but it seems that in functional quads the evaluation order makes no difference. The problem is not with the functional quads reduction system, but simply in what we consider a normal form.

In functional quads, computations (redexes) are never removed from the state, even when their values do not contribute to the final answer. To illustrate:

$$\Diamond \; = \; (\text{k } 5) \; \text{p; } p \; = \; (\text{loop}) \; 3; \; \text{loop } v \; = \; \{a \; = \; (\text{loop}) \; v \; \text{in } a\}; \; \text{k } x \; y \; = \; \{\text{in } x\};$$

This program has no normal form, because each attempt to reduce (loop x) adds another call to loop to the state. On the other hand, it is possible to reduce this program to a state that contains a binding $\Diamond$ = 5. So we can obtain states that are not normal forms but nevertheless have an answer. We call these states *weak normal forms*.

Definition 4.16 *A* weak normal form *in functional quads is a state containing a binding* $\Diamond = V$, *where* V *is any value.*

Unlike normal forms, weak normal forms are not necessarily unique. For example, the preceding program has the following two weak normal forms, among others:

$$\Diamond \; = \; 5; \; p \; = \; (\text{loop}) \; 3; \; \text{xx} \; = \; 5; \; \text{yy} \; = \; p; \; \text{loop } v \; = \; \{...\}; \; \text{k } x \; y \; = \; \{\text{in } x\};$$

$$\Diamond \; = \; 5; \; p \; = \; \text{aa; } \text{vv} \; = \; 3; \; \text{xx} \; = \; 5; \; \text{yy} \; = \; p; \; \text{aa} \; = \; (\text{loop}) \; \text{vv; } \text{loop } v \; = \; \{...\}; \; \dots$$

While weak normal forms are not unique, we certainly expect the answers contained in weak normal forms to be unique. This is expressed in the following theorem:

Theorem 4.17 (Unique Values) *Let* S_0, S_1, *and* S_2 *be states such that* $S_0 \vdash^* S_1$ *and* $S_0 \vdash^* S_2$, *where* S_1 *contains a binding* $x \; = \; V_1$; *and* S_2 *contains a binding* $x \; = \; V_2$; *for some identifier* x. *Then* $V_1 = V_2$ *(syntactic equality).*

Proof. By Corollary 4.9, there must be a state S_3 such that $S_1 \vdash^* S_3$ and $S_2 \vdash^* S_3$. Now there is no rewrite rule which modifies a binding of the form $x^{(0)} = V$; (see Figure 4.3), so S_3 must contain a binding $x = V_3$; and furthermore $V_1 = V_2 = V_3$. ∎

Corollary 4.18 *The answers contained in different weak normal forms of the same state are equal.*

Proof. Let x be $\Diamond$ in Theorem 4.17. ∎

We see, therefore, that it makes sense to stop evaluation when a weak normal form is reached, since the answer contained in a weak normal form will not be altered by further evaluation.[3] If a program has no normal form, however, there is no guarantee that a particular evaluation sequence will reach a weak normal form. So if we are interested in weak normal forms, evaluation order becomes significant. We generally specify an evaluation order through an *evaluation strategy*, which is an algorithm for choosing the next redex to reduce, given a state. At each step, the strategy either identifies a redex to reduce, or indicates that no further reduction is to be done.[4] We can give a characterization of program execution in terms of weak normal forms and evaluation strategies, as follows:

Definition 4.19 *An execution under strategy S of a program S_0 is a reduction sequence $S_0, S_1, \ldots$ where the redex chosen at each step is determined by the strategy S. A terminating execution under strategy S is a finite execution under strategy S $S_0, \ldots, S_n$ where strategy S identifies no redexes in S_n. Terminating executions are further classified as non-deadlocking, if S_n is a weak normal form, and deadlocking otherwise.*

In other words, deadlock means termination with no answer.

We will mainly concern ourselves with the *lenient strategy*, which simply says that at any step, *any* of the available redexes may be evaluated next, unless the state is already in weak normal form, in which case the strategy terminates. How does this correspond to lenient evaluation, which we described in Chapter 3? We recall that lenient evaluation scheduled a subexpression based on whether it was executable, in the sense of having enough of its input data available to proceed. Furthermore, an arm of a conditional is evaluated only after the predicate is known. Examining the rewrite rules for functional quads, we see that both of these requirements are met automatically by the construction of the $\vdash$ relation. Thus, choosing any available redex corresponds to lenient evaluation. Stopping at a weak normal form reflects the fact that we are only interested in answers.

The *lazy strategy* for functional quads chooses a redex that is required to produce an answer, and so models lazy evaluation. We can describe the lazy strategy as a case analysis on the current state:

$$\mathcal{L}[\![\Diamond = E; \ldots]\!] = \mathcal{N}[\![E]\!][\![\Diamond = E; \ldots]\!]$$

---

[3]If the answer in a weak normal form is a data structure, then the variables it contains may or may not have values. If desired, these can be further evaluated, and Theorem 4.17 guarantees their uniqueness.

[4]An alternative way of defining a strategy is as a function from an initial state to the sequence of states resulting from reducing according to the strategy [10].

54

$$\mathcal{N}[\![V]\!][\![S]\!] = [\text{Terminate}]$$
$$\mathcal{N}[\![E]\!][\![S]\!] = E, \quad \text{if } E \text{ is a redex, otherwise:}$$
$$\mathcal{N}[\![x^{(0)}]\!][\![\ldots; \ x^{(0)} = E; \ \ldots]\!] = \mathcal{N}[\![E]\!][\![\ldots; \ x^{(0)} = E; \ \ldots]\!]$$
$$\mathcal{N}[\![V_1 + P_2]\!][\![S]\!] = \mathcal{N}[\![P_2]\!][\![S]\!]$$
$$\mathcal{N}[\![P_1 + P_2]\!][\![S]\!] = \mathcal{N}[\![P_1]\!][\![S]\!]$$
$$\mathcal{N}[\![\texttt{if } P \texttt{ then } \ldots]\!][\![S]\!] = \mathcal{N}[\![P]\!][\![S]\!]$$
$$\mathcal{N}[\![P \ x]\!][\![S]\!] = \mathcal{N}[\![P]\!][\![S]\!]$$
$$\mathcal{N}[\![\texttt{sel\_}t\_i \ P]\!][\![S]\!] = \mathcal{N}[\![P]\!][\![S]\!]$$
$$\mathcal{N}[\![\texttt{is\_}t? \ P]\!][\![S]\!] = \mathcal{N}[\![P]\!][\![S]\!]$$

$\mathcal{L}$ basically traces its way back from the answer until it finds a redex needed to make further progress. The strategy has the same desirable termination property as lazy evaluation, namely:

Theorem 4.20 *If a program S_0 has a weak normal form, execution under the lazy strategy always terminates.*

Proof. At every step, $\mathcal{L}$ chooses a redex which must be reduced in any reduction sequence that ends in a weak normal form (demonstratable through case analysis). So any reduction sequence to a weak normal form is a superset of the sequence chosen by $\mathcal{L}$; if there is a finite sequence to a weak normal form, then the $\mathcal{L}$ sequence is finite too. (See [11] for a more general discussion of needed redexes.) ∎

The function $\mathcal{L}$ can be used to obtain a strategy for reducing any state variable to a value, not just $\diamond$.

To summarize, the behavior of a lenient or lazy implementation of a functional language is modeled in functional quads as finding weak normal forms under the lenient or lazy evaluation strategy, respectively.[5] Weak normal forms from the same program contain the same answers, so the choice of strategy does not affect the result of a program, as long as a weak normal form is found. Whether a weak normal form is found *does* depend on the strategy: the lazy strategy always finds one when one exists, while the lenient evaluation strategy is only guaranteed of finding a weak normal form when the program has a normal form, which is true as long as the program does not contain any infinite loops.

4.8 Substitutions, Contexts, and *newid*

This section formalizes concepts related to the function application rewrite rule, R8. We define exactly how α-renaming takes place in that rule, in such a way that the identifiers introduced for a given application are the same for all reduction sequences. We also introduce some definitions that will be useful later in talking about functions and function application.

The notion of substitution (renaming) is formalized as follows.

---

[5]For completeness, we point out that there is also an evaluation strategy for functional quads which models strict evaluation. We will not discuss it in detail, but as an example we point out that it will not select an R8 redex unless all of the identifiers y_1 through y_n are bound to values. Hence, there will be programs for which the lenient strategy terminates but the strict strategy deadlocks.

Definition 4.21 *A substitution is a function that maps identifiers to identifiers, notated as follows*

$$\sigma = [y_1/x_1, y_2/x_2, \ldots]$$

where

$$\sigma x = \begin{cases} y_i, & \text{if } x = x_i \\ x, & \text{if } x \text{ is not equal to any } x_i \end{cases}$$

Composition of substitutions, $\sigma_1 \circ \sigma_2$, has the obvious meaning. As a notational convenience, if $(\sigma_1 \circ \sigma_2) = (\sigma_2 \circ \sigma_1)$, we write $\sigma_1 \cup \sigma_2$ instead of $\sigma_1 \circ \sigma_2$.

By extension, a substitution σ maps sets of identifiers to sets of identifiers:

$$\sigma V = \{\, \sigma x \mid x \in V \,\}$$

and also maps functional quads syntax to syntax by applying the substitution to each identifier, regardless of its syntactic context (i.e., on both left and right hand sides of bindings, in formal parameter lists, within blocks, etc.).

When an R8 redex is reduced, the substitution that applies to the function body includes a substitution for each formal parameter, and a substitution for every *non-free variable* of the body.

Definition 4.22 *The non-free variables of a binding list, $\mathcal{NV}[\![B_1; \ldots; B_n;]\!]$, is the set of variables defined as follows:*

$$\mathcal{NV}[\![B_1; \ldots; B_n;]\!] = \mathcal{NV}[\![B_1]\!] \cup \cdots \cup \mathcal{NV}[\![B_n]\!]$$
$$\mathcal{NV}[\![x^{(0)} = E;]\!] = \{x\} \cup \mathcal{NV}[\![E]\!]$$
$$\mathcal{NV}[\![f^{(n)}\ x_1\ \ldots\ x_n = \{B_1; \ldots; B_m;\ \text{in}\ z_f\}]\!] = \{f^{(n)}, x_0, \ldots, x_n\} \cup \mathcal{NV}[\![B_1; \ldots; B_m]\!]$$
$$\mathcal{NV}\left[\!\!\left[\begin{array}{l}\text{if } P \text{ then } \{B_{t,1}; \ldots; B_{t,n};\ \text{in}\ y_t\} \\ \text{else } \{B_{e,1}; \ldots; B_{e,m};\ \text{in}\ y_e\}\end{array}\right]\!\!\right] = \mathcal{NV}[\![B_{t,1}; \ldots; B_{t,n};]\!]$$
$$\cup\, \mathcal{NV}[\![B_{e,1}; \ldots; B_{e,m};]\!]$$
$$\mathcal{NV}[\![E]\!] = \emptyset, \qquad \text{if } E \text{ is not a conditional}$$

We can now formally state the R8 rule. Given two bindings in the state of the following form:

$$x = (f^{(n)}\ z_1\ \ldots\ z_{n-1})\ z_n;$$
$$f^{(n)}\ y_1\ \ldots\ y_n = \{B_{f1}; \ldots; B_{fm}\ \text{in}\ z_f\};$$

they are rewritten to:

$$x = \sigma_{f,x} z_f;$$
$$f^{(n)}\ y_1\ \ldots\ y_n = \{B_{f1}; \ldots; B_{fm}\ \text{in}\ z_f\};$$
$$\sigma_{f,x} B_{f1}; \ldots \sigma_{f,x} B_{fm};$$
$$\sigma_{f,x} y_1 = z_1; \ldots; \sigma_{f,x} y_n = z_n;$$

56

where the substitution $\sigma_{f,x}$ is defined as follows:

$$\sigma_{f,x} = \bigcup_{i=1}^{n} [newid(x, y_i)/y_i] \cup \bigcup_{z \in NV[B_{f1}; \ldots ; B_{fm}]} [newid(x, z)/z]$$

When discussing properties of function definitions in Chapter ??, it will be useful to formalize the notion of a *context*, a program containing a particular R8 redex for a given function. A context is defined as follows.

Definition 4.23 *A context for a function f is a pair $\langle S, \alpha \rangle$ where S is a state containing a function definition binding for f of the form:*

$$f^{(n)} \ x_1 \ \ldots \ x_n = \{\ldots\};$$

and α is a redex specifier naming an R8 redex in S of the following form:

$$x = (f^{(n)} \ z_1 \ \ldots \ z_{n-1}) \ z_n;$$

For every context C there is a substitution σ_C, defined as follows:

$$\sigma_C = \sigma_{f,x} \cup [x/\Diamond]$$

This substitution maps identifiers in the body of the function definition to their corresponding identifiers in the new bindings added to the state when the R8 redex is reduced. It also includes a substitution that maps $\Diamond$ to the variable that receives the result of the function. The use of *newid* in the R8 rewrite rule insures that the substitution σ_C is unique for every context, no matter when the indicated R8 redex is actually reduced.

4.9 Appendix: The Structure of the Set *Identifier*

In Section 4.1 we stated that the syntactic set *Identifier* has a particular structure: it is partitioned into sets according to arity, and there is a function *newid* defined over it for producing new identifiers from old ones. In this appendix, which the reader may skip, we give a detailed account of this structure.

What exactly does the function *newid* do? Mathematically speaking, it does not actually "create" anything, but instead is just a ternary relation defined over the set *Identifier*. Given the set *Identifier*, all we require is that *newid* satisfy the following three axioms:

- (*Uniqueness*) If $newid(a, b) = newid(c, d)$, then $a = c$ and $b = d$. In other words, the same identifier cannot be constructed from two different pairs.

- (*Newness*) If $newid(a, b) = c$, then there is no way to obtain either a or b from c by successive applications of *newid*. That is, the following relation:

$$\{ (x, z) \mid \exists y \text{ s.t. } newid(x, y) = z \vee newid(y, x) = z \}$$

  is acyclic.

- (*Arity Preservation*) If $newid(a, b) = c$, then b and c have the same arity.

The easiest way to visualize $newid$ is as a pairing operation, so that $newid(\mathtt{a}^{(0)}, \mathtt{f}^{(3)}) = (\mathtt{a}, \mathtt{f})^{(3)}$. Formally, let $s_i = \{a_i, b_i, \ldots\}$ be disjoint sets of symbols for all $i \geq 0$. Then define sets $\sigma_0, \sigma_1, \ldots$ inductively as follows:

$$x \in s_i \;\Rightarrow\; x \in \sigma_i$$
$$\chi \in \sigma_0, v \in \sigma_i \;\Rightarrow\; \langle \chi, v \rangle \in \sigma_i$$

In this approach, each σ_i is the set of identifiers of arity i, the set of all identifiers is $\bigcup_{i \geq 0} \sigma_i$, and the $newid$ operation is simply defined as $newid(\chi, v) = \langle \chi, v \rangle$.

Of course, it is more palatable to think of identifiers just as symbols, not pairs; so what we are really asserting is that the set of symbols *Identifier* together with the $newid$ relation is isomorphic to the union of the σ_i sets and the pairing operation defined above. We also note that the easiest way to satisfy condition (3) of name-consistency (see page 35) is to construct programs only from the identifiers isomorphic to the sets $s_0, s_1, \ldots$; none of these identifiers are $newid(x, y)$ for any x or y.

5 Code Generation

The previous chapter introduced functional quads and showed how programs are executed abstractly, through rewrite rules. Now we show how to produce actual machine code that mimics the behavior of the rewrite system, and hence implements functional quads programs on real computers. The goal is to translate each function definition into code that correctly implements the function no matter in what context it is called. As discussed earlier, non-strictness will in general prevent generating a single sequential thread for a function; instead, compiled code for a function will be a collection of threads that are interleaved at run time in different ways depending on the context.

Before commencing code generation for a function, we assume that some analysis phase has computed a "partitioning" for that function. A partitioning is a set of "threads," where each thread is an ordered sequence of identifiers such that each identifier corresponds to a single functional quads statement in the original function definition. At a very high level, then, object code for a function is generated by first translating each functional quads statement into a corresponding piece of sequential code and then arranging those pieces according to the sequences given in the partitioning; the resulting code sequences collectively implement the function. It is the responsibility of the analysis phase to insure that for every context in which the function could be invoked, there is an interleaving of the threads such that computing the values of the identifiers in that interleaved order will respect all data dependences, *i.e.*, that all input data to a subexpression will be available when execution of that subexpression is attempted. If lazy evaluation is desired, it must also be the case that if one value computed by a thread is needed by some other thread, then every value computed by the first thread will eventually be needed by the answer. It is the responsibility of code generation to insure that, given a correct partitioning, run-time mechanisms will succeed in finding the correct interleaving for each invocation of the function. If lazy evaluation is desired, the run-time mechanisms must also refrain from executing a thread unless the values it computes are needed by the answer.

For most functions, there are many correct partitionings possible. The trivial partitioning that assigns every subexpression to a separate thread is always correct. At the end of this chapter (Section 5.7), a method of partitioning by coalescing the threads produced from the trivial partitioning is presented; this method produces partitionings that are correct for both lenient and lazy evaluation. A method for partitioning based on data dependence analysis is presented in Chapters 6, 7, and 8. This method is capable of finding partitionings that have fewer threads than the coalescing method, when lazy evaluation is not desired. In general, the larger the threads, the smaller the overhead of multi-threaded execution.

There are several factors which distinguish multi-threaded code generation from the conventional code generation problem. The most obvious of these is that each function is implemented by a collection of independent code segments, which therefore must communicate and synchronize with one another. For example, if thread 1 uses the value of a which is computed by thread 2, then thread 1 must include code to wait for thread 2 to finish computing a. Moreover, the location which holds the value of a must indicate to thread 1 whether a has been computed; it must be equipped with a presence bit, and thread 2 must include code to set the presence bit when it stores a.

The second factor stems from non-strictness: because function calls and data constructors are non-strict, it may be necessary to pass values to procedures or data constructors before they have been computed. For example, to execute the constructor (cons a b), two words of storage are allocated, and a and b are copied into them. This is easy if the values of a and b have already been computed, but tricky if they have not. We must somehow provide for copying values which do not yet exist.

The third factor relates to the compilation of conditional expressions. The statements comprising the "then" or "else" arm of a conditional may not necessarily be assigned to the same thread, and even within one thread they may be interspersed with statements appearing outside the conditional. This requires a special technique for the introduction of conditional branch instructions into the sequential threads.

To accommodate these factors, we will augment the usual sequential quads notation with a few primitives that deal with presence bits, inter-thread synchronization, and the copying of values not yet computed. These aspects are explicit in the notation, to allow reasoning about optimizations such as eliminating unnecessary presence bits and synchronization; nevertheless, the notation hides the details of how these mechanisms are actually implemented. There is considerable freedom here, and the appropriate choice will depend on the target architecture as well as design decisions relating to scheduling policy and parallelism: target architectures may or may not have hardware support for the presence bits, scheduling of threads may be on a demand driven basis (execution of a thread is not begun until at least one other thread is waiting for a value computed by that thread) or on an eager basis (all threads for a function are begun when the function is invoked), and threads may execute concurrently (as on a multiprocessor) or one at a time. With our notation, all of these choices are reflected simply by choosing an appropriate implementation of the primitives in terms of the instruction set provided by the target.

The basic plan of this chapter, then, is to describe how to generate object code by first showing how to produce sequential quads augmented with some special primitives, and then illustrating the way these primitives can be implemented for a variety of combinations of hardware and scheduling policy. Some of the implementations have additional partitioning restrictions and opportunities for optimizations, and we will explore these. Throughout, it will be clear that the quality of object code depends strongly on which partitioning is chosen from the many partitionings that are possible for a given function. One topic which we will *not* discuss is algorithms for choosing one partitioning over another; this is an important topic for future research. Nevertheless, we will draw some conclusions about what characterizes a "good" partitioning.

5.1   Code Generation Concepts

The behavior of a function is defined in terms of the reductions that take place when it is invoked in the functional quads reduction system, and so the goal of code generation is to produce target code which performs the same computations that take place during reduction. When a function is invoked in functional quads (via the rewrite rule R8), new bindings for each local variable are added to the state, and succeeding reductions eventually reduce the right hand sides of these bindings to values. At a high level, then, when the target code for a function is invoked it must allocate storage for the local variables and then compute their values. Of course, the target code for a function is actually several pieces of code, each of which is responsible for the computation of a subset of the local variables, according to the partitioning.

The first order of business is to analyze the program to obtain the partitioning to be used for code generation. A partitioning has the following general form:

$$\{(v_{1,1}, v_{1,2}, \ldots), (v_{2,1}, v_{2,2}, \ldots), \ldots\}$$

where each v stands for an identifier defined in the body of the function (one of the v's is $\Diamond$, representing the code that returns the result to the caller). Each sequence $(v_{i,1}, v_{i,2}, \ldots)$ is a thread, with an implied left-to-right ordering. In practice, there will be many possible partitionings of a function, and the partitioning chosen can have a large effect on the quality of object code produced. This implies that we may want to combine partitioning and code generation, or at least incorporate heuristics into partitioning that anticipate the needs of code generation. We will defer this point to the end of the chapter.

Each identifier in the partitioning represents the reduction of an identifier to a value, and will correspond to a segment of code which computes that value. For example, suppose we were compiling this function:

```
def example x y =
    {a = ...;
     b = f + d;
     c = ...;
     d = ...;
     e = x * y;
     f = ...;
     g = const <cons,c,e>;          %% i.e., (cons c e)
     in
        g};
```

and the partitioning phase chose the following three threads: $(\mathrm{b}, \mathrm{g}, \Diamond)$, $(\mathrm{a}, \mathrm{f}, \mathrm{e})$, and (c, d). The object code would be the following:

function example (x, y)	*thread* 2 *of* example	*thread* 3 *of* example
⟨*Initialization*⟩	⟨*Compute value of* a⟩	⟨*Compute value of* c⟩
⟨*Compute value of* b⟩	⟨*Compute value of* f⟩	⟨*Compute value of* d⟩
⟨*Compute value of* g⟩	⟨*Compute value of* e⟩	*stop*
⟨*Return g to caller*⟩	*stop*	
stop		

We assume that the caller of a function initiates and passes parameters to the thread which computes $\Diamond$ (*i.e.*, the thread that returns the result), which we will always call thread 1.

61

The initialization code in that thread allocates storage for the local variables a through g, and then starts up the second and third threads—exactly what this entails will be discussed later. Each of the "compute value of x" segments is the sequential quads equivalent of the corresponding functional quads statement x = *Simple*.

Some of the code segments which compute the value of a variable will contain special instructions needed to deal with multiple threads. Consider the statement b = f + d. It is not sufficient to merely include the statement b := f + d in thread 1, for when we reach it there is no guarantee that threads 2 and 3 will have progressed to the points where the values of f and d are computed. To synchronize properly, we must include presence bits in the locations allocated for the local variables, and generate the following code:

```
. . .
force f
force d
b  :=ᵥ  val(f) + val(d)
. . .
```

The statement *force* f tests the presence bit for f and halts execution of the thread until that presence bit turns on.[1] The *val* notation indicates that presence bits of f and d need to be stripped off before their values are added, while the *v* subscript in the assignment statement indicates that the presence bit for b should be turned on when the assignment is made (*v* stands for *value*). The need to force the operands of the addition is a direct consequence of the functional quads reduction system: an addition in functional quads (rule R4) must be preceded by R1b and R1c rewrites, which in turn can only take place when the operands of the addition have been reduced to values.

Another wrinkle in generating code for a functional quads statement arises because of non-strictness. Again referring to **example**, consider the binding g = const <cons,c,e>. To reduce g to a value we must create a two-element data structure with structure tag cons containing c and e, and as before the values of c and e may or may not have been computed yet. Unlike the earlier addition, though, it is *not* safe to force c and e; data constructors are non-strict, and must execute even if the component values are not yet evaluated. Specifically, it may not be possible to compute the value of c or e until after g has a value, so waiting for either to become a value before computing g could lead to deadlock (consider the case where the argument x, used to compute e, depends on the result of the call). We instead generate the following code:

```
. . .
temp     :=  allocate 2
temp[1]  :=_c  c
temp[2]  :=_c  e
g        :=ᵥ  temp
. . .
```

---

[1]The *force* statement used here should not be confused with the **force** operator of Henderson's transformation (Section 2.2), although there is a connection between them which will become apparent later in this chapter.

The c-subscripted assignment is a special kind of assignment which makes the left hand side location be a *copy* of the right hand side location: executing *force* temp[1] will have the same effect as executing *force* c, and a subsequent fetch *val*(temp[1]) will retrieve the value of c. Notice that this is more than merely copying the *contents* of c into temp[1]; we really mean that the two locations become equivalent for all time, so that when a value is stored into c it will effectively be stored in temp[1] as well.

The c-subscripted assignment is also used for procedure calls, for like data constructors, procedure calls are also non-strict. Thus, if the statement for g were a procedure call such as g = (foo$^{(2)}$ c) e, the code generated would be:

```
...
begincall foo
Arg₁ :=_c c
Arg₂ :=_c e
invoke foo
g     :=_v Res
endcall foo
...
```

The notation here hides the details of the calling convention: the *begincall* primitive does whatever is needed to begin a call for foo (*e.g.*, allocating space for the arguments on the stack or in registers), *invoke* actually transfers control to foo, and *endcall* performs any necessary cleanup. Between the *begincall* and *endcall* statements are allowed the special identifiers Arg$_i$ and Res which stand for whatever locations are to be used to pass arguments and receive the result from the function being called. The choice of a particular calling convention for each function is a topic adequately covered elsewhere [62, 44]; the important feature for our purposes is that the non-evaluating $:=_c$ operator is used to pass the arguments.

The upshot of all this is that memory locations in the target implementation can contain three classes of data:

1. A *value*, such as an integer, boolean, (pointer to a) data structure, *etc.*

2. A *promise* to receive the value computed by some thread. In the example above, f initially contains a promise to receive the value computed by thread 2, and after thread 2 executes it contains a value. In some implementations, a location holding a promise is just an empty location, while in others the location might contain some information, such as a pointer to the thread that will eventually store a value in that location.

3. A *copy* of some other location, such that forces and references to this location behave as if they were forces and references to the other location.

Because the target implementation will need tag bits or an equivalent mechanism to indicate which class of data a location holds, these locations will be called *tagged* locations. When a tagged location is created it may be initialized to any of the three classes, but the only subsequent write that is allowed is when a thread stores a value in a location that

Statement	::=	*UntaggedLoc* := *Expression* |
		TaggedLoc :=$_v$ *Expression* |
		TaggedLoc :=$_p$ *Closure* |
		TaggedLoc :=$_c$ *TaggedLoc* |
		force *TaggedLoc* |
		begincall *ProcedureName* |
		invoke *ProcedureName* |
		endcall *ProcedureName* |
		goto *Label* |
		if *Operand* goto *Label* |
		if ¬ *Operand* goto *Label* |
		stop
Expression	::=	*Operand* | allocate *Constant* |
		Operand + *Operand* | *Operand* > *Operand* | ...
Operand	::=	*Constant* | *UntaggedLoc* | val(*TaggedLoc*)
UntaggedLoc	::=	*Identifier*
TaggedLoc	::=	*Identifier* | arg$_i$ | Res | ◇ |
		UntaggedLoc[*Constant*]

Figure 5.1: Grammar of Sequential Quads

previously contained a promise (a location that contains a copy, however, may be implicitly overwritten with a value when the copied location receives a value). In contrast, *untagged* locations which can only contain values may be freely used within a thread; these are just ordinary memory locations that may be read and written at will, and are typically used as temporaries (*e.g.*, the location temp in the earlier example). The use of tagged locations typically requires more overhead than untagged locations.

With all this in mind, the complete grammar of the sequential quads notation we will use to describe object code is given in Figure 5.1, which apart from five constructs dealing with tagged locations is pretty much standard [2]. Three of the five tagged location constructs are assignments, :=$_v$, :=$_p$, and :=$_c$, corresponding to the three classes of data that can be stored in a tagged location; each stores an object of a particular class, and updates presence bits accordingly (depending on the implementation, a more complex operation may be called for). The fourth is *force*, which suspends execution until the indicated location holds a value, and the fifth is *val*, which extracts the data from a location known to hold a value. To clarify the remaining notation: a[c] assumes that the untagged location a contains the address of the first word of a contiguous block of memory, and refers to the cth location beyond that word.[2] The expression *allocate c* allocates c consecutive words of tagged locations and returns the address of the first word. Arg$_i$ and Res are only legal between a *begincall*/*endcall* pair, and correspond to the locations named by the formal

---

[2]This is slightly non-standard: in [2] it would refer to the cth consecutive location that follows a itself, as opposed to the address contained in a.

parameters and $\Diamond$ in the code for the function being called. The remainder of the notation should be evident from the earlier discussion.

To generate code for a particular target machine we must choose a representation for the three classes of tagged data (values, promises, and unevaluated copies) and convert the operators $:=_v$, $:=_p$, $:=_c$, *force*, and *val* into appropriate machine instructions. Many variations are possible, a few of which will be described in Section 5.4, but they all share the property that tagged locations are more expensive to use than untagged locations, and that storing a value in a tagged location ($:=_v$) is better than storing an unevaluated copy ($:=_c$).

5.2 Basic Code Generation

As outlined in the last section, the first cut at object code for a function is just the concatenation of code for each functional quads statement, in the order given by the partitioning. In this section we give the translations of each kind of functional quads statement into sequential quads, with examples. We will not be concerned with producing highly optimized code, as optimizations will be taken up in later sections.

Throughout this section, we will assume that Johnsson's lambda lifting transformation [38] has been performed to lift internal definitions to top level, converting their free variables to formal parameters. Our compilation method does not *require* that lambda lifting be used to handle internal definitions; for illustrative purposes it simply has the advantage of not introducing any new mechanisms for accessing variables in outer lexical scopes. A real compiler may choose to use Algol-style displays or some other environment structure, with the appropriate modifications to the schemata below.

5.2.1 First Order Constructs

The schemata for translating the majority of functional quads constructs into sequential quads are given in Figure 5.2. Most of these were discussed in the last section, and all are very straightforward. In these schemata it is assumed that n-tuple data structures are represented as a contiguous block of $(n + 1)$ words, where the first word contains the structure tag and the remaining words the components. Depending on the type system of the source language, it may be possible in some instances to omit the structure tag slot, with the obvious modifications to the translation. Notice that the rule for $x = y$ forces y; this is because the object code must reduce x to a value. On the other hand, it is probably better to simply eliminate the statement altogether by replacing all references to x by y in the original functional quads program.

5.2.2 Higher-Order Functions

Missing from Figure 5.2 are the schemata for handling higher-order functions. There are many ways of compiling such code; we will describe a method which employs a direct representation of partial application values, patterned after [67]. The form of a partial application object is depicted in the upper right corner of Figure 5.3: it is a 3-tuple containing the name of the function, the number of further applications needed to satisfy

$x = y$	*force* y $x :=_v val(y)$
$x = y_1 + y_2$	*force* y_1 *force* y_2 $x :=_v val(y_1) + val(y_2)$
$x = $ const C	$x :=_v C$
$x = $ const $<t, y_1, \ldots, y_n>$	temp $:= allocate \ n+1$ temp[0] $:=_v t$ temp[1] $:=_c y_1$ $\ldots$ temp[n] $:=_c y_n$ $x \qquad :=_v$ temp
$x = $ sel_t_i y	*force* y temp $:= val(y)$ *force* temp[i] $x \qquad :=_v val(\text{temp}[i])$
$x = $ is_t? y	*force* y temp1 $:= val(y)$ temp2 $:= val(\text{temp1}[0])$ $x \qquad :=_v$ temp2 $== t$
$x = (f^{(n)} \ y_1 \ldots y_{n-1}) \ y_n$	*begincall* f Arg$_1$ $:=_c y_1$ $\ldots$ Arg$_n$ $:=_c y_n$ *invoke* f $x \qquad :=_v val(\text{Res})$ *endcall* f

Figure 5.2: Basic Code Generation Schemata

the arity, and the arguments already applied in the form of a linked list. Applying this to an argument does one of two things depending on whether the arity is satisfied. If it is not, then a new partial application is constructed with a decremented arity count and a new entry added to the front of the argument chain (this is why the arguments in the chain appear in reversed order). If it is, the function is invoked by sending the chain and the final argument to a special entry point created for the function, which unpacks the chain and performs an ordinary call to the function. Having a separate piece of entry code for each function allows the first-order calling convention to be customized on a per-procedure basis, while still presenting a uniform interface to the general apply in which the identity of the function is not known at compile time.

Figure 5.3 content:

$x = y_1\ y_2$		

```
force y₁
ap       :=   val(y₁)
entry    :=   val(ap[0])
rem      :=   val(ap[1])
chn      :=   val(ap[2])
rdy      :=   rem == 1
if rdy goto L1
n_ap     :=   allocate 3
n_ap[0]  :=ᵥ  entry
n_rem    :=   rem - 1
n_ap[1]  :=ᵥ  n_rem
n_chn    :=   allocate 2
n_chn[0] :=_c y₂
n_chn[1] :=ᵥ  chn
n_ap[2]  :=ᵥ  n_chn
x        :=ᵥ  n_ap
goto L2
```

```
L1:  begincall (entry)
     Arg₁      :=ᵥ  chn
     Arg₂      :=_c y₂
     invoke (entry)
     x         :=ᵥ  val(Res)
     endcall (entry)
L2:  ...
```

$x = \text{const}\ (f^{(n)})$

```
temp     :=   allocate 3
temp[0]  :=ᵥ  f_hof_entry
temp[1]  :=ᵥ  n
temp[2]  :=ᵥ  nil
x        :=ᵥ  temp
```

Representation of $(f^{(n)}\ y_1\ \ldots y_i)$

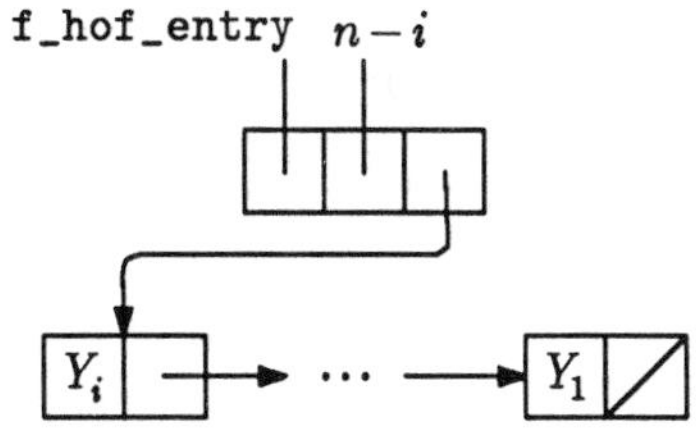

f_hof_entry $n-i$

H.O.F. entry code for $f^{(n)}$

```
function f_hof_entry (chn, last)
begincall f
Argₙ     :=_c last
temp     :=   val(chn)
Arg_{n-1} :=_c temp[0]
temp     :=   val(temp[1])
Arg_{n-2} :=_c temp[0]
temp     :=   val(temp[1])
...
Arg₁     :=_c temp[0]
invoke f
temp     :=   val(Res)
endcall f
◇        :=ᵥ  temp
```

Figure 5.3: Basic Code Generation Schemata for Higher Order Functions

The remainder of Figure 5.3 shows sequential quads code to accomplish all this (in the code for application, some temporaries have been given names other than temp to aid in readability). The noteworthy aspect of the code for application is that y_1 is forced, while y_2 is copied unevaluated; this is consistent with the fact that in the reduction system y_1 must be a value before either rule R7 or rule R8 applies, while y_2 need not. Also in the figure is code for creating an empty partial application, generated when a procedure is used as a value in the source program. This could be generalized to directly compile a statement like

$$x = \text{const}\ (f^{(n)}\ y_1\ \ldots\ y_i)$$

by building the appropriate partial application structure.

```
def cond_example x y q =
  {p = x > y;
   a = if p then
       {r = x + 8;
        s = c + 7;
        t = const <cons,r,s>;
        in
          t}
       else
       {q = const <cons,x,y>;
        in
          q};
   b = sel_cons_1 a;
   c = b + 9;
   d = sel_cons_2 a;
   in
     d};
```

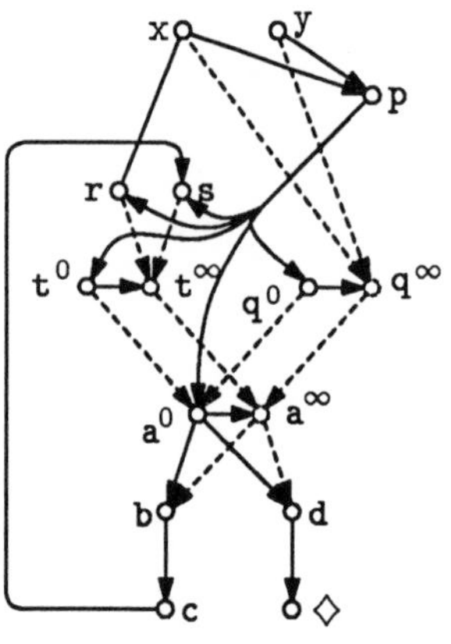

Figure 5.4: Program Illustrating Non-Contiguous Conditional

5.2.3 Conditionals

The translation for the conditional statement completes the description of basic code generation. In the functional quads reduction system, conditionals serve two roles: they select one of two values to which the conditional's left hand side is bound, and they prevent the execution of bindings appearing in the arm not selected by the predicate. Thus we would like to surround the code generated for the arms of a conditional with conditional branches, but in practice this is somewhat involved because after partitioning there is no guarantee that statements taken from a given "then" or "else" arm will be assigned to the same thread, or even in contiguous segments in different threads.

The program in Figure 5.4 illustrates the problem. The value of r computed in the "then" arm of the conditional is fed back into the conditional through the variable c, computed outside the conditional. Analysis of the dependence graph shows that this program can be compiled into a single sequential thread only if c occurs between r and s, for example, $(p, r, t, q, a, b, c, s, d, \diamond)$ (for reference, Figure 5.4 includes the dependence graph computed for the function by the methods of Chapter 7). We cannot, therefore, simply generate a single conditional branch which branches around the code for r, s, and t, because they cannot occur contiguously.

The solution to this problem annotates the partitioning with *control strings* that indicate the control conditions governing the execution of each statement. For each variable in the original functional quads program, we compute a control string by considering the innermost block which encloses the binding defining it:

1. If the block is not in the arm of a conditional, the control string is the empty string.

2. If the block is the "then" arm in the binding x = if p then {...} else {...}, the control string is Ap, where A is the control string of x.

3. If the block is the "else" arm in the binding x = if p then {...} else {...}, the control string is $A\overline{p}$, where A is the control string of x.

The control string of a variable x can be interpreted as a boolean formula which must be true in order for the binding defining x to be executable; the set of statements corresponding to each unique control string comprise a *basic block* as defined in [67].

Annotating the thread $(\mathrm{p}, \mathrm{r}, \mathrm{t}; \mathrm{q}, \mathrm{a}, \mathrm{b}, \mathrm{c}, \mathrm{s}, \mathrm{d}, \Diamond)$ with control strings gives:

$$
\begin{array}{ll}
& function \ \texttt{cond\_example (x, y)} \\
& \langle Initialization \rangle \\
& \langle Code \ for \ \texttt{p = x > y} \rangle \\
p & \langle Code \ for \ \texttt{r = x + 8} \rangle \\
p & \langle Code \ for \ \texttt{t = const <cons,r,s>} \rangle \\
\overline{p} & \langle Code \ for \ \texttt{q = const <cons,x,y>} \rangle \\
& \langle Code \ for \ \texttt{a = if p then t else q} \rangle \\
& \langle Code \ for \ \texttt{b = sel\_cons\_1 a} \rangle \\
& \langle Code \ for \ \texttt{c = b + 9} \rangle \\
p & \langle Code \ for \ \texttt{s = c + 7} \rangle \\
& \langle Code \ for \ \texttt{d = sel\_cons\_2 a} \rangle \\
& \Diamond \ :=_v \ val\texttt{(d)} \\
& stop
\end{array}
$$

Notice that the fragment corresponding to code for the conditional itself (the code for a) simply selects one variable or another as the value of a. This in turn can be expressed as a pair of assignments with control strings mutually exclusive in p:

$$
\begin{array}{ll}
& function \ \texttt{cond\_example (x, y)} \\
& \langle Initialization \rangle \\
& \langle Code \ for \ \texttt{p = x > y} \rangle \\
p & \langle Code \ for \ \texttt{r = x + 8} \rangle \\
p & \langle Code \ for \ \texttt{t = const <cons,r,s>} \rangle \\
\overline{p} & \langle Code \ for \ \texttt{q = const <cons,x,y>} \rangle \\
p & \langle Code \ for \ \texttt{a = t} \rangle \\
\overline{p} & \langle Code \ for \ \texttt{a = q} \rangle \\
& \langle Code \ for \ \texttt{b = sel\_cons\_1 a} \rangle \\
& \langle Code \ for \ \texttt{c = b + 9} \rangle \\
p & \langle Code \ for \ \texttt{s = c + 7} \rangle \\
& \langle Code \ for \ \texttt{d = sel\_cons\_2 a} \rangle \\
& \Diamond \ :=_v \ val\texttt{(d)} \\
& stop
\end{array}
$$

The following algorithm converts control strings to conditional branches:

1. Find a maximal group of adjacent statements whose control string begins with the same term (either x or $\overline{x}$, where x is an identifier).

2. Generate a conditional branch statement to bypass the group if the condition represented by the common term is false. A conditional branch must force the predicate variable.

3. Remove the common term from the control strings of the group's statements.

4. Repeat steps 1 through 3 until only empty control strings remain.

This algorithm ends up processing nested conditionals from the outside in. Applying it to the thread above yields:

```
         function cond_example (x, y)
         ⟨Initialization⟩
         ⟨Code for p = x > y⟩
         force p
         if ¬val(p) goto L1
         ⟨Code for r = x + 8⟩
         ⟨Code for t = const <cons,r,s>⟩
  L1:    force p
         if val(p) goto L2
         ⟨Code for q = const <cons,x,y>⟩
  L2:    force p
         if ¬val(p) goto L3
         ⟨Code for a = t⟩
  L3:    force p
         if val(p) goto L4
         ⟨Code for a = q⟩
  L4:    ⟨Code for b = sel_cons_1 a⟩
         ⟨Code for c = b + 9⟩
         force p
         if ¬val(p) goto L5
         ⟨Code for s = c + 7⟩
  L5:    ⟨Code for d = sel_cons_2 a⟩
         ◇ :=ᵥ val(d)
         stop
```

Obviously, fewer branches are generated when the groups of adjacent statements with common control prefixes are as large as possible, and this is one criterion which should guide the analysis that computes the partitioning. On the other hand, adjacent statements with mutually exclusive control strings can always be exchanged safely without referring back to the analysis, as there cannot possibly be any dependence between them. This is particularly helpful in placing the pair of assignment statements created for the conditional (a = t and a = q in the example above):

```
     function ...                     function ...                           function ...
     ⟨Init⟩                           ⟨Init⟩                                 ⟨Init⟩
     ⟨Code for p⟩                     ⟨Code for p⟩                           ⟨Code for p⟩
  p  ⟨Code for r⟩                  p  ⟨Code for r⟩                           force p
  p  ⟨Code for t⟩                  p  ⟨Code for t⟩                           if ¬val(p) goto L1
  p̄  ⟨Code for q⟩                  p  ⟨Code for a = t⟩                       ⟨Code for r⟩
  p  ⟨Code for a = t⟩   ⟶         p̄  ⟨Code for q⟩         ⟶               ⟨Code for t⟩
  p̄  ⟨Code for a = q⟩              p̄  ⟨Code for a = q⟩                       ⟨Code for a = t⟩
     ⟨Code for b⟩                     ⟨Code for b⟩                  L1:      force p
     ⟨Code for c⟩                     ⟨Code for c⟩                           if val(p) goto L2
  p  ⟨Code for s⟩                  p  ⟨Code for s⟩                           ⟨Code for q⟩
     ⟨Code for d⟩                     ⟨Code for d⟩                           ⟨Code for a = q⟩
     ◇ :=ᵥ val(d)                     ◇ :=ᵥ val(d)                  L2:      ⟨Code for b⟩
     stop                             stop                                   ⟨Code for c⟩
                                                                             force p
                                                                             if ¬val(p) goto L3
                                                                             ⟨Code for s⟩
                                                                    L3:      ⟨Code for d⟩
                                                                             ◇ :=ᵥ val(d)
                                                                             stop
```

Flow analysis techniques [2] can be used to improve the code by removing branches or converting them to unconditional branches. Opportunities for this most often arise between adjacent groups of statements with mutually exclusive control prefixes. To illustrate:

```
            ...                                          ...
            if ¬val(p) goto L1                           if ¬val(p) goto L1
            ⟨Code for r⟩                                 ⟨Code for r⟩
            ⟨Code for t⟩                                 ⟨Code for t⟩
            ⟨Code for a = t⟩                             ⟨Code for a = t⟩
     L1:    force p                                      goto L2
            if val(p) goto L2       ⟶            L1:     ⟨Code for q⟩
            ⟨Code for q⟩                                 ⟨Code for a = q⟩
            ⟨Code for a = q⟩                     L2:     ⟨Code for b⟩
     L2:    ⟨Code for b⟩                                 ⟨Code for c⟩
            ⟨Code for c⟩                                 ...
            ...
```

The control string technique works regardless of whether the arms of a conditional are contiguous or separated, in one thread or many.

5.2.4 Initialization

We assume that invoking a function initiates execution of its first thread, so it is that thread's responsibility to allocate space for and initialize the local variables and to initialize the other threads (if any). As we have discussed, the initial contents of each local variable

71

is a promise to receive the value computed by a particular thread, the identity of the thread being determined by the partitioning. Initializing a thread entails creating an environment by which it can access local variables, formal parameters, and variables imported from enclosing lexical scopes.

To illustrate the form of initialization code, suppose we are compiling a function f which is partitioned into three threads: $(\texttt{a1}, \texttt{a2}, \Diamond)$, $(\texttt{b1}, \texttt{b2})$, and $(\texttt{c1}, \texttt{c2}, \texttt{c3})$. Suppose further that it has two formal parameters p1 and p2, and imports the variable i from a surrounding scope (if lambda lifting is used, i will actually appear as a formal). The beginning of the code for thread 1 is as follows:

function f (p1, p2)
⟨*Allocate location for* a1⟩
. . .
⟨*Allocate location for* c3⟩
temp1 := ⟨*Null Closure*⟩
temp2 := ⟨*Close thread 2 over* p1, p2, i, a1, . . ., c3⟩
temp3 := ⟨*Close thread 3 over* p1, p2, i, a1, . . ., c3⟩
a1 $:=_p$ temp1
a2 $:=_p$ temp1
b1 $:=_p$ temp2
b2 $:=_p$ temp2
c1 $:=_p$ temp3
c2 $:=_p$ temp3
c3 $:=_p$ temp3
⟨*Initiate thread 2*⟩
⟨*Initiate thread 3*⟩
⟨*Code for* a1⟩
. . .

We will discuss each of the phases of initialization code in turn.

Allocating local variable locations. The first step allocates a tagged location for each local variable. We take no position on where each location is allocated—it may be in a register, on the stack, or in the heap—the only restriction is that the location must continue to exist as long as there are threads which may refer to it. A suitable lifetime analysis can be used to choose an appropriate storage class [62, 44]. We do not show allocation code for untagged (temporary) locations used within threads, as this is accommodated through standard register/stack allocation technology.

Creating closures. Each of the other threads associated with a given function invocation will need access to some or all of the formal parameters, local variables, and other variables imported from enclosing lexical scopes, and so the addresses of these must be passed to the threads by creating a *closure*. In effect, a closure is a structure containing a pointer to the code for the thread along with enough pointers for that thread to gain access to all of the locations to which it refers; the latter group of pointers are collectively called the *environment*. Packaging the code pointer and environment into a closure allows the thread to be initiated at an arbitrary time in the future, as is required by demand-driven scheduling. Although the code above shows each thread closed over all formals, locals,

```
gen_fact_list fact_list i n =
  {p = i > n;
   a =
     if p then
       {e = const <nil> in e}
     else
       {im1 = i - 1;
        prev = (nth im1) fact_list;
        this = i * prev;
        ip1 = i + 1;
        nfl = (gen_fact_list fact_list ip1) n;
        b = const <cons,this,nfl>;
        in
          b};
   in
     a}
```

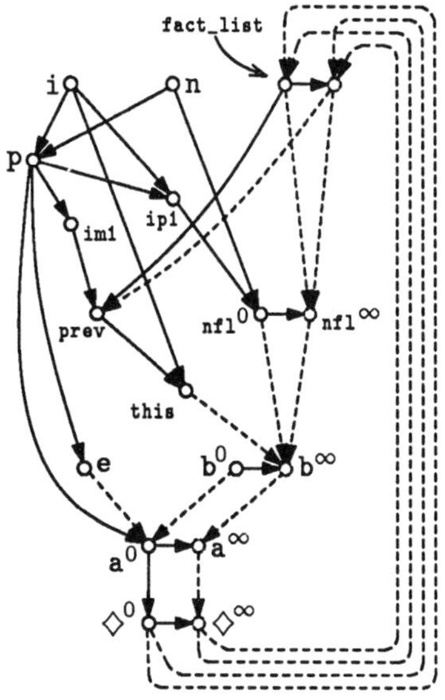

Figure 5.5: gen_fact_list Program and Dependence Graph

and imports, of course it is only necessary to close a thread over the variables to which it actually refers. Again, we take no position on the layout of an environment, as these issues are adequately discussed elsewhere [44].

A point of notation: if **x** is a tagged location, then ⟨*Close thread 2 over* **x**⟩ means that the environment for thread 2 contains the *address* of **x**; thread 2 can store a value in **x**, or read it after some other thread stores a value. If **x** is an untagged location, or if we write ⟨*Close thread 2 over val*(**x**)⟩, then the environment contains only the *value* of **x**, thread 2 is limited to using the value of **x** as an operand, and within thread 2 **x** will be notated as an untagged location. Naturally, this is only possible if **x** is known to contain a value at the time the closure is built.

Storing promises and initiating threads. With the threads closed over appropriate environments, the local variables are initialized with promises (using the $:=_p$ operator) and the threads are initiated. Exactly what these two steps entail depends on the scheduling policy and on how tagged locations are implemented, as will be discussed in Section 5.4. In demand-driven implementations, for example, thread execution is initiated by the *force* operator, and the "initiate" code shown in the initialization will actually be omitted. In parallel eager implementations, on the other hand, the initiate code will begin the concurrent execution of the other threads, but the $:=_p$ operator will have a simpler implementation.

5.2.5 Examples

We now illustrate the basic code generation method with two of the programs from Section 3.1. The first of these is the gen_fact_list subroutine from the make_fact_list example in Section 3.1.2, whose functional quads equivalent and dependence graph (according to the methods of Chapter 7) are shown in Figure 5.5. (`Gen_fact_list` has been lambda lifted from the body of `make_fact_list`, making `fact_list` appear as a formal parameter.) For readers returning to this example after reading Chapters 7 and 8, notice that feedback dependences have been introduced (Section 7.5), but because `gen_fact_list` is strict in `i` and `n` feedback to them is inadmissible (Section 8.4).

One possible partitioning of this program is into the two threads $(\mathtt{p}, \mathtt{ip1}, \mathtt{nfl}, \mathtt{b}, \mathtt{e}, \mathtt{a}, \Diamond)$ and $(\mathtt{im1}, \mathtt{prev}, \mathtt{this})$, which the reader may verify are consistent with the constraint graphs obtained by the methods of Chapter 8 (in fact, it is possible to produce a single thread, which will appear in a later section). This partitioning yields the following object code:

```
function gen_fact_list (fact_list, i, n)              thread 2 of gen_fact_list
⟨Allocate locations for p, ip1, nfl, b, a,            force p
  e, im1, prev, this⟩                                 if val(p) goto L1
temp1    :=  ⟨Null Closure⟩                           force i
temp2    :=  ⟨Close thread 2 over i, p, im1,          im1  :=_v val(i) - 1
             fact_list, prev, this⟩                   begincall nth
p        :=_p temp1                                   Arg₁ :=_c im1
...                                                    Arg₂ :=_c fact_list
e        :=_p temp1                                   invoke nth
im1      :=_p temp2                                   prev :=_v val(Res)
prev     :=_p temp2                                   endcall nth
this     :=_p temp2                                   force i
⟨Initiate thread 2⟩                                   force prev
force i                                               this :=_v val(i) * val(prev)
force n                                      L1:       stop
p        :=_v val(i) > val(n)
force p
if val(p) goto L1
force i
ip1      :=_v val(i) + 1
begincall gen_fact_list
Arg₁     :=_c fact_list
Arg₂     :=_c ip1
Arg₃     :=_c n
invoke gen_fact_list
nfl      :=_v val(Res)
endcall gen_fact_list
temp     := allocate 3
temp[0]  :=_v ⟨Tag for cons⟩
temp[1]  :=_c this
temp[2]  :=_c nfl
b        :=_v temp
force b
a        :=_v val(b)
goto L2
L1:  temp     := allocate 1
     temp[0]  :=_v ⟨Tag for nil⟩
     e        :=_v temp
     force e
     a        :=_v val(e)
L2:  force a
     ◊        :=_v val(a)
     stop
```

In creating this code we have applied some of the branch elimination optimizations discussed earlier (in particular, the code computing e was permuted with one of the assignments to a), but no other optimizations have been applied. There are ample opportunities for eliminating redundant *force* statements and the like, as discussed in the next section.

The second program we shall consider is the conditional dependence program from Section 3.1.3, shown with its dependence graph in Figure 8.1. As will be discussed in Section 8.2, for lenient evaluation this program requires at least two threads, for example $(p, a, aa, c, \Diamond)$ and (b, bb):

function cond_examp (x)
⟨*Allocate locations for* p, a, aa, b, bb, c⟩
temp1 := ⟨*Null Closure*⟩
temp2 := ⟨*Close thread 2 over* p, aa, b, bb⟩
p   :=$_p$ temp1
a   :=$_p$ temp1
aa   :=$_p$ temp1
c   :=$_p$ temp1
b   :=$_p$ temp2
bb   :=$_p$ temp2
⟨*Initiate thread 2*⟩
force x
p   :=$_v$ *val*(x) > 0
force p
if *val*(p) *goto* L1
a   :=$_v$ 3
goto L2

L1:   *force* bb
a   :=$_v$ *val*(bb)
L2:   *force* a
aa   :=$_v$ *val*(a) + 5
force aa
force bb
c   :=$_v$ *val*(aa) + *val*(bb)
force c
$\Diamond$:=$_v$ *val*(c)
stop

thread 2 of cond_examp
force p
if *val*(p) *goto* L1
force aa
b   :=$_v$ *val*(aa)
goto L2
L1:   b   :=$_v$ 4
L2:   *force* b
bb :=$_v$ *val*(b) + 6
stop

5.3 Optimizations

Object code produced by the basic code generation schemata leaves much room for improvement. In addition to the usual sort of peephole optimization that can be applied to sequential quads, there are a number of optimizations which reduce the overhead of using tagged locations. We discuss these below.

5.3.1 Deferring Thread Initialization

The initialization code at the beginning of the first thread allocates storage for all local variables and initializes all other threads, according to Section 5.2.4. While workable, this may needlessly allocate storage for local variables defined in the arms of conditionals, some of which will never be used depending on the predicates. Similarly, threads which only compute the values of variables appearing within one arm of a conditional will do nothing if the conditional goes the other way. We can save some overhead, therefore, by conditionalizing the initialization of local variables and threads on the same predicates that control whether they will be needed at all.

Optimization 5.1 (Thread Initialization Deferment)

INSTANCE: A thread T such that the control strings of all its statements are prefixed by Ax, where A is a control string and x a control term; and the set of initialization statements S which closes thread T, stores the promises for the variables it computes, and initiates the thread.

ACTION:

1. Move the initialization statements S to a point immediately following the computation of the predicate variable **x** corresponding to the control term x (this may move S to a different thread).

2. Take Ax as the control string for each statement in S.

3. Strip the prefix Ax from each statement in T.

We described this optimization using the control strings discussed in Section 5.2.3; in terms of conditional branches the assertion that the control strings of all statements of T are prefixed by Ax says that there is a conditional branch which branches around the whole of T, Step 2 says that a branch around the statements of S is to be inserted, and Step 3 says that the branch around the whole of thread T is removed. By describing it in terms of control strings, we are allowing the conditional branch around S to be merged with similar conditional branches which are likely to follow the computation of **x**.

Applying this optimization to `gen_fact_list` yields the following:

Applying this optimization to `gen_fact_list` yields the following:

```
function gen_fact_list (fact_list, i, n)        thread 2 of gen_fact_list
⟨Allocate locations for p, ip1, nfl, b, a,      force i
  e, im1, prev, this⟩                           im1   :=ᵥ val(i) - 1
temp1 := ⟨Null Closure⟩                         begincall nth
p       :=ₚ temp1                               Arg₁  :=꜀ im1
...                                             Arg₂  :=꜀ fact_list
e       :=ₚ temp1                               invoke nth
force i                                          prev  :=ᵥ val(Res)
force n                                          endcall nth
p       :=ᵥ val(i) > val(n)                      force i
force p                                          force prev
if val(p) goto L1                               this :=ᵥ val(i) * val(prev)
temp2 := ⟨Close thread 2 over i, im1,           stop
          fact_list, prev, this⟩
im1   :=ₚ temp2
prev  :=ₚ temp2
this  :=ₚ temp2
⟨Initiate thread 2⟩
force i
ip1   :=ᵥ val(i) + 1
...
```

Notice, too, that by eliminating the conditional branch from the second thread we eliminate all of that thread's references to p, so that p need no longer be included in thread 2's environment.

After applying Optimization 5.1, the following optimization may be used to condition-alize local variable allocation:

Optimization 5.2 (Local Variable Initialization Deferment)

INSTANCE: A local variable y whose control string is Ax, allocated by statement s, and such that the control strings of all thread initialization code which refers to y (*i.e.*, during closure creation) are prefixed by Ax.

ACTION: Move s to a point immediately following the computation of the predicate x, and take Ax as its control string.

Even though there can be no computation which refers to y before the predicate x is computed, there might be thread initialization code which does: if a thread refers to both y and some other variable z computed outside the conditional governed by x, the code which closes that thread over y and z may need to occur before x is computed. This accounts for the restriction given above.

In `gen_fact_list`, the variables ip1, nfl, b, e, im1, prev, and this are subject to this optimization, with e allocated if p is false, the rest if p is true:

```
function gen_fact_list (fact_list, i, n)     thread 2 of gen_fact_list
⟨Allocate locations for p and a⟩             force i
temp1 :=  ⟨Null Closure⟩                     im1  :=ᵥ val(i) - 1
p      :=ₚ temp1                             begincall nth
a      :=ₚ temp1                             Arg₁ :=_c im1
force i                                      Arg₂ :=_c fact_list
force n                                      invoke nth
p      :=ᵥ val(i) > val(n)                   prev :=ᵥ val(Res)
force p                                      endcall nth
if val(p) goto L1                            force i
⟨Allocate locations for ip1, nfl, b,        force prev
  im1, prev, this⟩                           this :=ᵥ val(i) * val(prev)
ip1   :=ₚ temp1                              stop
nfl   :=ₚ temp1
b     :=ₚ temp1
temp2 :=  ⟨Close thread 2 over i, im1,
             fact_list, prev, this⟩
im1   :=ₚ temp2
prev  :=ₚ temp2
this  :=ₚ temp2
⟨Initiate thread 2⟩
force i
ip1   :=ᵥ val(i) + 1
. . .
goto L2
L1:   ⟨Allocate location for e⟩
e      :=ₚ temp1
temp  :=  allocate 1
. . .
```

5.3.2 Eliminating Redundant Forces and Excess Copies

A *force* statement suspends execution of a thread until the indicated location contains a value, and for the remainder of the thread's execution that location will contain a value. Subsequent forces of that location are therefore unnecessary. Similarly, it is not necessary to force a location previously assigned with a $:=_v$ assignment. In addition to removing a *force* when a location is known to be a value, a $:=_c$ assignment can be converted to a cheaper $:=_v$ assignment if the right hand side location is known to be a value. Finally, if a thread is closed over a location known to contain a value, only the value need be included in the environment.

To describe these optimizations, we generalize slightly the notion of a *dominator* as used in conventional compilers [2]. The conventional definition says that in a sequential piece of code with conditional branches, a statement A dominates another statement B if all possible flow paths from the beginning of the code to B pass through A. Using this definition, a statement *force* x can be eliminated if dominated by another statement *force* **x** or by a statement **x** $:=_v$ *Exp.* This is a bit too restrictive, however, for it does not handle the case where all paths to a *force* **x** statement include another *force* **x** statement, but not necessarily the *same force* **x** statement. We therefore define *value-domination* as follows:

Definition 5.3 *In a thread, a statement A is* value-dominated *for* **x***, where* **x** *is a variable, if all possible flow paths from the beginning of the thread to A pass through either a statement force* **x** *or* **x** $:=_v$ *Exp.*

If the code which initializes some thread is value-dominated for **x***, then all statements in that thread are considered value-dominated for* **x** *as well.*

Given this definition, we give three optimizations:

Optimization 5.4 (Redundant Force Removal)

INSTANCE: A statement *s* of the form *force* **x** that is value-dominated for **x**.

ACTION: Remove statement *s*.

Optimization 5.5 (Copy Assignment Conversion)

INSTANCE: A statement *s* of the form *Loc* $:=_c$ **x** that is value-dominated for **x**.

ACTION: Replace *s* by the statement *Loc* $:=_v$ *val*(**x**).

Optimization 5.6 (Environment Assignment Conversion)

INSTANCE: A statement *s* of the form *ULoc* := ⟨*Close thread i over* ..., **x**, ...⟩ that is value dominated for **x**.

ACTION: Replace *s* by the statement *ULoc* := ⟨*Close thread i over* ..., *val*(**x**), ...⟩, and replace all occurrences of *val*(**x**) in thread *i* by just **x**.

Applying these optimizations to the code from the last section gives:

```
    function gen_fact_list (fact_list, i, n)      thread 2 of gen_fact_list
    ⟨Allocate locations for p and a⟩               im1   :=ᵥ i - 1
    temp1    :=  ⟨Null Closure⟩                     begincall nth
    p          :=ₚ temp1                            Arg₁  :=ᵥ val(im1)
    a          :=ₚ temp1                            Arg₂  :=_c fact_list
    force i                                         invoke nth
    force n                                         prev  :=ᵥ val(Res)
    p          :=ᵥ val(i) > val(n)                  endcall nth
    if val(p) goto L1                               this  :=ᵥ i * val(prev)
    ⟨Allocate locations for ip1, nfl, b,           stop
     im1, prev, this⟩
    ip1      :=ₚ temp1
    nfl      :=ₚ temp1
    b        :=ₚ temp1
    temp2    :=  ⟨Close thread 2 over val(i),
                   im1, fact_list, prev, this⟩
    im1      :=ₚ temp2
    prev     :=ₚ temp2
    this     :=ₚ temp2
    ⟨Initiate thread 2⟩
    ip1      :=ᵥ val(i) + 1
    begincall gen_fact_list
    Arg₁     :=_c fact_list
    Arg₂     :=ᵥ val(ip1)
    Arg₃     :=ᵥ val(n)
    invoke gen_fact_list
    nfl      :=ᵥ val(Res)
    endcall gen_fact_list
    temp     :=  allocate 3
    temp[0]  :=ᵥ ⟨Tag for cons⟩
    temp[1]  :=_c this
    temp[2]  :=ᵥ val(nfl)
    b        :=ᵥ temp
    a        :=ᵥ val(b)
    goto L2
L1: ⟨Allocate location for e⟩
    e        :=ₚ temp1
    temp     :=  allocate 1
    temp[0]  :=ᵥ ⟨Tag for nil⟩
    e        :=ᵥ temp
    a        :=ᵥ val(e)
L2: ◇        :=ᵥ val(a)
    stop
```

and applying them to `cond_examp` gives:

function `cond_examp` `(x)`
⟨*Allocate locations for* `p, a, aa, b, bb, c`⟩
`temp1` `:=` ⟨*Null Closure*⟩
`temp2` `:=` ⟨*Close thread 2 over* `p, aa, b, bb`⟩
`p`   `:=`$_p$ `temp1`
`a`   `:=`$_p$ `temp1`
`aa`   `:=`$_p$ `temp1`
`c`   `:=`$_p$ `temp1`
`b`   `:=`$_p$ `temp2`
`bb`   `:=`$_p$ `temp2`
⟨*Initiate thread 2*⟩
force `x`
`p`   `:=`$_v$ `val(x) > 0`
if `val(p)` *goto* `L1`
`a`   `:=`$_v$ `3`
goto `L2`
`L1:`   *force* `bb`
`a`   `:=`$_v$ `val(bb)`
`L2:`   `aa`   `:=`$_v$ `val(a) + 5`
force `bb`
`c`   `:=`$_v$ `val(aa) + val(bb)`
`◇`   `:=`$_v$ `val(c)`
stop

thread 2 *of* `cond_examp`
force `p`
if `val(p)` *goto* `L1`
force `aa`
`b`   `:=`$_v$ `val(aa)`
goto `L2`
`L1:`   `b`   `:=`$_v$ `4`
`L2:`   `bb` `:=`$_v$ `val(b) + 6`
stop

Notice that the second *force* `bb` in the first thread could not be eliminated, since it can be reached without passing through the first *force* `bb`.

5.3.3   Converting Tagged Locations to Untagged Locations

Tagged locations include presence bits which are needed to synchronize their use among multiple threads, and can be copied even before they have received a value. Many of a function's local variables, however, only appear in one thread, and furthermore are always assigned a value before use. These locations could just as well be untagged.

The following optimization should be applied only after optimizations 5.4 and 5.5.

Optimization 5.7 (Untagging)

INSTANCE: Local variable `x` allocated by statement `s` and which, ignoring initialization code, only appears in one thread, and furthermore does not appear on the right hand side of a `:=`$_c$ assignment.

ACTION:

1. Replace every statement of the form `x` `:=`$_v$ `Exp` by `x` `:=` `Exp`.

2. Replace every occurrence of `val(x)` by just `x`.

82

3. Remove statement *s*.

4. Remove x from any statements which create thread closures (it should have only appeared in one thread's closure to begin with).

Applying this to `gen_fact_list` gives:

```
function gen_fact_list (fact_list, i, n)       thread 2 of gen_fact_list
temp1    :=  ⟨Null Closure⟩                    im1   :=  i - 1
force i                                         begincall nth
force n                                         Arg₁  :=ᵥ im1
p        :=  val(i) > val(n)                    Arg₂  :=_c fact_list
if p goto L1                                    invoke nth
⟨Allocate location for this⟩                    prev :=  val(Res)
temp2    :=  ⟨Close thread 2 over val(i),       endcall nth
             fact_list, this⟩                   this :=ᵥ i * prev
this     :=ₚ temp2                              stop
⟨Initiate thread 2⟩
ip1      :=  val(i) + 1
begincall gen_fact_list
Arg₁     :=_c fact_list
Arg₂     :=ᵥ ip1
Arg₃     :=ᵥ val(n)
invoke gen_fact_list
nfl      :=  val(Res)
endcall gen_fact_list
temp     :=  allocate 3
temp[0]  :=ᵥ ⟨Tag for cons⟩
temp[1]  :=_c this
temp[2]  :=ᵥ nfl
b        :=  temp
a        :=  b
goto L2
L1:      temp     :=  allocate 1
         temp[0]  :=ᵥ ⟨Tag for nil⟩
         e        :=  temp
         a        :=  e
L2:      ◇        :=ᵥ a
         stop
```

and applying it to `cond_example` gives:

function `cond_examp` (`x`)
⟨*Allocate locations for* `p, aa, bb`⟩
`temp1 :=` ⟨*Null Closure*⟩
`temp2 :=` ⟨*Close thread 2 over* `p, aa, bb`⟩
`p       :=ₚ temp1`
`aa      :=ₚ temp1`
`bb      :=ₚ temp2`
⟨*Initiate thread 2*⟩
force `x`
`p       :=ᵥ val(x) > 0`
if `val(p)` *goto* `L1`
`a       := 3`
goto `L2`
`L1:` *force* `bb`
`a       := val(bb)`
`L2:` `aa    :=ᵥ a + 5`
force `bb`
`c       := val(aa) + val(bb)`
`◇       :=ᵥ c`
stop

thread 2 *of* `cond_examp`
force `p`
if `val(p)` *goto* `L1`
force `aa`
`b   := val(aa)`
goto `L2`
`L1:`   `b  := 4`
`L2:`   `bb :=ᵥ b + 6`
stop

5.3.4 Using Strictness Analysis

If a function is strict in the top-level value of some argument, it is always safe to force that argument before making a call to that function. If we require that *every* call to a function force its strict arguments before making the call, then the function body never need force those arguments, and in fact they can be passed in untagged locations. In the worst case, this simply moves the *force* statements from the function body to the callers and allows untagged argument-passing locations. Often, however, the call will be value-dominated for some or all of the strict arguments, so that no extra forcing need be inserted in the caller, with a resulting net savings.

Optimization 5.8 (Argument Untagging)

INSTANCE: Function `f` strict in the top-level value of its *i*th argument (let `x` be the corresponding formal parameter), along with all code which makes first-order calls to `f`.

ACTION:

1. In each first-order call to `f`, replace a statement of the form `Arg`ᵢ `:=ᵥ` *Exp* by `Arg`ᵢ `:=` *Exp*.

2. In each first-order call to `f`, replace a statement of the form `Arg`ᵢ `:=`*c* *Loc* by the following two-statement sequence:

   force Loc
   `Arg`ᵢ `:= val(`*Loc*`)`

3. In all threads comprising the body of f, remove any statement of the form *force* x.

4. In all threads comprising the body of f, replace all occurrences of *val*(x) by just x.

To illustrate, here is `gen_fact_list` again, where we note that `gen_fact_list` is strict in i and n, and `nth` is strict in all arguments.

function `gen_fact_list (fact_list, i, n)`
```
temp1   :=  ⟨Null Closure⟩
p       :=  i > n
```
if p *goto* L1
⟨*Allocate location for* `this`⟩
```
temp2   :=  ⟨Close thread 2 over i, fact_list,
                this⟩
this    :=ₚ temp2
```
⟨*Initiate thread 2*⟩
```
ip1     :=  i + 1
```
begincall `gen_fact_list`
```
Arg₁    :=c fact_list
Arg₂    :=  ip1
Arg₃    :=  n
```
invoke `gen_fact_list`
```
nfl     :=  val(Res)
```
endcall `gen_fact_list`
```
temp    :=  allocate 3
temp[0] :=ᵥ ⟨Tag for cons⟩
temp[1] :=c this
temp[2] :=ᵥ nfl
b       :=  temp
a       :=  b
```
goto L2

thread 2 *of* `gen_fact_list`
```
im1  :=  i - 1
```
begincall `nth`
```
Arg₁ :=  im1
```
force `fact_list`
```
Arg₂ :=  val(fact_list)
```
invoke `nth`
```
prev :=  val(Res)
```
endcall `nth`
```
this :=ᵥ i * prev
```
stop

```
L1:    temp    :=  allocate 1
       temp[0] :=ᵥ ⟨Tag for nil⟩
       e       :=  temp
       a       :=  e
L2:    ◇       :=ᵥ a
```
       stop

Notice that aside from a *force* `fact_list` statement in the second thread, no other additional *force* statements were needed.

We note that one of the first-order calls into which force statements must be inserted is the higher-order entry code created for the function (see Figure 5.3). Passing strict arguments as values and the entry code method for making it work in the presence of higher-order functions are due to [13].

5.3.5 Code Motion

One of the advantages of the sequential quads notation is that standard flow analysis and code motion techniques [2] can be applied to it. Here is an example of how code motion can be employed to reduce tagged location overhead.

In gen_fact_list from the last section, the tagged variable this is copied into the cons cell created in thread 1, but is not used elsewhere:

function gen_fact_list (fact_list, i, n)	*thread* 2 *of* gen_fact_list
...	...
⟨*Allocate location for* this⟩	this $:=_v$ i * prev
temp2 := ⟨*Close thread 2 over* i, fact_list, this⟩	*stop*
this $:=_p$ temp2	
⟨*Initiate thread 2*⟩	
...	
temp := *allocate* 3	
temp[0] $:=_v$ ⟨*Tag for cons*⟩	
temp[1] $:=_c$ this	
temp[2] $:=_v$ nfl	
b := temp	
...	
stop	

This is a fairly common situation, as the conversion from the source language to functional quads introduces a variable when the argument to a data constructor is an expression, and non-strictness often requires it to be tagged. But a structure location is a perfectly good tagged location, and so we would like the second thread above to store directly into the cons cell, as follows:

function gen_fact_list (fact_list, i, n)	*thread* 2 *of* gen_fact_list
...	...
⟨*Allocate location for* b⟩	*force* b
temp2 := ⟨*Close thread 2 over* i, fact_list, b⟩	temp3 := i * prev
⟨*Initiate thread 2*⟩	b[1] $:=_v$ temp3
...	*stop*
temp := *allocate* 3	
temp[0] $:=_v$ ⟨*Tag for cons*⟩	
temp[1] $:=_p$ temp2	
temp[2] $:=_v$ nfl	
b $:=_v$ temp	
...	
stop	

This has eliminated the variable this, but b had to be made tagged, since thread 2 now refers to it, and is closed over it before it becomes a value. A better approach is to recognize that in the original program, the code which initializes this and thread 2 can be moved to a point just before the first reference to this:

```
function gen_fact_list (fact_list, i, n)          thread 2 of gen_fact_list
  ...                                               ...
  temp      :=  allocate 3                          this  :=ᵥ i * prev
  temp[0]   :=ᵥ ⟨Tag for cons⟩                      stop
  ⟨Allocate location for this⟩
  temp2     :=  ⟨Close thread 2 over i, fact_list, this⟩
  this      :=ₚ temp2
  ⟨Initiate thread 2⟩
  temp[1]   :=ᶜ this
  temp[2]   :=ᵥ nfl
  b         :=  temp
  ...
  stop
```

Now `this` can be removed by closing thread 2 over the value of `temp`, which holds the pointer to the structure:

```
function gen_fact_list (fact_list, i, n)          thread 2 of gen_fact_list
  ...                                               ...
  temp      :=  allocate 3                          temp3   := i * prev
  temp[0]   :=ᵥ ⟨Tag for cons⟩                      temp[1] :=ᵥ temp3
  temp2     :=  ⟨Close thread 2 over i, fact_list, temp⟩  stop
  temp[1]   :=ₚ temp2
  ⟨Initiate thread 2⟩
  temp[2]   :=ᵥ nfl
  b         :=  temp
  ...
  stop
```

The net result is the elimination of both tagged location `this` and the $:=_c$ assignment. We have also duplicated the behavior of Heller's L-structures [25], where a data structure slot initially points to a thread which ultimately stores a value directly into that slot.

5.4 Implementing Tagged Locations

An explanation of how to implement tagged locations completes the description of code generation. There are a limitless number of possible schemes, but we will try to illustrate a few of the more interesting ones. Each scheme is described by defining the representation of values, promises, and unevaluated copies, and giving five procedures corresponding to the five operations on tagged locations: $:=_v$, $:=_p$, $:=_c$, *force*, and *val*. To avoid being tied to any particular instruction set, we will use a "pseudo-algol" notation to describe these procedures. An example:

procedure $loc :=_v value$
  $[loc] \leftarrow V.value$

Brackets indicate indirection, so that [*loc*] means the location to which *loc* points. The contents of a tagged location are indicated as *tag.data*, so the above procedure stores the tag *V* in the tag part of the location to which *loc* points, and *value* in the data part. If the target architecture has hardware support for tagged locations this might be a single instruction, otherwise it might require some shifting and masking operations.

In taking a position on how tagged locations are to be implemented, we will also have to take a position on the thread scheduling policy, that is, when does the execution of a thread begin and end in relation to the execution of other threads. The object code itself sets boundaries on the scheduling policy: the earliest time at which thread 1 of a function can begin execution is when the function is invoked, and similarly the other threads of a function cannot begin until their initialization code has been executed. On the other hand, the latest time a thread can begin is when one of the locations it computes is forced, if the forcing thread is to make further progress. We will consider various points along this spectrum.

5.4.1 Demand-Driven Uniprocessor Implementations

By uniprocessor, we mean a conventional von Neumann machine, which can only execute one thread at a time and has no special hardware support for switching among threads. To accommodate multi-threaded code, then, we must either simulate multi-processor task switching in software, or have the threads explicitly transfer control between one another. The schemes we describe in this section all fall into the latter category, as this is likely to be the most efficient method (in any event, the multi-processor schemes described in Section 5.4.3 can all be adapted for the former approach, if desired).

The natural point at which to switch threads is at the *force* operator: forcing a location which does not yet contain a value transfers control to the thread which is to compute that value, with the forcing thread regaining control when the other thread reaches its *stop* statement. The *force* operator is thus a kind of procedure call, where the procedure to be called is indicated by the promise stored in the forced location.[3] The resulting scheduling is termed *demand-driven*, as a thread is not executed until another thread needs one of the values it computes. Demand-driven scheduling should not be confused with lazy evaluation; the connection between the two is the topic of Section 8.6.

In uniprocessor demand-driven schemes, a *force* statement invokes a thread through a form of procedure call, and so the *stop* statement is compiled as a return to the point at which the *force* occurred. Similarly, the *invoke* statement found in the function call schema is compiled as a call to thread 1 of the function being called, differing from *force* only in that arguments are passed and a result returned. Because threads are initiated by *force* statements, the "initiate" portion of thread initialization (Section 5.2.4) is omitted.

The procedure call behavior of *force* constrains the way threads will be interleaved at run time; in particular, the forcing thread does not regain control until the forced thread terminates. The impact of this on partitioning is discussed in Section 5.5.

Scheme 1

---

[3]In these implementations, therefore, the sequential quads *force* behaves exactly like Henderson's `force`.

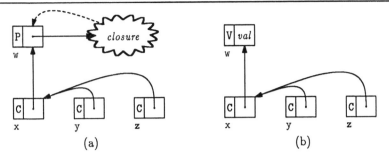

Figure 5.6: Tagged Location Scheme 1

The simplest scheme uses three tags to indicate which of the three classes of data a tagged location contains:

V.value The value given by *value*.

P.closure A promise to have a value stored by the code to which *closure* points.

C.addr A copy of the location to which *addr* points, where that location may contain a value, promise, or another copy.

Figure 5.6 illustrates this representation. Part (a) of the figure shows four locations after the following code sequence is executed:

```
w  :=ₚ closure
x  :=c w
y  :=c x
z  :=c x
```

The dotted line from the closure to w indicates that the closure will have a pointer to w in its environment. Part (b) shows the same four locations after one of them is forced, and the thread has stored a value in w and terminated.

The definition of the five tagged location operations is as follows:

procedure $loc :=_v value$
   $[loc] \leftarrow V.value$

procedure $loc :=_p closure$
   $[loc] \leftarrow P.closure$

procedure $loc_1 :=_c loc_2$
   $[loc_1] \leftarrow C.loc_2$

function $val(loc)$
   $a \leftarrow followindir(loc)$
   if $[a] = V.value$ **then**
     return *value*
   else error

procedure $force(loc)$
   $a \leftarrow followindir(loc)$
   if $[a] = P.closure$ **then**
     call *closure*

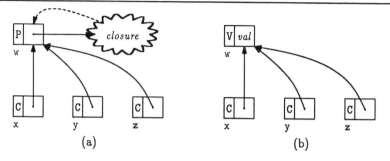

Figure 5.7: Variation on Tagged Location Scheme 1

The subroutine *followindir* follows a chain of C pointers and returns a pointer to the location at the end of the chain:

function *followindir(loc)*
    if $[loc] = C.addr$ **then**
        return *followindir(addr)*
    else
        return *loc*

The *val* operator shows a test to make sure a points to a value. This test can be eliminated, as it only detects bugs in the compiler: a *val* operator can only be used when the indicated location is known to be a value, with the compiler inserting a *force* operator prior to it if necessary.

The assignment operators are all very cheap in this scheme, but *force* and *val* are expensive because the chains of C pointers may be arbitrarily long. This can be remedied by a small change to $:=_c$:

procedure $loc_1 :=_c loc_2$
    if $[loc_2] = C.addr$ **then**
        $[loc_1] \leftarrow [loc_2]$
    else
        $[loc_1] \leftarrow C.loc_2$

With this modification, a location containing $C.addr$ only points to locations containing either values or promises, never copies, as illustrated in Figure 5.7. The *followindir* subroutine can then be simplified to check for a single indirection:

function *followindir(loc)*
    if $[loc] = C.addr$ **then**
        return *addr*
    else
        return *loc*

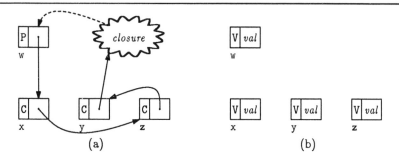

Figure 5.8: Tagged Location Scheme 2

Even with this variation, an indirection is created when a copy of a location containing a value is made. But because the contents of a location never change once it is assigned a value, there is no reason why the value itself cannot be copied. Again, this is a small modification to $:=_c$:

> **procedure** $loc_1 :=_c loc_2$
>> **if** $[loc_2] = P.closure$ **then**
>>> $[loc_1] \leftarrow C.loc_2$
>> **else**
>>> $[loc_1] \leftarrow [loc_2]$

Scheme 2

In Scheme 1 and its variations, a copy of an unevaluated location is represented by an indirection, and the indirection remains even after the location to which it points receives a value. All subsequent fetches of the copy location, therefore, must follow the indirection. This can be eliminated, however, if we arrange for the $:=_v$ operation to store the value in all locations which contain copies of the location to be stored.

One way to accomplish this would be to keep a "notifier" list with each location, containing the addresses of other locations which need copies. The operation **x** $:=_c$ **w** would add the address of **x** to the notifier list for **w**, and the operation **w** $:=_v$ *value* would store *value* in **w** and in every other location on the list. This is akin to the method for handling deferred reads in I-structure memory [8].

A better method requiring no additional storage is reported in [41]. The idea is to form the notifier list by chaining together the copy locations themselves, with the head of the chain stored in the location which originally contained the promise. An $:=_c$ operation simply splices in the new copy location into the chain, carrying the original closure pointer to the end of the chain, and the $:=_v$ operation stores the value in every location along the chain, beginning at the head. We again need three tags, but their interpretation differs slightly from Scheme 1:

V.value The value given by *value*.

P.closure A promise to have a value stored by the code to which *closure* points.

C.addr A promise to have a value stored by the code to which the closure found at the end of the *C* pointer chain points.

The representation is depicted in Figure 5.8 (which illustrates the same code sequences as before), and the definition of the five operations is as follows:

procedure $loc :=_v value$
    $old \leftarrow [loc]$
    $[loc] \leftarrow V.value$
    if $old = C.addr$ **then**
        $addr :=_v value$

procedure $loc :=_p closure$
    $[loc] \leftarrow P.closure$

procedure $loc_1 :=_c loc_2$
    $[loc_1] \leftarrow [loc_2]$
    if $[loc_2] \neq V.value$ **then**
        $[loc_2] \leftarrow C.loc_1$

function $val(loc)$
    if $[loc] = V.value$ **then**
        return $value$
    else error

procedure $force(loc)$
    if $[loc] = P.closure$ **then**
        call $closure$
    else if $[loc] = C.addr$ **then**
        $force(addr)$

Notice the recursive calls in $:=_v$ and *force*, which follow the chains as needed. The main attraction of this scheme is the simplicity of the *val* operator, which presumably is the most frequently used of the five.

5.4.2   Implementations Requiring Only Two Tags

The main drawback shared by the schemes presented in the last section is that a location may have one of three tags, resulting in fairly complex definitions of some operators tagged operators. Here we present two schemes which only require two tags. Any scheme will require at least two tags, of course, because any implementation of a non-strict programming language will have to distinguish between evaluated and unevaluated expressions.

Scheme 3

In the basic code generation schemata given in Section 5.2, the left hand sides of $:=_v$ and $:=_p$ operators were always local variables, while the left hand sides of $:=_c$ operators were always the elements of data structures or arguments to procedures.[4] If we stick to these schemata, then, local variables can only contain values or promises, and structure elements and arguments can only contain copies; locations for local variables need only one bit to encode the tag, while other locations need none at all.

    The appearance of this representation is the same as in Figure 5.7, but we need to translate the $:=_c$, *force*, and *val* operators two different ways, depending on whether their operands are local variables or arguments/structure elements:

---

[4]The structure tag slots of data structures (offset 0) appear on the left hand sides of $:=_v$ operators, but since these locations always receive a value immediately upon creation we can treat them as untagged.

```
procedure varloc :=_v value                    function val(strloc)
    [varloc] ← V.value                              if [strloc] = C.addr then
                                                        if [addr] = V.value then
procedure varloc :=_p closure                               return value
    [varloc] ← P.closure                                else error
                                                    else error
procedure strloc :=_c varloc
    [strloc] ← C.varloc                         procedure force(varloc)
                                                    if [varloc] = P.closure then
procedure strloc_1 :=_c strloc_2                        call closure
    [strloc_1] ← [strloc_2]
                                                procedure force(strloc)
function val(varloc)                                if [strloc] = C.addr then
    if [varloc] = V.value then                          if [addr] = P.closure then
        return value                                        call closure
    else error                                      else error
```

(*varloc* refers to a local variable location, while *strloc* is a structure element or argument location.)

This scheme has the overall most efficient implementation of the five operators: there is no looping, and if error-checking is eliminated only the *force* operator tests tag bits (again, the error-checking in the code really only detects compiler bugs). The main disadvantage is that it precludes Optimization 5.5 (Copy Assignment Conversion), because that optimization violates the restriction that structure locations and arguments can only contain copies. The code motion optimization illustrated in Section 5.3.5 is also ruled out.

This scheme is essentially that used by the Yale ALFL compiler [13], and is also the same as what goes on in a graph reduction implementation such as the G-machine LML compiler [39].

Scheme 4

Another two-tag scheme has no restrictions on what any tagged location may contain, but instead eliminates the need for a copy tag by using a promise to simulate a copy. To perform x :=_c w, a small thread which forces w and stores its value into x is created, and a promise for that thread is placed in x. Forcing x, therefore, also forces w, and a subsequent *val*(x) will obtain the value of w. Since there are now only promises and values, only two tags are needed. This scheme is illustrated in Figure 5.9, and the code is as follows:

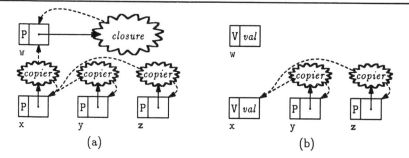

(a)   (b)

Figure 5.9: Tagged Location Scheme 4

procedure $loc :=_v value$
    $[loc] \leftarrow V.value$

procedure $loc :=_p closure$
    $[loc] \leftarrow P.closure$

procedure $loc_1 :=_c loc_2$
    $[loc_1] \leftarrow P.(\lambda\,().$
        $force(loc_2)$
        $[loc_1] \leftarrow [loc_2])$

function $val(loc)$
    if $[loc] = V.value$ **then**
        return $value$
    else error

procedure $force(loc)$
    if $[loc] = P.closure$ **then**
        call $closure$

A drawback of this scheme is the overhead of an extra procedure call when a copy is forced. It also fails to implement completely the definition of an unevaluated copy, which says that if x contains a copy of w then all operations performed on x should behave as if they were performed on w. In particular, if a value is stored in w then a subsequent $val(\text{x})$ should fetch w's value, without having to perform a *force* operation on x. In the present scheme, storing a value in w does not affect the promise stored in x, so a force of x is needed before any attempt to do $val(\text{x})$. This is not a problem, however, for even with all the optimizations described earlier copies are only stored in structure elements and arguments, and we never generate code which fetches the value from such a location without first forcing it.

The code generated from Henderson's force and delay transformation [26] often resembles this scheme, for if a delayed expression is just an identifier the thread corresponding to that delay is just like a copier thread as defined above.

5.4.3   Multiprocessor Implementations

Moving from a uniprocessor to a multiprocessor implementation does not appreciably affect the way tagged data is represented; all of the schemes described above can be adapted for multiprocessors without much change. If threads are to execute concurrently, however, there must be some changes in the scheduling policy, for the policy described earlier results in only one thread executing at a time. One possibility is to retain demand-driven scheduling but relax it so that threads can start a little earlier, and so that the forcing thread can resume execution a little earlier as well. Another possibility is to abandon demand-driven scheduling in favor of eager scheduling.

Parallel Demand-Driven Scheduling

In the demand-driven schemes described for uniprocessors, a forcing thread suspends until the thread it forced terminates execution, even if the forced thread stores a value in the location long before it terminates. One way to obtain some concurrency, then, is to have the forcing thread initiate the concurrent execution of the thread named in the promise, and then wait until a value is stored in the forced location. When a value is stored, the forcing thread and the remainder of the forced thread can proceed in parallel. When a thread reaches its *stop* statement, it just dies rather than returning to the thread which initiated it.

Any of the schemes described earlier can be adapted to this scheduling policy simply by modifying the *force* operator. For scheme 1, the modification would be as follows:

> **procedure** *force(loc)*
>   *a* ← *followindir(loc)*
>   **if** $[a] = P.closure$ **then**
>   **initiate** *closure*
>   **wait until** $[a] = V.value$

The *invoke* statement used for function calls needs a similar modification: it should initiate the concurrent execution of thread 1 of the called function, then wait for Res to receive a value.

Unfortunately, allowing concurrent execution of threads opens up the possibility that a second force of a location may occur between the time the first force initiates the corresponding thread and the time the location receives a value. With the code for *force* above, this results in two concurrent executions of the same thread, a wasteful and possibly hazardous occurrence. The solution is to include a bit in each closure which indicates whether the closure has already been invoked:

> **procedure** *force(loc)*
>   *a* ← *followindir(loc)*
>   **if** $[a] = P.closure$ **then**
>   **begin critical section**
>   **if** ¬*Executing?(closure)* **then**
>   *Executing?(closure)* ← *True*
>   **initiate** *closure*
>   **end critical section**
>   **wait until** $[a] = V.value$

Notice the use of the critical section to avoid the race that would result if two *force* statements could test the closure's bit at the same time (all that is really needed is an atomic test-and-set instruction). We have to associate the bit with the closure rather than with the forced location because the same thread can be forced through two different locations, if the thread computes more than one local variable. An analog of the executing bit can be found in every parallel demand-driven functional language implementation (see [66] and [19], as well as the *d-union* operator in [52]).

"Sparking"

The parallel demand-driven scheduling policy given above gains some concurrency, but there is still a lot of room for improvement. Consider a common code sequence like:

```
...
force y
force z
x :=ᵥ val(y) + val(z)
...
```

Under the previous policy, there will be no concurrency at all between the thread for y and the thread for z, except to the degree that the thread for y computes other values after storing the value of y. There is no reason, however, why the two threads cannot be started at the same time. To achieve this, we define an operator called *spark* that performs the initiating part of *force* but not the waiting part (the term *spark* is due to [19]):

```
procedure spark(loc)
    a ← followindir(loc)
    if [a] = P.closure then
        begin critical section
            if ¬Executing?(closure) then
                Executing?(closure) ← True
            initiate closure
        end critical section
```

Using *spark* we can rephrase the earlier code to completely overlap the computation of y and z:

```
...
spark y
spark z
force y
force z
x :=ᵥ val(y) + val(z)
...
```

A more aggressive use of *spark* tries to move the *spark* statements to the earliest point possible while still insuring that every location that is sparked is eventually forced. Within a thread, this says that a *spark* x statement can be moved to the earliest point where it is *post-dominated* by a statement *force* x. Post-domination [3] is the mirror image of domination: a statement A is post-dominated by B if every control flow path from A to the end of the thread also includes B.

96

Eager Scheduling

Even with liberal use of *spark*, demand-driven scheduling policies will only initiate a thread if there is (or will be) at least one force of that thread, *i.e.*, at least one of the values the thread computes is definitely needed by some other computation. In contrast, any scheduling policy which may initiate a thread even if none of its values are ultimately used is called an *eager* policy.

The simplest eager scheduling policy initiates every thread as soon as possible, that is, immediately following the initialization code which creates the closure for it and initializes the local variables it computes. Since every thread starts executing right after creation, when a location is forced the thread which is to compute its value will already be executing concurrently, if the location does not already contain a value. This considerably simplifies the job of the *force* operator:

$$\textbf{procedure } force(loc)$$
$$a \leftarrow followindir(loc)$$
$$\textbf{wait until } [a] = V.value$$

The *force* operator does not even need to examine the promise stored in an unevaluated location, and so there is no reason for $:=_p$ to store a promise at all, but instead it just needs to clear the presence bit. In dataflow architectures [49, 4] and in Iannucci's architecture [36] this simplified *force* and the *val* operator are combined into a single instruction—essentially it is just a blocking read which waits for the presence bit to turn on.

Because eager scheduling may result in executing threads none of whose values are forced, it is sometimes termed "speculative" [17]. We stress, however, that it is only speculative in the sense that it may do more work than is necessary to produce the program's ultimate answer; in other words, it may do some work not done by a *lazy* evaluation of the same program. Eager scheduling does *not* do any extra work relative to *lenient* evaluation (Section 4.7), since conditional branches which prevent the execution of the unselected arm of a conditional expression are still obeyed. As we will explore in Section 8.6, even demand-driven scheduling may do extra work relative to lazy evaluation if the program is not specially partitioned for laziness.

5.5 Partitioning for Uniprocessor Demand-Driven Execution

Implementing *force* as a procedure call (Sections 5.4.1 and 5.4.2) is a very efficient method for uniprocessors, but its correct operation imposes additional constraints upon partitioning beyond merely insuring that there is an interleaving of the threads that respects the data dependences. The difficulty is that the procedure call implementation of *force* does not allow all possible interleavings to be achieved at run-time.

During execution, the *force* operator dynamically interleaves threads, by transferring control to another thread when an uncomputed location is forced. In order to achieve an arbitrary interleaving, then, *force* must be able to transfer control to an arbitrary thread. More precisely, control transfers to a *runnable* thread, either beginning the execution of a recently initialized thread or resuming a thread which recently suspended while forcing a location that now contains a value. A *force* which suspends the current thread must be able to transfer control to at least one of these runnable threads, otherwise the computation deadlocks. Executing a *stop* statement causes a similar transfer of control.

The parallel schemes for implementing *force* (Section 5.4.3) can accommodate an arbitrary interleaving, for when a thread suspends (indicated by the **wait** statement in the definition of *force*) any of the other threads may continue in parallel. Similarly, in a uniprocessor simulation of a parallel method the suspending thread can select any of the runnable threads maintained in the simulated task queue. The uniprocessor demand-driven schemes of Sections 5.4.1 and 5.4.2, on the other hand, are much more limited: when a thread suspends it always goes to the beginning of the thread indicated by the forced location's promise, resuming only when that thread terminates. This rules out certain kinds of interleavings, as illustrated by the following program:

```
def nest x =
    {a = x + 2;
     b = a + 3;
     c = a + 4;
     d = a + 5;
     e = b + 6;
     f = e * d;
     g = f * a;
     h = f * c;
     i = h * g;
    in
        i};
```

If this program is partitioned into the two threads $(e, h, i, \Diamond)$ and (a, b, c, d, f, g), the following code results:[5]

<table>
<tr><td>

function nest (x)
⟨*Initialize* b, c, e, f, g⟩
force b
e :=$_v$ *val*(b) + 6
force f
force c
h := *val*(f) * *val*(c)
force g
i := h * *val*(g)
$\Diamond$:=$_v$ i
stop

</td><td>

thread 2 of nest
force x
a := *val*(x) + 2
b :=$_v$ a + 3
c :=$_v$ a + 4
d := a + 5
force e
f :=$_v$ *val*(e) * d
g :=$_v$ *val*(f) * a
stop

</td></tr>
</table>

Using one of the parallel schemes of Section 5.4.3, the dependence among b, e, f, and h will cause a "coroutining" execution path, as illustrated in Figure 5.10a. When the first thread starts, the *force* b statement immediately transfers control to the second thread, which suspends at the *force* e statement. But since b has been computed, the first thread

---

[5]Of course, this simple program would normally be partitioned into only one thread—the partitioning shown is only for purposes of illustration.

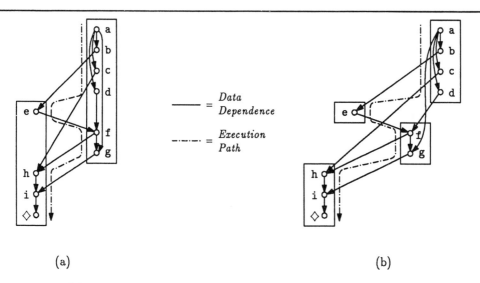

(a)   (b)

Figure 5.10: (a) "Coroutining" Interleaving; (b) Proper Partitioning for Uniprocessor Demand-Driven Implementations

can resume execution until it forces f, at which point the second thread can resume and terminate, which then allows the first thread to complete as well.

Now consider the execution of this program using one of the demand-driven uniprocessor schemes of Section 5.4.1. As before, the first thread suspends at the *force* b statement and calls the second thread. When the second thread reaches *force* e, there is a problem: the thread which is to compute e has already been activated, and the second thread has no way of transferring control back to it. If the second thread simply invokes the closure stored in e it will effectively create a duplicate instance of the first thread, so that e, h, i, and ◇ will be computed twice. This is clearly not satisfactory, especially considering how the duplication would multiply in the presence of recursion.

To prevent duplicated computation in uniprocessor demand-driven implementations, the *force* of an uncomputed location must always transfer control to a thread that is not already suspended. We now prove a sufficient condition on a partitioning to insure that this is the case, but first we need to introduce some terminology to help describe execution under demand-driven uniprocessor schemes. We distinguish between *threads*, which are static pieces of code comprising function definitions, and *thread instances*, which are the dynamic instances of threads created each time a function is invoked at run time. Let l_1 be an uncomputed tagged location, which therefore contains either a promise or a copy of some other uncomputed location l_2. Define l_1' to be either l_1 if the former, or l_2' if the latter. In other words, l_1' is the location found by following the chain of copies, if any, until a location containing a promise is found. When l_1 is forced, l_1' is the location which actually appears on the left hand side of $:=_v$ in the forced thread instance. The thread instance forcing l_1 is the *parent* of the thread instance which stores l_1', and location l_1' is the *requestor* of the latter thread instance. If a thread computes the value of more than one tagged location, then different instances of it may have different requestors. Finally,

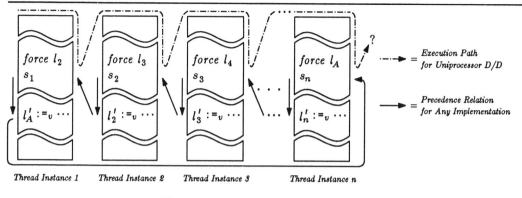

Figure 5.11: Proof of Theorem 5.11

ancestor is the transitive closure of parent.

Lemma 5.9 *In uniprocessor demand-driven implementations, a thread instance which forces an uncomputed location l transfers control to the thread instance containing a statement of the form $l' :=_v$ Exp.*

Proof. True because of the implementation of *force* as a procedure call. ∎

Lemma 5.10 *Given a statement force l, let s be the next statement executed by the thread containing the force. Then in* any *implementation, uniprocessor demand-driven or not, thread instances are interleaved such that s is always executed after the statement $l' :=_v$ Exp.*

Proof. The definition of *force* says that *force l* suspends the current thread until a value is stored in l'. ∎

Theorem 5.11 *If a partitioning is correct in the sense that for every context there is an interleaving of the threads that respects the data dependences, and furthermore in a demand-driven uniprocessor implementation no thread instance executes a force statement after storing a value in its requestor, then no thread instance forces an ancestor.*

Proof. At any point during demand-driven uniprocessor execution, the set of thread instances consists of an active thread instance and its ancestors, where each ancestor is suspended at a *force* statement. Now suppose a thread instance (call it thread instance n) forces an ancestor n generations back by forcing the location l_A. A snapshot of the thread instances is as shown in Figure 5.11, which shows all ancestors from the instance being forced (thread instance 1) through the instance doing the forcing. The uniprocessor demand-driven implementation of force results in the execution path as shown by the dot-and-dashed line. Now the theorem says that no thread instance executes a force after storing its requestor, so the statements storing l'_2 through l'_n must follow the force statements in thread instances 2 through n. Furthermore, while l'_A is not necessarily the

100

requestor of thread instance 1, it nevertheless must follow the statement *force* l_2; if it did not, the *force* l_A statement in thread instance n would simply fetch a value rather than trying to force an ancestor. These precedence relations are shown by the downward-pointing solid lines in the figure. But by the previous lemma, in any interleaving of these threads execution of each statement s_i must follow the statement storing l'_{i+1}, and s_n must follow the storing of l'_A; this is indicated by the upward-pointing solid lines. No interleaving can simultaneously satisfy all of these precedence relations, so the partitioning cannot be correct. Contradiction. ∎

On the basis of this theorem, .then, to partition for uniprocessor demand-driven execution we must insure that no thread instance executes a *force* statement after storing its requestor. It is sufficient, therefore, to verify statically that no thread can execute a force statement after executing an $:=_v$ statement. This can be achieved either by a suitable partitioning algorithm, or by splitting the threads produced by the usual partitioning algorithm. We discuss the latter approach in further detail.

To split a thread for uniprocessor demand-driven execution, consider all execution paths from the beginning of the thread. If a *force* statement follows a $:=_v$ assignment, split the thread somewhere between the *force* and the $:=_v$. Note that an *invoke* statement must be treated as if it were a *force*, since it effectively forces Res. Continue this process on the remaining threads until no further splitting is needed. When a thread is split in two, there may be untagged local variables which are defined in the first thread and referenced in the second; these must be converted back to tagged locations by replacing the := assignment by $:=_v$, inserting *val* () as needed, and by forcing the location at the beginning of the second thread. This force is perfectly safe, as it simply reconstructs the sequential ordering of the original single thread.

Applying the splitting algorithm to the earlier example program, nest, yields the following four threads, whose execution is depicted in Figure 5.10b.

function nest (x)	*thread* 2 *of* nest	*thread* 3 *of* nest	*thread* 4 *of* nest
⟨Initialization⟩	*force* b	*force* a	*force* x
force f	e $:=_v$ *val*(b) + 6	*force* d	a $:=_v$ *val*(x) + 2
force c	*stop*	*force* e	b $:=_v$ *val*(a) + 3
h := *val*(f) ∗ *val*(c)		f $:=_v$ *val*(e) ∗ *val*(d)	c $:=_v$ *val*(a) + 4
force g		g $:=_v$ *val*(f) ∗ *val*(a)	d $:=_v$ *val*(a) + 5
i := h ∗ *val*(g)		*stop*	*stop*
◇ $:=_v$ i			
stop			

Notice that a and d were converted to tagged locations. There is some freedom in choosing the split points; if the second thread had been split *before* the statement computing d, then d could have remained untagged.

The preceding algorithm assumed that any $:=_v$ assignment might store the requestor of the thread. In fact, certain $:=_v$ assignments are easily shown "safe" in that they cannot possibly store the requestor. Assignments to Arg_i fall into this category, as do assignments which initialize structure slots, where the pointer to the structure has not been stored in a tagged location (no other thread instance could possibly have access to the structure slot).

101

These assignments can be ignored when finding split points. Finally, we always know that the requestor of thread 1 for any function is the location $\Diamond$, and so thread 1 need only be split at points following the assignment to $\Diamond$. In the previous example, this would have allowed three threads instead of four. These improvements also show that both examples given in Section 5.3.3 will run on uniprocessor demand-driven implementations.

5.6   Partitioning Heuristics

Throughout this chapter we have assumed that the graph has been partitioned and ordered before code generation takes place, but by now the reader should realize that the quality of object code can vary dramatically depending on the partitioning and ordering chosen. Usually large threads are more desirable than small (this is not so clear in parallel implementations), but there are other ways that quality is affected. We list below some partitioning heuristics that can lead to improved code.

- It is generally undesirable to mix instructions from different basic blocks as it leads to excessive conditional branching. On the other hand, it *is* desirable to embed both arms of a conditional in the thread containing its left hand side.

- Vertices with only one outgoing dependence arc should be placed in the same thread as their target so that untagged locations can be used. Preferably they should be placed as close to their successors as possible to minimize the variable's lifetime.

- Arguments of data constructors and non-strict procedures should be placed before the call to minimize the use of $:=_c$ assignments.

- The number of dependence arcs crossing thread boundaries should be minimized, to reduce the number of tagged locations.

Finding efficient algorithms which incorporate these and other heuristics is a topic for future research. Some of these have already been addressed by others in the context of both strict and lazy evaluation [56, 57, 29].

5.7   Partitioning via Coalescing

For most of this chapter, we have assumed that prior to code generation an analysis phase produced a partitioning, describing the grouping of the function's subexpressions into threads. We remarked, though, that it is possible to generate code using the trivial partitioning (one subexpression per thread), and then coalesce the resulting threads. We now describe this technique in detail. This technique, first reported in the author's paper [68], results in threads that implement lazy evaluation if a demand-driven implementation of tagged locations is chosen.

The rule for coalescing threads is very simple:

- If, among all a function's threads, there is a single statement of the form *force* x for some variable x, and x does not appear on the right hand side of a $:=_c$ assignment in any thread, then the *force* statement can be replaced by the body of the thread which computes x (has a statement of the form x :=$_v$ ...).

To illustrate, consider the following function:

```
f x y = {w = x + 1; z = w / x; a = const <cons,z,y>; in a}
```

Using the trivial partitioning, the code produced is:

function f (x, y)	*thread 2 of* f	*thread 4 of* f
⟨*Allocate* w, z, a⟩	*force* w	temp := *allocate* 3
temp1 := ⟨*Close thread 2 over* x, w, z⟩	*force* x	temp[0] :=$_v$ cons
temp2 := ⟨*Close thread 3 over* x, w⟩	z :=$_v$ *val*(w) / *val*(x)	temp[1] :=$_c$ z
temp3 := ⟨*Close thread 4 over* z, y, a⟩	*stop*	temp[2] :=$_c$ y
z :=$_p$ temp1		a :=$_v$ temp
w :=$_p$ temp2	*thread 3 of* f	*stop*
a :=$_p$ temp3	*force* x	
force a	w :=$_v$ *val*(x) + 1	
◇ :=$_v$ *val*(a)	*stop*	
stop		

Applying the coalescing rule, thread 3 can be merged into thread 2, and thread 4 into thread 1, yielding:

function f (x, y)		*thread 2 of* f
⟨*Allocate* w, z, a⟩		*force* x
temp1 := ⟨*Close thread 2 over* x, w, z⟩		w :=$_v$ *val*(x) + 1
z :=$_p$ temp1		*force* x
w :=$_p$ temp1		z :=$_v$ *val*(w) / *val*(x)
temp := *allocate* 3		*stop*
temp[0] :=$_v$ cons		
temp[1] :=$_c$ z		
temp[2] :=$_c$ y		
a :=$_v$ temp		
◇ :=$_v$ *val*(a)		
stop		

The Untagging optimization (Optimization 5.7) can now be applied to a and w, and the Redundant Force Removal optimization (Optimization 5.4) can be applied to the second *force* x in thread 2. The final result is as follows.

```
function f (x, y)                              thread 2 of f
⟨Allocate z⟩                                   force x
temp1    :=   ⟨Close thread 2 over x, z⟩       w  :=   val(x) + 1
z        :=ₚ temp1                             z :=ᵥ w / val(x)
temp     :=   allocate 3                       stop
temp[0]  :=ᵥ cons
temp[1]  :=꜀ z
temp[2]  :=꜀ y
a        :=   temp
◇        :=ᵥ a
stop
```

The Redundant Force Removal optimization can often expose new opportunities for coalescing. If the Argument Untagging optimization (Optimization 5.8) is used to insert *force* statements in function invocation code, threads computing unshared strict arguments will be coalesced into the thread making the call. The resulting code is typical of what existing lazy compilers achieve.

6 A Syntactic Theory of Data Dependence

To use the code generation methods presented in the last chapter, a function must first be partitioned into a set of threads. In this and the next two chapters, we develop a method for partitioning any function into threads, by analyzing data dependences. The goal is to produce a partitioning such that no matter how the function is invoked there is an interleaving that corresponds to a valid reduction sequence.

The culmination of this chapter will be the development of the *function dependence graph*, which summarizes the data dependences that may exist among a function's subexpressions in all contexts in which it could be invoked. Chapter 7 will show how to compute a function dependence graph for any function through compile-time analysis. Chapter 8 will describe how to use the function dependence graph to guide the creation of a legal partitioning of the function.

The development of the theory of function dependence graphs proceeds in three steps. The first step is concerned with complete programs, that is, a complete state in functional quads, consisting of a number of function definitions and all the input data for the initial call. We define the *program requirement graph*, which is a partial order on the identifiers (hence, on the subexpressions) that appear in the state in any reduction sequence starting with the given program. The requirement graph is defined in terms of observing all possible reduction sequences from the given program. The main theorem is that a reduction sequence is valid if and only if the order in which subexpressions are reduced is consistent with the partial order expressed in the requirement graph.

In the next step, we define another partial order on identifiers, called the *program dependence graph*. Rather than being defined in terms of all possible reduction sequences, however, a dependence graph is the composition of separate observations made about each of the subexpressions in the program. It is therefore a collection of local information, rather than a set of global information. The relationship between the program dependence graph and the program requirement graph is established in a theorem stating that the requirement graph equals the transitive closure of the dependence graph.

Finally, the function dependence graph is defined, which gives information about a single function in isolation, rather than a complete program with all input data. It is shown that the dependence graph among the identifiers resulting from the invocation of the function in any context may be extracted from its function dependence graph.

6.1 Required Reductions

Definition 6.1 *Let* $A^{S_0 \vdash^* S_1}$ *be the set of reductions for a program* S_0 *to some derivable form* S_1, $S_0 \vdash^* S_1$. *Then for* $\alpha, \beta \in A^{S_0 \vdash^* S_1}$, β *requires* α *if* α *is reduced before* β *in every* *reduction sequence from S_0 to S_1.*

We note that requirement is transitive and antisymmetric, and so requirement forms a partial order on the set $\mathrm{A}^{S_0 \vdash^* S_1}$.

Theorem 6.2 *Let $\alpha_1, \ldots, \alpha_n$ be a permutation of $\mathrm{A}^{S_0 \vdash^* S_1}$. Then $S_0 \vdash_{\alpha_1} \cdots \vdash_{\alpha_n} S_1$ is a valid reduction sequence if and only if the permutation is consistent with the partial order expressed by the requirement relation on $\mathrm{A}^{S_0 \vdash^* S_1}$.*

Proof. The only if side is true by definition. To prove the if side, suppose $S_0 \vdash_{\alpha_1} \cdots \vdash_{\alpha_n} S_1$ is consistent with the requirement relation but not a valid reduction sequence. Let α_i $(1 \leq i \leq n)$ delimit the valid prefix of this sequence; that is, let i be such that $S_0 \vdash_{\alpha_1} \cdots \vdash_{\alpha_{i-1}} S' \vdash^* S_1$ is a valid sequence but $S_0 \vdash_{\alpha_1} \cdots \vdash_{\alpha_i} S'' \vdash^* S_1$ is not. Now by Theorem 4.13 the former sequence must be of the form

$$S_0 \vdash_{\alpha_1} \cdots \vdash_{\alpha_{i-1}} S' \vdash_{\alpha_{a_1}} \cdots \vdash_{\alpha_{a_{k-1}}} S_a \vdash_{\alpha_{a_k}} S_b \vdash_{\alpha_i} S_c \vdash^* S_1$$

where $i < a_1, \ldots, a_k \leq n$. But because the original sequence is consistent with the requirement relation, for all a_j it is not the case that α_{a_j} must precede α_i, and so by the contrapositive of Theorem 4.15 (strong dependence), α_i must exist in S_a, and we can commute α_{a_k} and α_i to obtain:

$$S_0 \vdash_{\alpha_1} \cdots \vdash_{\alpha_{i-1}} S' \vdash_{\alpha_{a_1}} \cdots \vdash_{\alpha_{a_{k-1}}} S_a \vdash_{\alpha_i} S_d \vdash_{\alpha_{a_k}} S_c \vdash^* S_1$$

Continuing this process eventually leads to a valid sequence $S_0 \vdash_{\alpha_1} \cdots \vdash_{\alpha_i} S'' \vdash^* S_1$. Contradiction. ∎

We therefore see that the requirement relation gives a necessary and sufficient ordering condition for the construction of an execution sequence from one state to another. Naturally, we are particularly interested in the case of the requirement relation from an initial program to its normal form. We are also interested in the requirement relation from an initial program to some weak normal form, but given that a program has many weak normal forms we need to establish some connection between their respective requirement relations. The following theorem does the trick:

Theorem 6.3 *Let $S_0 \vdash^* S_1 \vdash^* S_2$ and let $\mathrm{A}^{S_0 \vdash^* S_1}$ and $\mathrm{A}^{S_0 \vdash^* S_2}$ be the set of redexes reduced in an execution $S_0 \vdash^* S_1$ and $S_0 \vdash^* S_2$, respectively, with associated requirement relations $\Pi^{S_0 \vdash^* S_1}$ and $\Pi^{S_0 \vdash^* S_2}$. Then (a) $\mathrm{A}^{S_0 \vdash^* S_2} \supseteq \mathrm{A}^{S_0 \vdash^* S_1}$; and (b) $\Pi^{S_0 \vdash^* S_1}$ is equal to the restriction of $\Pi^{S_0 \vdash^* S_2}$ onto $\mathrm{A}^{S_0 \vdash^* S_1}$.*

Proof. (a) Choose any path from S_0 to S_1 and any path from S_1 to S_2. The first path consists of elements of $\mathrm{A}^{S_0 \vdash^* S_1}$; the concatenation of the paths give the elements of $\mathrm{A}^{S_0 \vdash^* S_2}$, which therefore contains $\mathrm{A}^{S_0 \vdash^* S_1}$.

(b) Suppose there were $\beta_1, \beta_2 \in \mathrm{A}^{S_0 \vdash^* S_1}$ such that $(\beta_1, \beta_2) \in \Pi^{S_0 \vdash^* S_2}$ but $(\beta_1, \beta_2) \notin \Pi^{S_0 \vdash^* S_1}$. Then there exists a sequence $S_0 \vdash^* S_1$ where β_2 precedes β_1, and so β_2 precedes β_1 in some sequence $S_0 \vdash^* S_1 \vdash^* S_2$. But then $(\beta_1, \beta_2) \notin \Pi^{S_0 \vdash^* S_2}$; contradiction. Conversely, suppose there were $\beta_1, \beta_2 \in A^{S_0 \vdash^* S_1}$ such that $(\beta_1, \beta_2) \notin \Pi^{S_0 \vdash^* S_2}$ but $(\beta_1, \beta_2) \in \Pi^{S_0 \vdash^* S_1}$. So there is a sequence from S_0 to S_2 that looks something like this:

$$\beta\alpha\beta\beta_2\beta\alpha\beta\beta_1\alpha\alpha\beta\alpha$$

where each β denotes an element of $A^{S_0 \vdash^* S_1}$ and each α denotes an element of $A^{S_1 \vdash^* S_2}$. Now because $S_0 \vdash^* S_1$ and by the contrapositive of Theorem 4.15 (strong dependence), we can always commute a β with an α, so that we get construct a sequence of all β's followed by all α's, with β_2 preceding β_1. By Theorem 4.14, the β portion of this sequence is $S_0 \vdash^* S_1$. Contradiction. ∎

This theorem says that additional execution of a program adds no new requirement relationships between the redexes that were already reduced.

Corollary 6.4 *The same requirement relationship holds between two redexes α and β in any execution sequence beginning with a state S_0 that includes them both.*

Proof. Immediate by applying Corollary 4.9 (confluence). ∎

6.2 Program Requirement Graphs

When constructing object code, we do not really care about all of the reductions performed by the functional quads reduction system, only those that result in an identifier becoming bound to a value. This is a consequence of the interaction of rewrite rules as expressed in Figure 4.3: the only reductions in one binding that have any effect on the reducibility of another binding are those that introduce a new binding of the form $x = V$, as this results in new substitution redexes in other bindings. These interactions between bindings are the things that vary from program to program; the ordering of redexes within a given sort of binding are the same for all programs, as expressed in Figure 4.3. To focus our attention on the interactions between bindings, we introduce the following definitions:

Definition 6.5 *The reduced identifiers in state S, notation reduced(S), is the set of arity zero identifiers*

$$\{ x \mid S \text{ contains a binding of the form } x^{(0)} = V \}$$

where V is a value.

Fact 6.6 (Monotonicity of reduced) *For all S_i and S_j such that $S_i \vdash^* S_j$, reduced(S_j) $\supseteq$ reduced(S_i).*

This is a consequence of the particular rewrite rules in functional quads, which provide no way of altering a binding of the form $x^{(0)} = V$.

Definition 6.7 *Identifier $x^{(0)}$ is reduced at step i in a reduction sequence $S_0, S_1, \ldots$ if $x^{(0)} \in$ reduced(S_i) but $x^{(0)} \notin$ reduced(S_{i-1}). By convention, $x^{(0)}$ is reduced at step 0 if $x^{(0)} \in$ reduced(S_0).*

Alternatively, by considering Figure 4.3 we can say that x is reduced at step i in a sequence $S_0 \vdash_{\alpha_1} S_1 \vdash_{\alpha_2} \cdots$ if $\alpha_i = \langle x, \rho \rangle$, where ρ is either R1a, R2, R4, R6, or R7. The terminology is a little funny here: when we say x is reduced at step i, we really mean that the expression on the right hand side of the binding for x is reduced at step i. Because functional quads requires a separate binding for each subexpression, this terminology gives us a way of saying when each subexpression of the program is reduced to a value. Thus do we use identifiers as proxies for the expressions to which they are bound.

Definition 6.8 x_1 *precedes* x_2 *in an execution sequence* $S_0, S_1, \ldots$ *if there exists* i, j *such that* x_1 *is reduced at step* i, x_2 *is reduced at step* j, *and* $i < j$. x_2 *follows* x_1 *if and only if* x_1 *precedes* x_2.

Given that, we redefine requirement as a relation on identifiers instead of on redexes:

Definition 6.9 x_2 *requires* x_1 *in a program* S_0 *if for every execution of* S_0 *in which* x_2 *is reduced,* x_1 *precedes* x_2. *By convention, if there is* no *execution of* S_0 *in which* x_2 *is reduced,* x_2 *does* not *require any* x_1.

Notice that both precedence and requirement on identifiers are transitive, antisymmetric relations. This new definition of requirement is really nothing more than the restriction of the original requirement relation, as defined in Definition 6.1, to R1a, R2, R4, R6, and R7 redexes. Therefore, Theorem 6.3 and its corollary still hold, and so we can determine requirement relations between identifiers without reducing a program to normal form. This implies that requirement between identifiers is a well-defined notion even for programs which have no normal form.

To illustrate these concepts, Figure 6.1 shows all possible reductions of a small program. Each path from the top to the bottom of the figure is a possible reduction sequence, and a step is labeled with an identifier if that identifier is reduced at that step. Now there are some paths for which **y** precedes **z**, and some where the reverse is true, but in every path, **y** and **z** precede **x**, and **x** precedes $\Diamond$. So **x** requires **y** and **z**, and $\Diamond$ requires **x**, **y**, and **z**. We can summarize these results in a *requirement graph*, a directed graph whose vertices correspond to variables (*i.e.*, arity 0 identifiers), and whose edges comprise the requirement relation between those variables.

Definition 6.10 *The* requirement graph *of program* S_0 *with respect to a set of variables* V *is a directed graph* $\vec{R}^{S_0} = (V, R^{S_0}|V)$, *where* $R^{S_0}|V$ *is the requirement relation between the identifiers in* V. *That is,* $(u, v) \in R^{S_0}|V$ *iff* v *requires* u *in the program* S_0.

The requirement graph for the program in Figure 6.1, with respect to $\{x, y, z, \Diamond\}$, is shown in that figure's inset.

Before moving on, we should address a small technical detail in our definition of program requirement graphs. If a program starts out with a binding $x = V$, where V is a value, then every other identifier will appear to require x, simply because x is a value in step 0. Similarly, if such a binding appears in an inner block, any binding that becomes a value after the block is added to the state will appear to require it. We remedy this with a restriction: programs for which we construct requirement graphs should not contain a binding of the form $x = V$ either in a state or in an inner block. This restriction is easily met by changing such bindings to $x = $ const V.

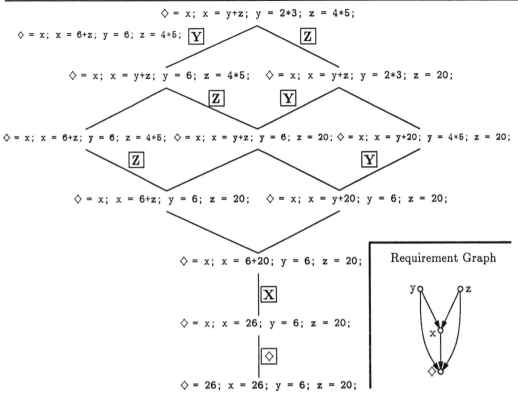

Figure 6.1: Lenient Rewritings of a Program

6.3 Program Dependence Graphs

The requirement graph is defined in terms of all possible reduction sequences from a given program. In a practical compiler, we would like to obtain this information by static analysis of the program, preferably one in which we can consider different parts of the program separately, combining the observations afterward. To that end, in this section we define the *dependence graph*; the dependence graph is obtained through static analysis, and we show that the requirement graph is easily computed from it.

We start by defining a *dependence set* for a variable, which says what other variables need to be reduced before the given variable can be.

Definition 6.11 *Let V be a set of arity zero identifiers, and let $x \in V$. Then $\Upsilon \subseteq V$ is a dependence set for x with respect to V in program S_0 if both of the following are true:*

- *(Necessity)   For all non-empty reduction sequences $S_0 \vdash S_1 \vdash^* S_i$ such that $x \in reduced(S_i)$, $\exists j < i$ s.t. $\Upsilon \subseteq reduced(S_j)$.*

- *(Sufficiency) $\forall S_i$ s.t. $S_0 \vdash^+ S_i \wedge \Upsilon \subseteq reduced(S_i)$, $\exists S_j$ s.t. $S_i \vdash^* S_j \wedge reduced(S_j) \cap V = (reduced(S_i) \cap V) \cup \{x\}$.*

The necessity condition says that all of the identifiers in the dependence set Υ must be reduced before x can be reduced. The sufficiency condition says that if all the identifiers in Υ are already reduced, it is always possible to arrive at a state where x is reduced and no other identifier in V has been reduced in the process. In other words, with respect to the set of identifiers V, the reduction of the identifiers in the dependence set are necessary and sufficient to obtain the reduction of x.

To illustrate dependence sets, consider the following program:

```
x = const 5; y = const 6; z = x + y; ◊ = z;
```

A dependence set for z, with respect to $\{x, y, z, \Diamond\}$, is $\{x, y\}$. This set is sufficient, for if x and y are both values we can reduce z to a value by applying the substitution rules R1b and R1c, followed by the arithmetic rule R4. The set is necessary, for if one of x or y is not a value, it is impossible to substitute into the binding for z, and therefore impossible to obtain an R4 redex in that binding, which is the only way to reduce z to a value.

A given identifier in a given program may have more than one dependence set. Consider the identifier $\Diamond$ in the above program. One dependence set with respect to $\{x, y, z, \Diamond\}$ is simply $\{z\}$. But $\{x, z\}$, $\{y, z\}$, and $\{x, y, z\}$ are also dependence sets. Note, however, that $\{x, y\}$ is *not* a dependence set for $\Diamond$ with respect to $\{x, y, z, \Diamond\}$: while it meets the necessity criterion, it is not sufficient, as it is impossible to reduce $\Diamond$ without first reducing z. On the other hand, $\{x, y\}$ *is* a dependence set for $\Diamond$ *with respect to* $\{x, y, \Diamond\}$, and in fact is the only dependence set with respect to $\{x, y, \Diamond\}$.

A somewhat more interesting example of multiple dependence sets is provided by the following program:

```
x = const 5; y = x + 6; z = x + y; ◊ = z;
```

As before, $\{x, y\}$ is a dependence set for z with respect to $\{x, y, z, \Diamond\}$. But in this case, $\{y\}$ is also a dependence set. This is true because in this particular case, y's being reduced implies that x is reduced also, so $\{y\}$ is a sufficient set for z. This leads one to question whether a notion of "minimal dependence set" is of any use. In fact, one could define the minimal dependence set, but it turns out not to be very useful, as determining the minimal set may require global analysis, and is in general undecidable. On the other hand, one can give a general rule of the following form: if the binding z = x + y occurs in any context, a dependence set for z is $\{x, y\}$. This rule is always valid, but whether it yields the minimal set depends on whether there are dependences between x and y. The next chapter will be devoted to finding general rules of this kind, which form the basis of compile-time analysis of programs.

We can summarize the dependence sets for a program in a *dependence graph*.

Definition 6.12 (V, D^{S_0}) *is a dependence graph for program* S_0 *if* $D^{S_0} \subseteq V \times V$ *and*

$$D^{S_0} = \bigcup_{x \in V} \bigcup_{y \in \Upsilon_x} (y, x)$$

where each Υ_x *is a dependence set for* x *with respect to* V *in* S_0.

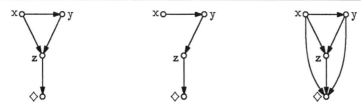

Figure 6.2: Example Dependence Graphs for a Program

Note that because there may be many dependence sets for a given identifier, there may be many dependence graphs for a given program, even for a single choice of V. Note, too, that for a given program the edges in a dependence graph for that program can differ depending on the choice of V, as the choice of V affects the sufficiency criterion of the dependence sets that comprise the graph.

Figure 6.2 shows some possible dependence graphs for the program

```
x = const 5; y = x + 6; z = x + y; ◇ = z;
```

with respect to the set $\{x, y, z, \Diamond\}$.

We now proceed to the main theorem of this section, which establishes the relationship between the dependence graph and the requirement graph.

Theorem 6.13 *If (V, D^{S_0}) is an acyclic dependence graph for a program S_0, $(D^{S_0})^+ = R^{S_0}|V$.*

Proof. $((D^{S_0})^+ \subseteq R^{S_0}|V)$ We must show that if $x_0 \xrightarrow{D^{S_0}} \cdots \xrightarrow{D^{S_0}} x_n$, $(x_0, x_n) \in R^{S_0}$ (and hence $\in R^{S_0}|V$). Now, $(x_i, x_{i+1}) \in D^{S_0}$ means x_i is in a dependence set for x_{i+1} with respect to V. By necessity, for all paths $S_0 \vdash^+ S_i$, if $x_{i+1} \in reduced(S_i)$ then $\exists j < i$ s.t. $x_i \in reduced(S_j)$; that is, x_i is always reduced before x_{i+1} whenever x_{i+1} is reduced. So by definition of requirement, $(x_i, x_{i+1}) \in R^{S_0}$, and by transitivity of the requirement relation, $(x_0, x_n) \in R^{S_0}$.

$((D^{S_0})^+ \supseteq R^{S_0}|V)$ We must show that if $(y, x) \in R^{S_0}|V$, $y \xrightarrow{D^{S_0}}^+ x$. Suppose not: let $(y, x) \in R^{S_0}|V$ be such that there is no path $y \xrightarrow{D^{S_0}}^+ x$. Then there is a topological sort $x_0, \ldots, x_n$ of (V, D^{S_0}) such that x occurs before y. We can construct a reduction sequence which follows the order given by the topological sort, by applying the sufficiency condition of dependence sets inductively, as follows. Suppose a prefix $x_0, \ldots, x_i$ of the topological sort has been reduced. Because the sequence is a topological sort of the dependence graph, the dependence set for x_{i+1} with respect to V contained in the graph is a subset of $\{x_0, \ldots, x_i\}$. By the sufficiency property, then, we can reduce x_{i+1} next, without reducing any other member of V. The base case is that x_0 can be reduced without reducing any other element of V, as its dependence set with respect to V must be empty. The net result is that we construct a reduction sequence for S_0 in which x is reduced before y. But that contradicts $(y, x) \in R^{S_0}|V$. ∎

This theorem only applies to acyclic dependence graphs. As the next few theorems establish, cycles in dependence graphs indicate identifiers that cannot be reduced. Consequently, cycles in dependence graphs are not terribly interesting in partitioning a program into threads, as we are mainly concerned with the proper scheduling of identifiers that *do* get reduced. For completeness, though, the remainder of this section establishes the relationship between arbitrary dependence graphs and requirement graphs. The reader may skip to the next section, if desired.

Lemma 6.14 *Let (V, D^{S_0}) be a dependence graph for S_0 with $(x_0, x_1), (x_1, x_2) \in D^{S_0}$. Then $(V, D^{S_0} \cup \{(x_0, x_2)\})$ is also a dependence graph for S_0.*

Proof. We must show that if Υ_1, $x_0 \in \Upsilon_1$, is a dependence set for x_1, and if Υ_2, $x_1 \in \Upsilon_2$, is a dependence set for x_2, then $\Upsilon_2' = \Upsilon_2 \cup \{x_0\}$ is also a dependence set for x_2 (all dependence sets taken with respect to V). Clearly Υ_2' is still sufficient. To show that it is necessary, first note that by necessity of Υ_2 for x_2, for all paths $S_0 \vdash^+ S_i$ such that $x_2 \in reduced(S_i)$, $\exists j < i$ s.t. $\Upsilon_2 \subseteq reduced(S_j)$. In particular, $x_1 \in reduced(S_j)$. But then by necessity of Υ_1 for x_1, $\exists k < j$ s.t. $\Upsilon_1 \subseteq reduced(S_k)$, and in particular $x_0 \in reduced(S_k)$. But by the monotonicity of $reduced()$, we also have $x_0 \in reduced(S_j)$, and therefore Υ_2' is necessary for x_2. ∎

Corollary 6.15 *If there is a cycle $x_0 \xrightarrow{D^{S_0}} \cdots \xrightarrow{D^{S_0}} x_n \xrightarrow{D^{S_0}} x_0$ in a dependence graph for S_0, then $x_0, \ldots, x_n$ are not reduced in any reduction sequence $S_0 \vdash^+ S_i$.*

Proof. From the previous lemma, x_a is in a dependence set for x_a, for all $0 \le a \le n$. Now suppose that x_a is reduced in some reduction sequence $S_0 \vdash^+ S_i$, say at step j. So $x_a \in reduced(S_j)$ but $x_a \notin reduced(S_k)$ for all $k < j$. But this contradicts the necessity of the dependence set of which x_a is a member. ∎

Corollary 6.16 *If there is a path $x \xrightarrow{D^{S_0}}{}^* y$ in a dependence graph for S_0, and x is part of a cycle, then y is not reduced in any reduction sequence $S_0 \vdash^+ S_i$.*

Proof. Immediate by applying necessity inductively along the path, given that the prior lemma shows that x is never reduced. ∎

We can summarize the preceding proposition and its corollaries by saying that the identifiers along a dependence graph cycle, along with their descendants in the dependence graph, are never reduced in any execution of the program. Cycles arise in the following programs, for example:

```
x = const 5; y = x + z; z = x + y; ◊ = z;
```

and

```
x = const 5; y = y + x; ◊ = y;
```

Recall that for any binding of the form `x = y + z`, $\{y, z\}$ is always a dependence set for `x` with respect to a set including `x`, `y`, and `z`. So in the first program above, a dependence set for `y` is $\{x, z\}$ and a dependence set for `z` is $\{x, y\}$; there is a cycle between `y` and `z`. Therefore, neither `y` nor `z` nor `◊` (whose dependence set includes `y`) are ever reduced. The reader can verify this by applying the reduction rules.

112

Note that $\{x, y\}$, for example, is a proper dependence set for z despite z's never being reduced, as it satisfies the definition of a dependence set vacuously. It satisfies necessity vacuously because there are *no* reduction sequences $S_0 \vdash^+ S_i$ such that $z \in reduced(S_i)$, as z is never reduced; it satisfies sufficiency vacuously because there are *no* reduction sequences $S_0 \vdash^+ S_i$ such that $\{x, y\} \subseteq reduced(S_i)$, as y is never reduced. A curious fact is that if an identifier is never reduced, any set that contains at least one other identifier that is never reduced is a dependence set, even if the members of that set have no apparent relation to the given identifier. This is just a mathematical artifact, which has no importance.

We can now show how to obtain the requirement relation from an arbitrary dependence graph.

Theorem 6.17 *Let* (V, D^{S_0}) *be a dependence graph for the program* S_0, *and define*

$$V_{cyc} = \{ y \mid x \xrightarrow{D^{S_0}}{}^* y \text{ for some } x \text{ that is part of a cycle} \}$$

Then $R^{S_0} | V = (D^{S_0} | (V - V_{cyc}))^+$.

Proof. By the previous lemma and its corollaries, none of the identifiers in V_{cyc} are ever reduced, and so by definition the requirement relation has no edges to or from them. None of the dependence sets for the remaining identifiers have elements of V_{cyc} as members, and so they are still proper dependence sets with respect to $(V - V_{cyc})$. Therefore, $(V - V_{cyc}, D^{S_0} | (V - V_{cyc}))$ is a dependence graph, and Theorem 6.13 gives the remaining edges in $R^{S_0} | V$. ∎

6.4   Function Dependence Graphs

A dependence graph contains all the information needed to construct the requirement relation for a complete program, an initial state containing all input data. Our goal, however, is not to analyze complete programs but to analyze function definitions, so that a function can be compiled in a way that works no matter how it is called. In this section, we define the *function dependence graph*, which summarizes dependence information about a function body for all possible contexts in which a function could be called. There will be two kinds of dependence edges: one that represents dependence for some but not necessarily all contexts, and another that represents dependence that holds for all contexts.

Now when considering all possible contexts, we will inevitably include some contexts in which certain variables are never reduced to a value. Such contexts yield no useful information for those variables; in particular, the dependence sets for those variables will be fairly arbitrary, as discussed in the previous section. Furthermore, if a variable is never reduced in some context it does not matter what compile-time decisions were taken with regard to its scheduling, and therefore it does not matter what the dependence graphs had to say about that variable in that context. So in defining function dependence graphs, we want to restrict our attention to contexts in which the variables of interest are actually reduced. We formalize this notion as follows. (At this point, the reader may wish to review the definitions of substitutions and contexts given in Section 4.8.)

Definition 6.18 *A context C for a function f in a state S is a* live context *for a variable x if there is a reduction sequence for S in which $\sigma_C x$ is reduced to a value, where σ_C is the substitution associated with context C.*

For example, given the following function definition

```
f x y z = {
    a = if x then {
            p = y + z;
            in p}
         else {
            in y};
    in a}
```

the only contexts that are live for `p` are those in which the variable $\sigma_C x$ is reduced to the value `true`. On the other hand, any context is live for `a` regardless of $\sigma_C x$'s value, as long as $\sigma_C x$ and $\sigma_C y$ are reduced to some value, and as long as $\sigma_C z$ is also reduced to some value in those contexts where $\sigma_C x$ is reduced to `true`.

We now extend the notion of dependence sets to describe dependence among the variables within function definitions.

Definition 6.19 *Let f be a function, x an identifier in that function, and V a set of identifiers including x. Further, let $C_1, C_2, \ldots$ include all possible live contexts of f for x, and for each C_i let $\sigma_{C_i} \Upsilon_i$ be a dependence set for $\sigma_{C_i} x$ with respect to $\sigma_{C_i} V$ in C_i's state. Then a* certain *dependence set for x is*

$$\Upsilon_{C,x}^f = \bigcap_i \Upsilon_i$$

and a full *dependence set for x is*

$$\Upsilon_{F,x}^f = \bigcup_i \Upsilon_i$$

(We omit V from the notation because we will always be taking function dependence sets with respect to a particular set V determined by f, to be described shortly.)

Informally, the certain dependence set gives the dependences that hold for all live contexts, while the full dependence set gives the dependences that hold for some, but not necessarily all, live contexts.

Now in general, it may be undecidable to determine whether a particular context is live for a given variable: determining whether there is any reduction sequence that reduces that variable to a value is tantamount to solving the halting problem. This is why in the definition above it is stated that $C_1, C_2, \ldots$ must *include* all live contexts, rather than *be* exactly the live contexts. When analysis fails to conclusively rule out a specific context, it must be included in the certain and full dependence sets. Thus, the full dependence set is guaranteed to have a subset corresponding to the actual dependence set for any live context, even if that context could not be proved live at compile time. This fact is central to the proof of Theorem 6.22, below.

In the same way we constructed dependence graphs from dependence sets, we construct function dependence graphs from function dependence sets. The vertices in a function dependence graph include vertices for each of the function's *local variables*, which are the identifiers bound within the function body, and therefore correspond to the subexpressions inside the function. Formally, the local variables are defined as follows.

Definition 6.20 *The* local variables *of a binding list,* $\mathcal{LV}[\![B_1;\dots;B_n;]\!]$, *is the set of variables defined as follows:*

$$
\begin{aligned}
\mathcal{LV}[\![B_1;\dots;B_n;]\!] &= \mathcal{LV}[\![B_1]\!] \cup \cdots \cup \mathcal{LV}[\![B_n]\!] \\
\mathcal{LV}[\![x^{(0)} = E;]\!] &= \{x^{(0)}\} \cup \mathcal{LV}[\![E]\!] \\
\mathcal{LV}[\![f^{(n)}\ x_1\ \dots\ x_n = \{\dots\}]\!] &= \emptyset \\
\mathcal{LV}\left[\!\!\left[\begin{array}{l}\texttt{if}\ P\ \texttt{then}\ \{B_{t,1};\dots;B_{t,n};\ \texttt{in}\ y_t\} \\ \texttt{else}\ \{B_{e,1};\dots;B_{e,m};\ \texttt{in}\ y_e\}\end{array}\right]\!\!\right] &= \mathcal{LV}[\![B_{t,1};\dots;B_{t,n};]\!] \cup \mathcal{LV}[\![B_{e,1};\dots;B_{e,m};]\!] \\
\mathcal{LV}[\![E]\!] &= \emptyset, \qquad \text{if } E \text{ is not a conditional}
\end{aligned}
$$

The local variables of a function body include all variables defined in the body, including blocks nested inside conditionals, but not the formals and bodies of internal function definitions. Now let

$$f^{(n)}\ x_1\ \dots\ x_n = \{B_1;\dots;B_m;\ \texttt{in}\ z_f\};$$

be a function definition; then the complete vertex set for its function dependence graphs is defined as follows:

$$V^f = \{x_1,\dots,x_n\} \cup \mathcal{LV}[\![B_1;\dots;B_m]\!] \cup \mathcal{FV}[\![B_1;\dots;B_m]\!] \cup \{\Diamond\}$$

($\mathcal{FV}$ denotes the free variables of the body.) There is a vertex for each input to the function (the formals and free variables), for each subexpression (the local variables), and the answer ($\Diamond$). Notice that for every context C, the substitution σ_C maps every identifier in V^f to the corresponding identifier in the state after the redex named by the context is reduced (including a mapping from $\Diamond$ to the identifier that receives the result of the function).

We now proceed to the definition of the function dependence graphs.

Definition 6.21 *Let f be a function and V^f be the set of identifiers for that function as defined above. Then a* function dependence graph *is a triple* (V^f, D_C^f, D_F^f) *where*

$$D_C^f = \bigcup_{x \in V^f}\ \bigcup_{y \in \Upsilon_{C,x}^f} (y, x)$$

and

$$D_F^f = \bigcup_{x \in V^f}\ \bigcup_{y \in \Upsilon_{F,x}^f} (y, x)$$

For convenience, we also define the certain dependence graph $\vec{D}_C^f$ *and the* full dependence graph $\vec{D}_F^f$:

$$
\begin{aligned}
\vec{D}_C^f &= (V^f, D_C^f) \\
\vec{D}_F^f &= (V^f, D_F^f)
\end{aligned}
$$

and also the potential dependence graph $\vec{D}_P^f$:

$$
\begin{aligned}
\vec{D}_P^f &= (V^f, D_P^f) \\
D_P^f &= D_F^f - D_C^f
\end{aligned}
$$

Most of the time, we will omit the f superscript when obvious from context. Informally, the graphs $\vec{D}_C$, $\vec{D}_F$, and $\vec{D}_P$ encode the dependences that hold for all contexts, some contexts, and some but not all contexts, respectively. Graphically, we will depict dependence graphs with a solid line for edges in D_C and a dashed line for edges in D_P (*i.e.*, for edges in D_F but not in D_C).

Function dependence graphs are one way of summarizing the dependences among a function's variables for all contexts in which it can be invoked. It is a particularly compact representation, since it only requires two graphs. It is also convenient for program analysis, as it is constructed by considering all contexts for each variable in isolation, afterwards combining the summaries obtained from each variable.

The latter fact leads to question whether a function dependence graph does in fact contain a dependence graph for every context, since it is not defined as the union of complete dependence graphs for each context. Because non-live contexts are excluded, the answer is not an unqualified yes, but it turns out that a function dependence graph does contain enough dependence information to order the computation of live variables for any context.

Theorem 6.22 *Let (V, D_C, D_F) be a function dependence graph for a function f. For any context C for that function, let $L \subseteq V$ be the live variables for that context (the variables such that every $l \in \sigma_C L$ is reduced in some execution sequence of the context's state). Then there exists a subset $D \subseteq D_F$, $D \subseteq (L \times L)$, such that $\sigma_C D$ is a dependence graph for the context's state with respect to $\sigma_C L$. Furthermore, $D \supseteq D_C$, and D is acyclic.*

Proof. Let $X_l = \{\, x \mid (x, l) \in D_F \,\}$ for any $l \in L$. By construction of D_F, for every $l \in L$ there is a subset $X_l' \in X_l$ such that $\sigma_C X_l'$ is a dependence set for $\sigma_C l$ in the context's state with respect to $\sigma_C V$. But because l is live, the variables on which it depends must also be live; that is, $X_l' \subseteq L$. So $\sigma_C X_l'$ is also a dependence set for $\sigma_C l$ with respect to $\sigma_C L$. Taking this fact over all $l \in L$ gives the desired result. By construction of D_C, it must also be the case that $X_l' \supseteq \{\, x \mid (x, l) \in D_C \,\}$, and so the result about D_C follows immediately. From Theorem 6.15, D must be acyclic because it only includes edges between live variables. ∎

The upshot is that for every context there is an acyclic subset of D_F, which is also a superset of D_C, that gives the ordering relationships between the function's variables that are live in that context.

7 Dependence Analysis

Having defined the function dependence graph and shown how it encodes ordering relationships between the subexpressions of a function definition, we describe how to analyze any function definition to obtain a function dependence graph. As we remarked in the last chapter, determining what contexts might be live for a given variable may be undecidable. Therefore, the analysis techniques we present can at best be an approximation to the best possible function dependence graph. As an approximation, a graph produced from analysis may have edges in the full dependence graph when none are necessary, or edges absent from the certain dependence graph when such an edge is possible. Both of these approximations are safe, in that for any context there is still a subset $D_C \subseteq D \subseteq D_F$ such that D is a dependence graph for the live variables of the function in that context.

If it is always safe to include edges in the full dependence graph and omit them from the certain dependence graph, why do we not in every case simply include all possible edges in the full dependence graph and no edges at all in the certain dependence graph? The answer comes in the next chapter, where it is shown how to partition a function based on the dependence graphs. The more certain edges there are, and the fewer non-certain full edges there are, the fewer constraints upon partitioning there will be, and therefore the more there will be the freedom to produce the largest possible threads.

For the most part, the analysis presented here is composed of simple rules for each type of binding in the functional quads grammar, where each rule gives the certain and full dependence sets for the identifier on the left hand side, in terms of the identifiers on the right hand side. In some cases, where more elaborate rules yield better results (as discussed above, in the sense of more certain edges and fewer non-certain full edges), such rules are discussed.

The remainder of this chapter is in two parts, preceded by an introductory section. The first part, Sections 7.2 through 7.6, give the rules for programs that do not use data structures or higher-order functions. The first four of those sections give rules for computing certain and full dependence sets for each type of binding, and Section 7.6 summarizes all those rules in a single set of equations. Some readers may wish to look over the summary in Section 7.6 before reading Sections 7.2 through 7.5, or perhaps avoid the proofs in the sections preceding the summary, on first reading. The second part of the chapter, Sections 7.7 and 7.8, give dependence analysis rules for programs that do use data structures or higher-order functions. The last section in this chapter is an appendix, containing a somewhat tedious proof of a theorem used in the analysis of data structures.

7.1 Introduction: Examples of Function Dependence Graphs

As function dependence graphs play a central role in partitioning programs for lenient evaluation, it is important to understand them thoroughly. Despite the complexity of their formal definition, it is actually quite easy to understand them intuitively.

To illustrate function dependence graphs, consider the function f defined on page 114. The local variables of f are $\{a, p\}$ and the formals are $\{x, y, z\}$, so that the vertex set V^f is $\{x, y, z, a, p, \Diamond\}$. The function dependence graph for f is shown below.

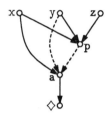

The dependence edges were obtained by considering all possible contexts for f. Any context for f will look like this (although perhaps with different variable names):

```
...; r = (f u v) w; ...
```

While there are an infinite number of such contexts, we can classify them into groups. An important group are those where the actual parameter u is reduced to a boolean value and the actuals v and w are reduced to a numeric value in some execution sequence; these can be further subdivided into those where u is reduced to **true** and those where it is reduced to **false**. Of these contexts, only the u = **true** contexts are live for p, while all of them are live for the other variables x, y, z, a, and $\Diamond$. Now, for each identifier, we analyze the contexts to obtain dependence sets. It turns out that a dependence set for σ_Cp for all of p's live contexts is $\sigma_C\{x, y, z\}$, and so we have $\Upsilon_{C,p} = \Upsilon_{F,p} = \{x, y, z\}$. This results in solid edges from x, y, and z to p in the function dependence graph. The dependence set for σ_Ca, on the other hand, depends on which side of the conditional is selected, so for some contexts the set is $\sigma_C\{p, x\}$ and for the others it is $\sigma_C\{y, x\}$. Thus, $\Upsilon_{C,a} = \{p, x\} \cap \{y, x\} = \{x\}$, and $\Upsilon_{F,a} = \{p, x\} \cup \{y, x\} = \{p, y, x\}$, yielding one solid and two dashed edges to a in the function dependence graph.

Remember, now, that there may be several possible dependence sets for a given identifier and state. In particular, in the previous example we said that in the u = **true** contexts the dependence set for σ_Ca is $\sigma_C\{p, x\}$. But another possible dependence set in those contexts is $\sigma_C\{p, y, x\}$. Using that set would lead to $\Upsilon_{C,a} = \{y, x\}$ and $\Upsilon_{F,a} = \{p, y, x\}$, and the dependence graph would have a solid edge from y to a instead of a dashed one.

What about those contexts where u, v, and w are not all reduced to boolean and numeric values? Some of those contexts are ones where those variables are reduced to values, but not of the proper type.[1] Such contexts will result in some of the function's local variables never being reduced; for example, if x is **true** and z is not a number, then no rewrite rule can succeed in reducing p to a value. (Of course, the relevance of this fact to code generation depends on run-time type errors being treated in the implementation in a manner consistent with the rewrite rules given.) Other contexts are ones where u, v, or w are not reduced to any value at all. Here are some possible contexts of this form:

---

[1] If the functional quads program was originally obtained from the translation of a program from a strongly typed language, then the type system guarantees that such contexts cannot arise, and so they need not be considered.

```
...; r = (f u v) w; u = v + 5; v = u + 7; ...
```

and

```
...; r = (f u v) w; u = r; ...
```

and

```
...; r = (f u v) w; u = (g 5); g b = {c = (g b) in c}; ...
```

In the first two examples u is never reduced to a value because of deadlock, in the third because of non-termination. Again, though, the effect on f's local variables is that some of them can never be reduced to values. In short, for a given variable in V^f, the contexts where u, v, and w are not reduced to boolean and numeric values either have the same behavior as the contexts already considered, or they are not live for that variable. Thus, they have no bearing on the dependence graph.

7.2 Identity Statements and Arithmetic, Outside Conditionals

We begin the analysis of programs with the simplest functional quads statements: arithmetic, identity statements, and the const statements, and furthermore only consider those statements when they appear in the top-level binding list of a function body, not nested in the "then" or "else" arms of any conditionals. In this section and the sections that follow, the general format is to present a dependence rule, followed by a proof of its correctness. The proofs may be skipped, if desired.

Given function f with a top-level binding of the form

```
x = y
```

then the dependence sets for x are:

$$\Upsilon^f_{C,x} = \{y\}$$
$$\Upsilon^f_{F,x} = \{y\}$$

Proof. In all contexts, reduction of the context results in a binding in the state of the form $\sigma x = \sigma y$. A dependence set for σx in all such contexts is $\{\sigma y\}$, as proved below. So $\Upsilon_C = \Upsilon_F = \{y\}$.

(Necessity) If σx is reduced to a value in some reduction sequence, it can only be because reduction of an R1a redex substituted for σy on the right hand side of the binding. For this to be possible, σy must have been reduced to a value in an earlier step.

(Sufficiency) If S_i is a state such that $\sigma y \in reduced(S_i)$, then either $\sigma x \in reduced(S_i)$, or σx can be reduced by applying rule $R1a$ to substitute a value into the right hand side of the binding for σx. In neither case are any other identifiers reduced. ∎

Given function f with a top-level binding of the form

```
x = y Op z
```

then the dependence sets for x are:

$$\Upsilon^f_{C,x} = \{y, z\}$$
$$\Upsilon^f_{F,x} = \{y, z\}$$

Proof. In all contexts, reduction of the context results in a binding in the state of the form $\sigma x = \sigma y \ Op \ \sigma z$. A dependence set for σx in all of those contexts that are live for x is $\{\sigma y, \sigma z\}$, as proved below. So $\Upsilon_C = \Upsilon_F = \{y, z\}$.

(Necessity) Reducing σx to a value requires that values be substituted for σy and σz (R1b and R1c redexes), which in turn requires that σy and σz were previously reduced to values.

(Sufficiency) Given a state S_i such that $\sigma y, \sigma z \in reduced(S_i)$, then σx can be reduced by performing (at most) the following steps: R1b to substitute σy's value into σx's binding, R1c to substitute σz's value, then R4. The last step might not be possible if σy or σz were not proper values (for example, if Op is + but σy or σz were not numbers), but in that case the context would not be live. ∎

Given function f with a top-level binding of the form

    x = const V

then the dependence sets for x are:

$$\Upsilon^f_{C,x} = \emptyset$$
$$\Upsilon^f_{F,x} = \emptyset$$

Proof. In all contexts, reduction of the context results in a binding in the state of the form $\sigma x = $ const V. A dependence set for σx in all of those contexts that are live for x is the empty set, as proved below. So $\Upsilon_C = \Upsilon_F = \emptyset$.

(Necessity) Satisfied trivially.

(Sufficiency) Given state S_i, if a state can be reached where the context is reduced, bringing $\sigma x = $ const V into the state, then rule R2 can be applied immediately, reducing σx to a value. On the other hand, if the context cannot be reduced, then the context is not live for x. ∎

7.3 Conditionals

Two rules describe the effects of conditionals on dependence graphs. First, there are the dependence sets for the conditional itself. Second, every binding appearing in the "then" or "else" arms of a conditional has additional dependences, compared to what its dependence set would be if the binding were at top level.

Given function f with a top-level binding of the form

    x = if y then {...in yₜ} else {...in yₑ}

120

then the dependence sets for x are:

$$\Upsilon^f_{C,x} = \{y\}$$
$$\Upsilon^f_{F,x} = \{y, y_t, y_e\}$$

Proof. All live contexts for x can be classified into two categories: those where σy is reduced to `true`, and those where σy is reduced to `false`. As proved below, in the "true" contexts a dependence set for σx is $\{\sigma y, \sigma y_t\}$, while in the "false" contexts a set is $\{\sigma y, \sigma y_e\}$. So $\Upsilon_C = \{y, y_t\} \cap \{y, y_e\} = \{y\}$, and $\Upsilon_F = \{y, y_t\} \cup \{y, y_e\} = \{y, y_t, y_e\}$.

(Necessity, "true" contexts) For σx to be reduced, an R3 redex must have been reduced, which in turn implies that y must have been reduced to a value (specifically, to `true` in the "true" contexts). Reduction of the R3 redex leaves the binding $\sigma x = \sigma y_t$ in the state, so for σx to be reduced to a value, so must σy_t.

(Sufficiency, "true" contexts) Given a state S_i in which both σy and σy_t have been reduced to values, σx can be reduced to a value by performing some or all of the following steps: rule R1d to substitute for σy in `if y` ..., then rule R3 to rewrite σx's binding to $\sigma x = \sigma y_t$, then rule R1a to substitute for σy_t in that binding. No identifiers besides σx become values in this sequence.

The necessity and sufficiency of $\{\sigma y, \sigma y_e\}$ for the "false" contexts is established through an analogous argument. ∎

At first glance, the inclusion of σy in the dependence sets for the "true" and "false" contexts may seem superfluous: if σy_t (or σy_e) has been reduced, does that not imply that the R3 redex has already been reduced? The answer is no, because σy_t (σy_e) could be an identifier defined *outside* the conditional. Even without this consideration, though, it is desirable to include σy in the dependence sets, since it results in a certain dependence.

Up to now, dependence rules have been given only for top-level bindings of a function: bindings that were not inside an arm of one or more conditionals. If a binding is nested in one or more conditionals, then it has the same dependence sets as if it appeared at top-level, with an additional certain dependence for each of the predicate variables of the conditionals in which it is nested.

Given function f with binding for x nested in n conditionals, where the predicate variables are $y_1, \ldots, y_n$, *i.e.*, a function of the form

```
f⁽ᵐ⁾ z₁ ... zₘ =
   {...
    x₁ = if y₁ then
            {...
             x₂ = if y₂ then
                    ...
                    ... xₙ = if yₙ then {... x = E; ...} else {...}; ...
                    ...
                  else {...};
            ...
          else {...};
    ...};
```

(in the illustration above, the binding $x = E$ is nested entirely in "then" arms, but the result holds for any mix of "then" and "else" arms) then the dependence sets for x are:

$$\Upsilon_{C,x}^f = \{y_1, \ldots, y_n\} \cup \Upsilon_{C,x_{top}}$$
$$\Upsilon_{F,x}^f = \{y_1, \ldots, y_n\} \cup \Upsilon_{F,x_{top}}$$

where $\Upsilon_{C,x_{top}}$ and $\Upsilon_{F,x_{top}}$ are what the certain and full dependence sets for x would be if x were at top level in the definition of f.

Proof. (Necessity) In any live context for x, $y_1, \ldots, y_n$ are necessary to bring the binding $\sigma x = \sigma E$ into the state; once in the state, it is as if the binding were top-level in the function, and so it still has necessary identifiers according to what kind of expression E is.

(Sufficiency) Given a live context for x, performing R1d and R3 reductions eventually brings $\sigma x = \sigma E$ into the state, at which point the same steps sufficient to reduce E if it were top level can be applied to reduce σx to a value. As this sequence does not reduce any other identifiers to values, the set is sufficient. ∎

For example, given the following function:

```
f x y z =
  {a = if x then
          {b = y < z;
           c = if b then
                  {in z}
               else
                  {d = z - y;
                   in d};}
       else
          {in y};
   in a};
```

the certain and full dependence sets for d, according to the rule given above, are $\Upsilon_{C,d} = \Upsilon_{F,d} = \{x, b, z, y\}$. All the dependences are certain, despite d's being defined within a conditional, because the dependences exist for all *live* contexts for d. The rules also give the dependence sets for b: $\Upsilon_{C,b} = \Upsilon_{F,b} = \{x, z, y\}$.

It may not be obvious why the predicate variables from all conditionals in which a statement is nested must be included in its dependence set, rather than just the nearest enclosing conditional's. Indeed, in the example above, $\{b, z, y\}$ is a valid certain and full dependence set for d (eliminating the outer conditional's predicate, x). But if the predicate variable b were defined outside the first conditional, or were a formal parameter, then x would have to be included in d's dependence set. This is just another case where the rules given for dependence sets do not necessarily yield the minimal sets. But the particular case of a predicate variable defined inside an enclosing conditional is noteworthy, because recognizing such cases may significantly reduce the size of the dependence graphs—in many cases, the number of edges need not be proportional to the nesting depth of conditionals. Using this trick cannot add or remove any *paths* in the dependence graphs, so it does not affect the quality of the analysis.

There is a case, however, where deviating from the above rules can lead to better quality dependence graphs. Consider the identifier a in the following function:

```
f x y z =
  {p = x < 0;
   a = if p then
           {b = y + z;
            in b}
       else
           {s = const 6;
            c = y + s;
            in c};
   d = a + 7
   in
     d};
```

According to the rules given earlier, the dependence set for σa in the "true" contexts is $\{\sigma p, \sigma b\}$, and in the "false" contexts $\{\sigma p, \sigma c\}$, giving certain and full dependence sets $\Upsilon_{C,a} = \{p\}$ and $\Upsilon_{F,a} = \{p, b, c\}$. But in the "true" contexts, $\{\sigma p, \sigma b, \sigma y\}$ is also a dependence set for σa; similarly, in the "false" contexts, $\{\sigma p, \sigma c, \sigma y\}$ is an alternative. These sets yield certain and full dependence sets $\Upsilon_{C,a} = \{p, y\}$ and $\Upsilon_{F,a} = \{p, b, c, y\}$, which are superior because they reveal an additional certain dependence.

The generalization of the case described above is that given a binding of the form

$$x = \text{if } y \text{ then } \{\dots \text{ in } y_t\} \text{ else } \{\dots \text{ in } y_e\}$$

for every identifier z such that there are paths in the certain dependence graph $z \xrightarrow{D_C}{}^* y_t$ and $z \xrightarrow{D_C}{}^* y_e$, the edge $z \xrightarrow{D_C} x$ may be added to the certain dependence graph. This result is easily proved by applying Lemma 6.14 to the "true" and "false" cases.

7.4   First-Order Function Calls

A first-order function call is a binding of the following form:

$$x = (f^{(n)} \ y_1 \ \dots \ y_{n-1}) \ y_n;$$

This is a special case of the general function call, in which the name of the function is known, and it is being applied to all of its arguments at once. To determine the dependence sets for x, something must be known about the behavior of the function f, specifically, which arguments to f must be reduced to a value before the result of f, and therefore x, can be.

At first glance, the function dependence graph for f would appear to hold the answer. If there is a path $(z_i, \Diamond) \in (D_C^f)^+$, where z_i is the ith formal parameter of f, then $y_i \in \Upsilon_{C,x}$. Similarly, if $(z_i, \Diamond) \in (D_F^f)^+$, then $y_i \in \Upsilon_{F,x}$. These rules are easy to justify formally; a formal proof is an exercise for the reader. But there is clearly a difficulty if the call to f is recursive, for then it is necessary to know about paths in f's dependence graph in order to compute that dependence graph. In principle, one could formulate a set of recursive graph

123

equations and solve them to obtain the function dependence graphs of all functions in the program. Preliminary studies by the author indicate that this approach is indeed feasible, but at the time of this writing it is still a topic for future research. In this section, we take a different approach.

Instead of obtaining the information needed about f from dependence graphs, we will rely on strictness analysis. Strictness is defined as follows:

Definition 7.1 *A function f of n arguments is* strict *in its ith argument if*

$$f(a_1, \ldots, a_{i-1}, \bot, a_{i+1}, \ldots, a_n) = \bot$$

for all $a_1, \ldots, a_{i-1}, a_{i+1}, \ldots, a_n$.

A related concept is *ignoring*, defined as follows:

Definition 7.2 *A function f of n arguments* ignores *its ith argument if*

$$f(a_1, \ldots, a_{i-1}, \bot, a_{i+1}, \ldots, a_n) = f(a_1, \ldots, a_{i-1}, a_i, a_{i+1}, \ldots, a_n)$$

for all $a_1, \ldots, a_n$.

Note that it is possible for a function to both be strict in its ith argument and ignore its ith argument, if the function returns $\bot$ for all inputs. Because functions in a functional quads program may have free variables other than formal parameters, for the purposes of strictness analysis the free variables will be considered as if they were additional formal parameters.

We will claim, without proof, that if a function f is strict in its ith argument (or free variable), then there is a certain dependence between the ith actual parameter (free variable) in a call to f and the identifier receiving the result, and similarly if f does *not* ignore its ith argument, then there is a full dependence between the actual parameter and the result. To actually prove these claims, it is necessary to establish the relationship between the denotational semantics of functional quads, from which strictness and ignoring are derived, and the operational (rewrite) semantics on which dependence analysis is based. Essentially, what needs to be established is that $\bot$ in the denotational semantics corresponds to a non-value in the operational semantics.

To give the dependence analysis rules for first-order function calls, suppose that a strictness analyzer is available, which computes the following two functions:

$$\begin{aligned} \textit{Strict}(\hat{f}) &= \{\, i \mid \hat{f} \text{ is inferred to be strict in its } i\text{th argument (or free variable)} \,\} \\ \textit{Ignored}(\hat{f}) &= \{\, i \mid \hat{f} \text{ is inferred to ignore its } i\text{th argument (or free variable)} \,\} \end{aligned}$$

In functional quads, function definitions are not necessarily closed. If the function f as it appears in functional quads has n formal parameters and k free variables, then the corresponding semantic function $\hat{f}$ has $n + k$ arguments, where the first n arguments $1 \le i \le n$ correspond to formal parameters, and the remaining k arguments $n + 1 \le i \le n + k$ correspond to free variables. The strictness analysis functions should be conservative: if

$\hat{f}$ cannot be conclusively proved to be strict in (ignore) its ith argument, i should not be a member of $Strict(\hat{f})$ $(Ignored(\hat{f}))$.

The rule for generating dependence sets for first-order function calls, then, is as follows. (In the following, let $y_{n+1}, \ldots, y_{n+k}$ stand for the free variables of f.)

Given function f with a top-level binding of the form

$$x = (f^{(n)}\ y_1\ \ldots\ y_{n-1})\ y_n$$

then the dependence sets for x are:

$$\Upsilon^f_{C,x} = \{\, y_i \mid i \in Strict(\hat{f}) \wedge i \notin Ignored(\hat{f}) \,\}$$
$$\Upsilon^f_{F,x} = \{\, y_i \mid i \notin Ignored(\hat{f}) \,\}$$

Justification. To justify these rules, first let us formalize the conjecture that relates the denotational and operational semantics. Let the semantic value of a functional quads expression E, notation $\mathcal{E}\llbracket E \rrbracket$, be $\bot$ if E is not a value, and the semantic equivalent of the value, otherwise. If S is a state containing the following bindings:

$$x = (f^{(n)}\ y_1\ \ldots\ y_{n-1})\ y_n;$$
$$y_1 = E_1;$$
$$\ldots$$
$$y_{n+k} = E_{n+k};$$

we conjecture that there is a reduction sequence $S \vdash^* S'$ such that S' contains the following bindings:

$$x = E';$$
$$y_1 = E_1;$$
$$\ldots$$
$$y_{n+k} = E_{n+k};$$

where $\mathcal{E}\llbracket E' \rrbracket = \hat{f}(\mathcal{E}\llbracket E_1 \rrbracket, \ldots, \mathcal{E}\llbracket E_{m+k} \rrbracket)$. Furthermore, there is no S'', $S \vdash^* S''$, such that S'' contains the following bindings:

$$x = E'';$$
$$y_1 = E_1;$$
$$\ldots$$
$$y_{m+k} = E_{m+k};$$

where $\mathcal{E}\llbracket E'' \rrbracket \sqsupset \hat{f}(\mathcal{E}\llbracket E_1 \rrbracket, \ldots, \mathcal{E}\llbracket E_{m+k} \rrbracket)$. In other words, x can be reduced to the semantic value of the function on the given arguments (and free variables) without further reduction of those arguments, and cannot be reduced further without further reduction of the arguments.

Now consider a live context for x. Any σy_i such that $i \in Strict(\hat{f})$ is necessary for σx. If it were not, then there would be an execution sequence in which σx is reduced to a value but σy_i is not, contradicting strictness according to the conjecture. On the other hand, any σy_i such that $i \in \text{Ignored}(\hat{f})$ cannot be necessary for σx. Ignoring says that $\hat{f}(\ldots, a_i, \ldots) = \hat{f}(\ldots, \bot, \ldots)$, so even if σy_i is not reduced the conjecture says it is still possible to find a reduction sequence in which σx is reduced. So for any live context, the set Υ is necessary, where Υ is some set satisfying:

$$\Upsilon \supseteq \{ \sigma y_i \mid i \in \text{Strict}(\hat{f}) \wedge i \notin \text{Ignored}(\hat{f}) \}$$
$$\Upsilon \subseteq \{ \sigma y_i \mid i \notin \text{Ignored}(\hat{f}) \}$$

(If both $i \in \text{Strict}(\hat{f})$ and $i \in \text{Ignored}(\hat{f})$, the context is not live; this justifies the second term in the first equation above.)

This set is also sufficient for σx: the conjecture insures that it is possible to reduce σx to a value without reducing further any of the σy_i; since none of the bindings introduced by the R8 rule (for the call to f) can refer directly to any of the other identifiers in the state, it is furthermore possible to reduce σx to a value without reducing any other identifier in σV. So some Υ satisfying the above equations is a dependence set for σx with respect to σV.

In the absence of any further information, we must assume that for every Υ satisfying the above two equations there might be a corresponding context where Υ is the dependence set for σx. So the certain and full dependence sets for x are as given. ∎

7.5   Formal Parameters, Free Variables, and the Result

The only vertices of the function dependence graph that we have not yet considered are the vertices for the formal parameters and free variables, and for the answer ($\Diamond$).

Given a function definition,

$$f^{(n)} \; x_1 \; \ldots \; x_n \; = \; \{B_1; \; \ldots; \; B_m; \; \text{in } x\};$$

then the dependence sets for $\Diamond$ are:

$$\Upsilon_{C,\Diamond}^f = \{x\}$$
$$\Upsilon_{F,\Diamond}^f = \{x\}$$

Proof. Any context for f is of the form $\langle S, \alpha,$ where α is a redex specifier $\langle y, R8 \rangle$. When the context is reduced, the state will contain a binding

$$y = \sigma x$$

But $\sigma \Diamond = y$, so this binding is equivalent to

$$\sigma \Diamond = \sigma x$$

So this is identical to the case of an identity binding, as discussed in Section 7.2, and so the reasoning in that section applies here as well. ∎

The dependence sets for the formal parameters and free variables are more interesting. Consider the following function:

126

```
f⁽³⁾ x y z =
   {a = x + y;
      b = x + z;
      in a};
```

called in the following context:

```
. . .
i = (f⁽³⁾ u v) j;
j = w + i;
. . .
```

where u, v, and w are defined elsewhere. Notice that the third actual parameter, j, depends on the result of the function call, i. When the R8 redex in i's binding is reduced, the state looks like this:

```
. . .
i = σ a;
σ x = u;
σ y = v;
σ z = j;
σ a = σ x + σ y;
σ b = σ x + σ z;
j = w + i;
. . .
```

With respect to the set $\sigma\{x, y, z, a, b, \Diamond\}$ (remember that $\sigma\Diamond = i$), a dependence set for σz is $\{\sigma a\}$. It is necessary, for if σa is not reduced, then i cannot be reduced, so that j cannot be reduced, preventing σz from being reduced. It is sufficient with respect to the given set, because if σa is reduced it is possible to apply various rules to reduce i, then j, then σz; this satisfies sufficiency because i and j are not members of the set with respect to which sufficiency is considered.

In general, statements in the surrounding context of a function call can feed back the answer into any of its formal parameters, resulting in a dependence between the result and that parameter. These represent legitimate constraints on ordering of subexpression evaluation; in the above example, f must be compiled in such a way that it returns its result before attempting to compute the value of b. Now it is difficult to construct compelling examples of feedback if we are limited to scalar programs. Indeed, if a function returns a scalar, then any computation inside the function that depends on the result being returned must be "dead code," in that it cannot contribute to the answer. The useful examples of feedback all occur when a function returns a data structure or partial application; the programs in Section 3.1 are all examples of useful feedback. Nevertheless, even in scalar-returning functions, feedback dependences lead to constraints on scheduling that must be obeyed, as the example above showed. (Of course, a real compiler should be able to eliminate the affected expressions by recognizing them as dead code.) Section 8.7 returns to a discussion of feedback dependences, after partitioning has been discussed.

Feedback dependences are slightly more complicated if a function has free variables, due to a mathematical artifact. So we first present the feedback rule in the case of functions with no free variables, and then in the case with free variables. Note that if a compiler chooses to lambda-lift internal functions, then they will not have free variables.

For scalar functions without free variables, the rule for computing the dependence sets for formal parameters is as follows. Given a function definition,

$$f^{(n)} \ x_1 \ \ldots \ x_n \ = \ \{B_1; \ \ldots; \ B_m; \ \text{in} \ x\};$$

The dependence sets for any x_i are:

$$\Upsilon^f_{C,x_i} \ = \ \emptyset$$
$$\Upsilon^f_{F,x_i} \ = \ \{\Diamond\}$$

Proof. As shown below, in any particular context, live for x_i, a dependence set for σx_i with respect to σV is either $\emptyset$ or $\{\sigma \Diamond\}$. Lacking more information about the contexts in which f can be invoked, we must assume that both dependence sets are possible, and so $\Upsilon^f_{C,x_i} = \emptyset$ and $\Upsilon^f_{F,x_i} = \{\Diamond\}$. The reason the dependence set can only contain $\sigma \Diamond$ is that among all of the bindings surrounding the context, $\sigma \Diamond$ is the only identifier in σV that can be referred to; this is because no other identifier in σV is in scope for those bindings. (The remainder of the proof is fairly long, and the reader may wish to skip it.)

Let Υ be a dependence set for σx_i with respect to σV. First we show that if $\Upsilon \neq \emptyset$, then $\sigma \Diamond \in \Upsilon$. Suppose that $\Upsilon \neq \emptyset$ but $\sigma \Diamond \notin \Upsilon$. Since the context is live for σx_i, there is a reduction sequence $S_0 \vdash^+ S_i$ such that $\sigma x_i \in reduced(S_i)$; let $S_0 \vdash^+ S_{i'}$ be the prefix of that sequence such that x_i is reduced in step i'. Since Υ is necessary, there exists $j < i'$ such that $\Upsilon \subseteq reduced(S_j)$. Now let j', where $j' \leq j$, be such that $\Upsilon \subseteq reduced(S_{j'})$ but $\Upsilon \not\subseteq reduced(S_{j'-1})$. But since Υ is sufficient, there exists k such that $S_{j'} \vdash^* S_k$ and σx_i is reduced in S_k, and where no identifier in σV other than σx_i is reduced in that sequence. But the very same reductions could have been applied to $S_{j'-1}$, as $S_{j'-1}$ differs from $S_{j'}$ only by having some identifier $y \in \Upsilon$, $y \neq \sigma \Diamond$, reduced, but all of the reductions in the $S_{j'} \vdash^* S_k$ sequence are surrounding the context and so could not be affected by the reduction of y. But that is a sequence that reduces σx_i without reducing y, contradicting the necessity of Υ. Hence, $\sigma \Diamond \in \Upsilon$.

It remains to show that if $\sigma \Diamond \in \Upsilon$, then $\{\sigma \Diamond\}$ is also a dependence set for σx_i with respect to σV. If Υ is necessary, then clearly $\{\sigma \Diamond\}$ is also necessary. To show that it is sufficient, consider any S_i such that $S_0 \vdash^+ S_i$ where $\sigma \Diamond \in reduced(S_i)$. Because the context is live for x_i, there exists a sequence $S_i \vdash^* S_j$ where $\sigma x_i \in reduced(S_j)$. From that sequence, one can be constructed where no $v \in \sigma V$ other than $\sigma \Diamond$ is reduced: starting from the end of the sequence, remove any step that reduces some identifier $v \in \sigma V$ other than $\sigma \Diamond$. Removing such a step cannot invalidate any following step, since it removes no redexes surrounding the context. The resulting sequence demonstrates the sufficiency of $\{\sigma \Diamond\}$. ∎

If a function has free variables, then the answer can feed back to any of the free variables, as well as to a formal parameter. So a potential dependence edge is called for between $\Diamond$ and each of the free variables. But there may be dependences among the free variables: for example, a function may have free variables **x** and **y**, but outside a call to the function there may be a binding **x** = **y**. Because the free variables are part of the function dependence graph, that dependence must be present in the graph to satisfy the definition of the function dependence graph. Similarly, if a free variable happens to also be an actual parameter to a call, there will be a dependence between the vertex representing the free variable and the vertex representing the formal.

The arcs from the free variable vertices to other free variables and the formals are in some sense a mathematical artifact. While the dependences they represent are real, they have no impact on code generation, since the formal parameter and free variable vertices do not correspond to any fragment of sequential code to be ordered. Any ordering constraints that would result from these dependences are adequately captured simply by including a feedback edge from the answer to each formal and free variable. Nevertheless, we state below the complete dependence set for formal parameter and free variable vertices, with proof. The rule reduces to the case described earlier, if there are no free variables.

Given a function definition,

$$f^{(n)} \; x_1 \; \ldots \; x_n = \{B_1; \; \ldots; \; B_m; \; \text{in } x\};$$

let the free variables be $x_{n+1}, \ldots, x_{n+k}$. The dependence sets for any formal parameter x_i, $1 \le i \le n$ are:

$$\Upsilon^f_{C,x_i} = \emptyset$$
$$\Upsilon^f_{F,x_i} = \{\Diamond, x_{n+1}, \ldots, x_{n+k}\}$$

For any free variable x_i, $n + 1 \le i \le n + k$, the dependence sets are:

$$\Upsilon^f_{C,x_i} = \emptyset$$
$$\Upsilon^f_{F,x_i} = \{\Diamond, x_{n+1}, \ldots, x_{i-1}, x_{i+1}, \ldots, x_{n+k}\}$$

Proof. As shown below, in any particular context, live for x_i, a dependence set Υ for σx_i with respect to σV satisfies $\Upsilon \subseteq (\{\sigma\Diamond, \sigma x_n, \ldots, \sigma x_{n+k}\} - \{\sigma x_i\})$. Lacking more information about the contexts in which f can be invoked, we must assume that all such dependence sets are possible, and so the certain and full sets are as given. Again, the reason the dependence set can only contain these identifiers is that among all of the bindings surrounding the context, they are the only identifiers in σV that can be referred to; this is because no other identifier in σV is in scope for those bindings.

To complete the proof, first consider the dependence set for σx_i not with respect to σV, but with respect to $\sigma V'$, where

$$V' = V - (\{\Diamond, x_n, \ldots, x_{n+k}\} - \{x_i\})$$

By the same argument used in the proof for functions having no free variables, the dependence set for σx_i with respect to $\sigma V'$ is either $\emptyset$ or $\{\sigma\Diamond\}$. (x_i is included in V' because a dependence set for an identifier must be taken with respect to a set that includes that identifier. Even so, σx_i cannot be a member of the dependence set, because if it were the context would not be live for x_i.)

Now consider taking the dependence set with respect to σV instead of $\sigma V'$. This can only add some or all of the identifiers in $\sigma V - \sigma V'$ to the dependence set. Hence, $\Upsilon \subseteq \{\sigma\Diamond\} \cup (\sigma V - \sigma V')$, which is the desired result. ∎

7.6 Summary of Dependence Analysis for Scalar Programs

We now summarize all the dependence rules given in the previous sections. Rather than just list all the rules, we give a pair of functions, $\mathcal{DC}$ and $\mathcal{DP}$, that map a function definition to edges in the function dependence graphs. For convenience, these functions give the certain and *potential* edges, and the full edges are obtained as the union of the two.

Given a function definition,

$$f^{(n)} \ x_1 \ \ldots \ x_n \ = \ \{B_1; \ \ldots; \ B_m; \ \text{in} \ x\};$$

let the free variables of the body be $x_{n+1}, \ldots, x_{n+k}$. Then the function dependence graph is (V, D_C, D_F), as given by the following equations.

$$V \ = \ \{x_1, \ldots, x_{n+k}\} \cup \mathcal{LV}[\![B_1; \ldots; B_m]\!] \cup \{\Diamond\}$$

$$D_C \ = \ \mathcal{DC}[\![B_1; \ldots; B_m]\!] \cup D_{C, answer}$$
$$D_F \ = \ D_C \cup D_P$$
$$D_P \ = \ \mathcal{DP}[\![B_1; \ldots; B_m]\!] \cup D_{P, feedback}$$

$$D_{C, answer} \ = \ \{(x, \Diamond)\}$$

$$D_{P, feedback} \ = \ \bigcup_{1 \le i \le n+k} (\Diamond, x_i) \cup \bigcup_{1 \le i \le n+k} \bigcup_{\substack{n \le j \le n+k \\ j \ne i}} (x_j, x_i)$$

$$\mathcal{DC}[\![B_1; \ \ldots; \ B_m]\!] \ = \ \mathcal{DC}[\![B_1]\!] \cup \cdots \cup \mathcal{DC}[\![B_m]\!]$$
$$\mathcal{DP}[\![B_1; \ \ldots; \ B_m]\!] \ = \ \mathcal{DP}[\![B_1]\!] \cup \cdots \cup \mathcal{DP}[\![B_m]\!]$$

$$\mathcal{DC}[\![x \ = \ \text{const} \ v]\!] \ = \ \emptyset$$
$$\mathcal{DP}[\![x \ = \ \text{const} \ v]\!] \ = \ \emptyset$$

$$\mathcal{DC}[\![x \ = \ y]\!] \ = \ \{(y, x)\}$$
$$\mathcal{DP}[\![x \ = \ y]\!] \ = \ \emptyset$$

$$\mathcal{DC}[\![x \ = \ y_1 \ Op \ y_2]\!] \ = \ \{(y_1, x), (y_2, x)\}$$
$$\mathcal{DP}[\![x \ = \ y_1 \ Op \ y_2]\!] \ = \ \emptyset$$

$$\mathcal{DC}\left[\!\!\left[\begin{matrix} x & \texttt{= if } y \texttt{ then } \{B_{t,1};\dots;B_{t,n};\texttt{ in } y_t\} \\ & \texttt{else } \{B_{e,1};\dots;B_{e,m};\texttt{ in } y_e\} \end{matrix}\right]\!\!\right] = \begin{array}{l} \{\,(y,z)\mid z\in\mathcal{LV}[\![B_{t,1};\dots;B_{t,n};]\!]\,\}\,\cup \\ \{\,(y,z)\mid z\in\mathcal{LV}[\![B_{e,1};\dots;B_{e,m};]\!]\,\}\,\cup \\ \mathcal{DC}[\![B_{t,1};\dots;B_{t,n};]\!]\,\cup \\ \mathcal{DC}[\![B_{e,1};\dots;B_{e,m};]\!]\,\cup \\ \{(y,x)\} \end{array}$$

$$\mathcal{DP}\left[\!\!\left[\begin{matrix} x & \texttt{= if } y \texttt{ then } \{B_{t,1};\dots;B_{t,n};\texttt{ in } y_t\} \\ & \texttt{else } \{B_{e,1};\dots;B_{e,m};\texttt{ in } y_e\} \end{matrix}\right]\!\!\right] = \begin{array}{l} \{(y_t,x),(y_e,x)\}\,\cup \\ \mathcal{DP}[\![B_{t,1};\dots;B_{t,n};]\!]\,\cup \\ \mathcal{DP}[\![B_{e,1};\dots;B_{e,m};]\!] \end{array}$$

$$\mathcal{DC}[\![x \;\texttt{=}\; (g^{(n)}\; y_1\;\dots y_{n-1})\; y_n;]\!] = \{\,(y_i,x)\mid i\in Strict(\hat{g})\wedge i\notin Ignored(\hat{g})\,\}$$
$$\mathcal{DP}[\![x \;\texttt{=}\; (g^{(n)}\; y_1\;\dots y_{n-1})\; y_n;]\!] = \{\,(y_i,x)\mid i\notin Strict(\hat{g})\wedge i\notin Ignored(\hat{g})\,\}$$

These equations are subject to the following explanatory notes:

1. The rules given for conditionals do not include certain edges that could be added by noting identifiers that have certain paths to both y_t and y_e.

2. In the rule for function application, $\hat{g}$ is the semantic function corresponding to g, and the functions *Strict* and *Ignored* are as described in Section 7.4.

3. In the rule for function application, it is assumed that the free variables of the function g are $y_{n+1}, y_{n+2}, \dots$.

These rules are straightforward adaptations of those given in previous sections. The first two terms in the $\mathcal{DC}$ equation for conditionals result in identifiers nested in conditionals to have a certain dependence on all relevant predicates, as discussed in Section 7.3.

7.7 Data Structures

Determining dependence sets when data structures are involved is not as straightforward as in the scalar case. Consider the following program fragment:

```
...
a = i + j;
b = i - j;
c = const <duple, a, b>;
d = c;
x = sel_duple_1 d;
...
```

What is a dependence set for x with respect to $\{a, b, c, d, i, j, x\}$? The singleton set $\{d\}$ is not a dependence set, because it is not sufficient: it is possible to reduce d without reducing a, but in that case x cannot be reduced without also reducing a. The set $\{d, a\}$,

131

```
{...
    a = const <duple,x,y>;
    b = a;
    i = is_duple? b;
    j = sel_duple_1 b;
    k = sel_duple_2 b;
    ...}
```

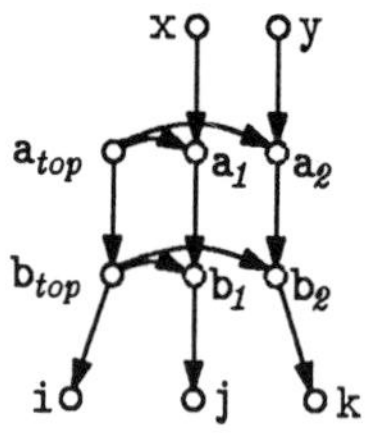

Figure 7.1: Program Illustrating Artificial Dependence Vertices

however, is a dependence set for x. Both d and a are necessary, since d must be a value in order to apply rule R5 to x's binding, and then a must be a value to apply rule R1a to the result of R5. The set is sufficient because once a and d are reduced, x can be reduced by applying (at most) an R5 rule followed by an R1a rule, and these two reductions do not reduce any other identifier.

This situation is different from all the dependence rules given so far, since a dependence set for x must include identifiers that do not appear on the right hand side of its binding. Determining x's dependence set required the examination of the bindings for d and c as well. This is not satisfactory, since the dependence graphs can no longer be constructed by a simple binding-by-binding examination of the function definition.

The situation can be remedied by introducing more vertices into the dependence graph. Suppose the value of an identifier, like d in the example above, is a two-tuple of integers. Then that identifier really represents *three* values: the top level structure value, and the value of each of two components. Corresponding to each is an event during reduction: the reduction that makes d be a value, the reduction that makes its first component a value (*i.e.*, the reduction that makes a a value), and the reduction that makes its second component a value. By having a vertex represent each of these events, a dependence graph can be formed through separate analysis of each binding, and the dependence graph will have correct paths between "top-level" vertices.

Figure 7.1 illustrates the technique. The two vertices with the *top* subscript represent "top-level" values; the shell of the data structure that just carries the information about its type. The other four subscripted vertices represent components of the data structures, with the lateral arcs reflecting the fact that a component cannot be accessed without also having the shell. In other words, for a component of b to have a value, b itself must have a value. The variables i, j, and k are sensitive to different combinations of the pieces of b: i only requires the type of b, j requires the first component but not the second, and vice versa for k. The paths between vertices representing the top-level values of identifiers give the expected dependence relationships: j depends on x but not y, and that i depends on neither x nor y. As before, for code generation all that matters is when identifiers are reduced to values, so once the dependence graph is constructed only the paths between top-level vertices will be relevant. For this reason, the other vertices are called *artificial* vertices.

132

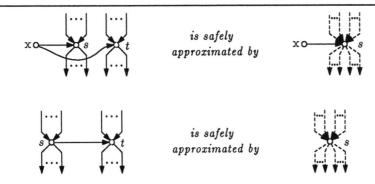

Figure 7.2: Collapsing Lemmas

To formally justify the use of artificial vertices, the definitions of dependence sets have to be extended to use a generalized form of the function *reduced*(S). We defer this justification to the end of the section, so that the reader who is willing to accept the intuition behind artificial vertices may skip the formal mathematics.

Adding a vertex for each distinct value within a data structure is feasible when the language is restricted to two-tuples of integers, but runs into difficulties with general data structures, whose components may themselves be any data structure. The problem of course, is that each variable can carry an unbounded number of atomic values, leading to an unbounded number of artificial vertices:

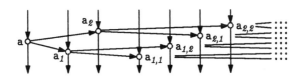

Of course, this figure only illustrates the case where the only kind of data structure is a two-tuple; the situation is correspondingly more complex as the number of data types increases.

The way around this problem is to collapse the infinite set of vertices for each variable into a finite set. Two lemmas, illustrated pictorially in Figure 7.2, accomplish this. The idea is to combine vertices of the dependence graph in a safe way, that is, so that the new graph has the same paths between the non-artificial vertices as the uncollapsed graph. More precisely, if there is an acyclic subset of the uncollapsed full dependence graph that includes all the certain edges and has a path between two non-artificial vertices u and v, then there is an acyclic subset of the collapsed full dependence graph that includes all the certain edges and has a path between u and v. A formal statement and proof of the safety of the collapsing lemmas can be found in the appendix to this chapter, Section 7.9.

One thing to note is that the edges leading to and away from collapsed vertices are always *potential* dependences, even if in the original graph some of the edges were certain dependences. This is not surprising; because collapsing makes one vertex track several independent values, there are no dependences that apply to all the values the vertex represents (an exception is illustrated in the first lemma; both collapsed vertices have a certain

133

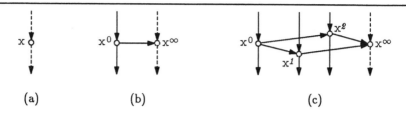

(a)   (b)   (c)

Figure 7.3: Some Possible Collapsings for Data Structure Variables

edge from the vertex **x**, and so this edge can remain as certain). It is safe for all of the
edges to be potential, however, because there are always subsets which correspond to the
dependences through each of the original vertices.

Of course, when vertices of the dependence graph are collapsed, information is inevitably lost; in this case, precision is lost in tracking the various values contained in data
structures. There is therefore a design decision as to what set of artificial vertices to collapse for each variable; Figure 7.3 shows some possibilities. Type information is valuable
here, for it may be desirable to tune the choice of artificial vertices for a variable to match
the type of that variable. If a variable is of type 2-tuple, for example, then the vertex
set shown in Figure 7.3c is a logical choice: each component is tracked separately, with
subcomponents collapsed if the components are themselves data structures. On the other
hand, for an array type it is infeasible to track each component separately since the number of components is not known until run time, and in fact may differ from one invocation
of the function to the next; Figure 7.3b seems the appropriate choice.[2] Recursive types
such as lists might benefit from yet a different approach, such as one that collapses all
"heads" into one point and all "tails" into another.[3] If no type information is available,
or if the language is not strongly typed, then the natural choice is a two-point approximation (Figure 7.3b), which just distinguishes between a top-level value and the components.
Using only a one-point approximation does not yield good results, because the collapsing
lemmas end up turning all dependence arcs into potential dependences (which we show
in Chapter 8 will lead to very bad code). Investigating the properties of various sets of
points is a topic for future research; for the remainder of this chapter we consider only
scalar/non-scalar type information and use the two-point approach.

We now present the complete set of rules for doing dependence analysis under a two-
point approximation for non-scalar variables. Given a function definition,

$$f^{(n)} \; x_1 \; \ldots \; x_n \; = \; \{B_1; \; \ldots; \; B_m; \; \text{in } x\};$$

let the free variables of the body be $x_{n+1}, \ldots, x_{n+k}$. Then the function dependence graph
is (V, D_C, D_F), as given by the following equations.

---

[2]Arrays admit a whole other class of analysis techniques generally referred to as *subscript analysis* [14].
The idea is to show that for no input can two array index expressions overlap; this information could be
used to eliminate potential dependence arcs in our framework. This is a good topic for future research.

[3]This is roughly what Wadler and Hughes are doing when they analyze "head strictness" and "tail
strictness" [74].

$$V_1 = \{x_0, \ldots, x_{n+k}\} \cup \mathcal{LV}[\![B_1; \ldots; B_m]\!] \cup \{\lozenge\}$$
$$V = \{z^0, z^\infty \mid z \in V_1\}$$

$$D_C = \mathcal{DC}_2[\![B_1; \ldots; B_m]\!] \cup D_{C,answer} \cup D_{C,lateral}$$
$$D_F = D_C \cup D_P$$
$$D_P = \mathcal{DP}_2[\![B_1; \ldots; B_m]\!] \cup D_{P,answer} \cup D_{P,feedback}$$

$$D_{C,answer} = \{(x^0, \lozenge^0)\}$$
$$D_{P,answer} = \{(x^\infty, \lozenge^\infty)\}$$

$$D_{C,lateral} = \{(z^0, z^\infty) \mid z \in V_1\}$$

$$D_{P,feedback} = \bigcup_{1 \le i \le n+k} \{(\lozenge^0, x_i^0), (\lozenge^\infty, x_i^0), (\lozenge^0, x_i^\infty), (\lozenge^\infty, x_i^\infty)\} \cup$$
$$\bigcup_{1 \le i \le n+k} \bigcup_{\substack{n \le j \le n+k \\ j \ne i}} \{(x_j^0, x_i^0), (x_j^\infty, x_i^0), (x_j^0, x_i^\infty), (x_j^\infty, x_i^\infty)\}$$

The vertex set has two vertices for each variable: the 0-superscripted vertex represents the top-level value, and the ∞-superscripted vertex the other values. If we have scalar/non-scalar type information, then we can eliminate the ∞-vertex for any variable that is known to be a scalar at compile time.

$$\mathcal{DC}_2[\![B_1; \ldots; B_m]\!] = \mathcal{DC}_2[\![B_1]\!] \cup \cdots \cup \mathcal{DC}_2[\![B_m]\!]$$
$$\mathcal{DP}_2[\![B_1; \ldots; B_m]\!] = \mathcal{DP}_2[\![B_1]\!] \cup \cdots \cup \mathcal{DP}_2[\![B_m]\!]$$

$$\mathcal{DC}_2[\![x = \texttt{const } v]\!] = \emptyset$$
$$\mathcal{DP}_2[\![x = \texttt{const } v]\!] = \emptyset$$

$$\mathcal{DC}_2[\![x = y]\!] = \{(y^0, x^0)\}$$
$$\mathcal{DP}_2[\![x = y]\!] = \{(y^\infty, x^\infty)\}$$

$$\mathcal{DC}_2[\![x = y_1 \texttt{ Op } y_2]\!] = \{(y_1^0, x^0), (y_2^0, x^0)\}$$
$$\mathcal{DP}_2[\![x = y_1 \texttt{ Op } y_2]\!] = \emptyset$$

In the rules for the const statement above, v denotes any scalar value. A simple binding has parallel edges between the 0 vertices and between the ∞ vertices, but the ∞ vertices must be potential because of the collapsing lemmas. The arithmetic expressions are treated in the same way as before. Conditionals are also treated as before:

$$\mathcal{DC}_2 \left[\!\!\begin{array}{l} x \ = \ \text{if } y \text{ then } \{B_{t,1};\dots;B_{t,n};\ \text{in } y_t\} \\ \qquad\quad \text{else } \{B_{e,1};\dots;B_{e,m};\ \text{in } y_e\} \end{array}\!\!\right] \ = \ \{\,(y^0,z^0) \mid z \in \mathcal{LV}[\![B_{t,1};\dots;B_{t,n};]\!]\,\} \cup$$

$$\{\,(y^0,z^0) \mid z \in \mathcal{LV}[\![B_{e,1};\dots;B_{e,m};]\!]\,\} \cup$$
$$\mathcal{DC}_2[\![B_{t,1};\dots;B_{t,n};]\!] \cup$$
$$\mathcal{DC}_2[\![B_{e,1};\dots;B_{e,m};]\!] \cup$$
$$\{(y^0,x^0)\}$$

$$\mathcal{DP}_2 \left[\!\!\begin{array}{l} x \ = \ \text{if } y \text{ then } \{B_{t,1};\dots;B_{t,n};\ \text{in } y_t\} \\ \qquad\quad \text{else } \{B_{e,1};\dots;B_{e,m};\ \text{in } y_e\} \end{array}\!\!\right] \ = \ \{(y_t^0,x^0),(y_e^0,x^0)\} \cup$$

$$\{(y_t^\infty,x^\infty),(y_e^\infty,x^\infty)\} \cup$$
$$\mathcal{DP}_2[\![B_{t,1};\dots;B_{t,n};]\!] \cup$$
$$\mathcal{DP}_2[\![B_{e,1};\dots;B_{e,m};]\!]$$

The interesting rules are the new ones for data structures:

$$\mathcal{DC}_2[\![x \ = \ \text{const } \langle t^{(n)},y_1,\dots,y_n\rangle]\!] \ = \ \emptyset$$
$$\mathcal{DP}_2[\![X \ = \ \text{const } \langle t^{(n)},y_1,\dots,y_n\rangle]\!] \ = \ \bigcup_{1\le i\le n} \{(y_i^0,x^\infty),(y_i^\infty,x^\infty)\}$$

$$\mathcal{DC}_2[\![x \ = \ \text{is\_}t?\ y]\!] \ = \ \{(y^0,x^0)\}$$
$$\mathcal{DP}_2[\![x \ = \ \text{is\_}t?\ y]\!] \ = \ \emptyset$$

$$\mathcal{DC}_2[\![x \ = \ \text{sel\_}t\_i\ y]\!] \ = \ \{(y^0,x^0)\}$$
$$\mathcal{DP}_2[\![x \ = \ \text{sel\_}t\_i\ y]\!] \ = \ \{(y^\infty,x^0),(y^\infty,x^\infty)\}$$

The rules for first-order procedure calls complete the definition of $\mathcal{DC}_2$ and $\mathcal{DP}_2$. As in Section 7.4, we will rely on a conjectured relationship between the denotational semantics and the operational semantics, so that some sort of strictness analysis technique may be used to determine the dependence edges. But ordinary strictness analysis is no longer sufficient, for we need to distinguish between strictness in the top-level value and strictness in subcomponents.

Two auxiliary functions are used to define the strictness properties we are after. The first is a predicate which identifies "top-level" values that are free of additional information.

$$toponly(a) = \begin{cases} true & \text{if } a = \bot,\ a \in C,\ a = \bot_S,\ \text{or } a = \langle t,\bot,\dots,\bot\rangle, \\ false & \text{otherwise.} \end{cases}$$

(In this definition, C is the semantic domain of scalars, including the bottom element $\bot_C$ of that domain, and $\bot_S$ is the bottom element of the semantic domain of data structures.) The second removes all information save the top-level value:

$$filter(a) = \begin{cases} \langle t,\bot,\dots,\bot\rangle & \text{if } a = \langle t,a_1,\dots,a_n\rangle, \\ a & \text{otherwise.} \end{cases}$$

Thus $toponly(filter(a)) = true$ for all a. Now define five properties, P1 through P5. A semantic function $\hat{f}$ has property P for its ith argument if the corresponding equation below is true for all $a_1,\dots,a_n$.

P1 : $\quad \hat{f}(\dots,\bot,\dots) = \bot$

$$P2: \quad filter(\hat{f}(\ldots, \bot, \ldots)) = filter(\hat{f}(\ldots, filter(a_i), \ldots))$$
$$P3: \quad filter(\hat{f}(\ldots, filter(a_i), \ldots)) = filter(\hat{f}(\ldots, a_i, \ldots))$$
$$P4: \quad toponly(\hat{f}(\ldots, a_i, \ldots)) \vee (\hat{f}(\ldots, \bot, \ldots) = \hat{f}(\ldots, filter(a_i), \ldots))$$
$$P5: \quad toponly(\hat{f}(\ldots, a_i, \ldots)) \vee (\hat{f}(\ldots, filter(a_i), \ldots) = \hat{f}(\ldots, a_i, \ldots))$$

These properties have the following interpretation:

P1 The top level of the ith argument is required to produce the top level of the result.

P2 The top level of the result completely ignores the top level of the ith argument.

P3 The top level of the result does not require any subcomponent of the ith argument.

P4 No subcomponent of the result requires the top level of the ith argument.

P5 No subcomponent of the result requires any subcomponent of the ith argument.

(Properties P1 and P2 reduce to ordinary strictness and ignoring, respectively, on flat domains.)

Now assume that we have a strictness analyzer which for every function of the program computes five sets corresponding to the five properties:

$$p_k(\hat{f}) = \{\, i \mid \text{Property P}k \text{ is inferred for } \hat{f} \text{ on its } i\text{th argument}\,\}$$

Then the rules for adding dependence edges for a first order call are:

$$\mathcal{DC}_2[\![x = (g^{(n)} \; y_1 \ldots y_{n-1}) \; y_n;]\!] = \{\, (y_i^0, x^0) \mid i \in p_1(\hat{g}) \wedge i \notin p_2(\hat{g})\,\}$$
$$\mathcal{DP}_2[\![x = (g^{(n)} \; y_1 \ldots y_{n-1}) \; y_n;]\!] = \{\, (y_i^0, x^0) \mid i \notin p_1(\hat{g}) \wedge i \notin p_2(\hat{g})\,\} \cup$$
$$\{\, (y_i^\infty, x^0) \mid i \notin p_3(\hat{g})\,\} \cup$$
$$\{\, (y_i^0, x^\infty) \mid i \notin p_4(\hat{g})\,\} \cup$$
$$\{\, (y_i^\infty, x^\infty) \mid i \notin p_5(\hat{g})\,\}$$

The Wadler and Hughes context analysis technique [74] is one kind of strictness analysis framework that is capable of inferring these five properties from functional quads programs.

The remainder of this section presents the mathematical formalization of artificial vertices. The reader may skip to the next section, if desired.

To define the precise meaning of artificial vertices, consider what the non-artificial (top-level) vertices represent. We started with a notion of requirement among all redexes (in Section 6.1), then restricted our attention to those redexes whose reduction caused an identifier to become bound to a value (in Section 6.2). The top-level vertices in dependence graphs represent those reductions.

To extend these concepts to artificial vertices, which are supposed to represent components of an identifier's value being reduced to values, the concept underlying the function $reduced(S)$ must be extended to recognize those events. Essentially, $reduced(S)$ is looking for bindings in S of a certain form, namely those of the form $x = v$, so we extend it to look for more complicated configurations.

137

Definition 7.3 *A* pattern *is a tuple* $\langle x, \mathcal{B} \rangle$, *where* x *is an arity zero identifier and* $\mathcal{B}$ *is a set of bindings, and where* x *is on the left hand side of one binding in* $\mathcal{B}$.

If we are limited to two-tuples of scalars, the patterns of interest are:

$$
\begin{aligned}
TopVal &= \langle x, \{x = v\} \rangle \\
HdVal &= \langle x, \{x = \texttt{<duple},y,z\texttt{>}, y = v\} \rangle \\
TlVal &= \langle x, \{x = \texttt{<duple},y,z\texttt{>}, z = v\} \rangle
\end{aligned}
$$

Definition 7.4 *A pattern* $\langle x, \mathcal{B} \rangle$ *is said to* match *in a state* S *if there is a substitution* σ *such that for every* $B \in \mathcal{B}$, σB *is a binding in* S. *Moreover, the pattern is said to match on* σx.

For example, in the following state:

```
a = 3;
b = a;
c = <duple, a, b>;
```

there are three matches: *TopVal* matches on a and also on c, and *HdVal* matches on c. (There is a technical point we are glossing over: in all patterns, the pattern variable v is supposed to match values in the state, not identifiers. The definition of matching did not formalize this; to do so requires a more elaborate notion of substitution.) The generalization of $reduced(S)$ is $matches(S)$, defined as follows.

Definition 7.5 *Given a state* S *and a set of patterns,* $matches(S)$ *is the set of pairs*

$$\{ (p, x) \mid Pattern \ p \ matches \ on \ x \ in \ S \}$$

In the previous example, $matches(S) = \{(TopVal, \text{a}), (TopVal, \text{c}), (HdVal, \text{c})\}$. The pairs returned by $matches(S)$ are called *match descriptors*.

Fact 7.6 (Monotonicity of *matches***)** *For all* S_i *and* S_j *such that* $S_i \vdash^* S_j$, $matches(S_j) \supseteq matches(S_i)$.

The definition of a dependence set, Definition 6.11, is extended by simply letting the set V be a set of match descriptors instead of identifiers, and by replacing *reduced* with *matches*. A small modification to the sufficiency part of the definition is required, though: the state S_j is allowed to have matches in the higher components of match descriptor x, as well as x itself. This modification is required because a single reduction step can simultaneously result in several new matches, though always on a single identifier.

Having extended the definition of a dependence set, the definition of dependence graphs and function dependence graphs follows analogously. The proofs of the central theorems, Theorems 6.13 and 6.22 generalize without significant modification. Thus, paths in dependence graphs with artificial vertices give the ordering relationships between subexpressions, and a dependence graph for every live context can be recovered from a function dependence graph with artificial vertices by considering acyclic subsets of the full graph that includes the edges of the certain graph.

We now use this machinery to prove correct some dependence sets for data structure constructs (in the case of two-tuples of integers).

Given function f with a top-level binding of the form

x = sel_duple_1 y;

then the dependence sets for $(Top\,Val, x)$ are:

$$\Upsilon^f_{C,(Top\,Val,x)} = \{(Top\,Val, y), (Hd\,Val, y)\}$$
$$\Upsilon^f_{F,(Top\,Val,x)} = \{(Top\,Val, y), (Hd\,Val, y)\}$$

Proof. In any context, a dependence set for $(Top\,Val, \sigma x)$ is $\{(Top\,Val, \sigma y), (Hd\,Val, \sigma y)\}$, as shown below. So $\Upsilon_C = \Upsilon_F = \{(Top\,Val, y), (Hd\,Val, y)\}$.

(Necessity) Suppose $(Top\,Val, \sigma y) \notin matches(S_i)$, then S_i contains no binding for σy, or it contains a binding where σy is not a value, so no R1e rule can be applied to the binding for σx. Suppose $(Top\,Val, \sigma y) \in matches(S_i)$ but $(Hd\,Val, \sigma y) \notin matches(S_i)$, then further reduction of S_i can arrive at a state containing σx = sel_duple_1 V where either (a) V is not a duple structure, in which case no further reduction of σx is possible, or (b) V is of the form <duple,σz_1,σz_2> but σy is not a value, in which case the binding can be reduced to σx = σy but no further.

(Sufficiency) Given a state S with $(Top\,Val, \sigma y), (Hd\,Val, \sigma y) \in matches(S)$, the following sequence can be performed (possibly omitting some steps): an R1e reduction resulting in σx = <duple,σz_1,σz_2>, an R5 reduction resulting in σx = σz_1, and finally an R1a reduction to substitute for σz_1. In the process, no new matches are created. ∎

Given function f with a top-level binding of the form

x = is_duple? y;

then the dependence sets for $(Top\,Val, x)$ are:

$$\Upsilon^f_{C,(Top\,Val,x)} = \{(Top\,Val, y)\}$$
$$\Upsilon^f_{F,(Top\,Val,x)} = \{(Top\,Val, y)\}$$

Proof. In any context, a dependence set for $(Top\,Val, \sigma x)$ is $\{(Top\,Val, \sigma y)\}$, as shown below. So $\Upsilon_C = \Upsilon_F = \{(Top\,Val, y)\}$.

(Necessity) If σy is not reduced to a value, no R1f reduction can substitute for σy, and so the binding for σx cannot be reduced further.

(Sufficiency) Given a state S with $(Top\,Val, \sigma y) \in matches(S)$, the following sequence can be performed (possibly omitting some steps): an R1f reduction resulting in substitution of a value for σy in σx's binding, then either an R6a or R6b reduction, reducing σx to a value. In the process, no new matches are created. ∎

Given function f with a top-level binding of the form

```
x = const <duple,y,z>;
```

then the dependence sets for $(TopVal, x)$ are:

$$\Upsilon^f_{C,(TopVal,x)} = \emptyset$$
$$\Upsilon^f_{F,(TopVal,x)} = \emptyset$$

the dependence sets for $(HdVal, x)$ are:

$$\Upsilon^f_{C,(HdVal,x)} = \{(TopVal, y)\}$$
$$\Upsilon^f_{F,(HdVal,x)} = \{(TopVal, y)\}$$

and the dependence sets for $(TlVal, x)$ are:

$$\Upsilon^f_{C,(TlVal,x)} = \{(TopVal, z)\}$$
$$\Upsilon^f_{F,(TlVal,x)} = \{(TopVal, z)\}$$

Proof. The dependence sets are the same for all contexts, so $\Upsilon_C = \Upsilon_F$ for all three cases. The dependence set for $(TopVal, \sigma x)$ is trivially shown to be the empty set: rule R2 applies to the const binding no matter what the state of other bindings. The sets for $(HdVal, \sigma x)$ and $(TlVal, \sigma x)$ are almost as easily derived: applying the R2 rule to σx's binding results in a match of the appropriate pattern, as long as σy (or σz) is also reduced to a value. ∎

All of the above results are reflected in Figure 7.1. It is straightforward to extend these results to other patterns and other kinds of bindings, if perhaps a bit tedious. Applying the collapsing lemma to them results in the rules for two-point dependence graphs given earlier.

7.8   Higher-Order Functions

The only remaining functional quads construct is general application, that is, bindings of the form $x = y\ z$. The easiest way to reason about this construct is as a call to a primitive binary function *apply*, which takes a function and a value and returns the result of applying that function to that value. Without any further information, then, *apply* is a function that is strict in its first argument and may or may not use its second argument, depending on what function is being applied. Higher-order strictness analysis techniques are still in their infancy [15, 32]; they attempt to determine for each instance of *apply* whether that application will always use or always ignore its second argument.

We shall not delve further into higher-order strictness analysis, but simply present the equations for the conservative case where nothing is inferred about a general application. Operationally, *apply* examines the function value y: if it is a partial application that needs more than one argument before the arity is satisfied, it just builds another partial application containing the new argument z; otherwise, it invokes the function over which y is closed, passing the arguments recorded in y along with the new argument z. These two cases correspond to Rules R7 and R8 in the functional quads reduction system, respectively.

140

The important feature to note is that the function value y may be a partial application, and because it may be closed over some identifiers it behaves like a data structure. Hence, the dependence analysis techniques presented for data structures also apply to general applications. In two-point analysis, a conservative treatment of *apply* behaves like a function with Property P1 for its first argument and none of properties P1 through P5 for its second. The dependence equations, therefore, are:

$$
\begin{aligned}
\mathcal{DC}_2[\![x = y\ z]\!] &= \{(y^0, x^0)\} \\
\mathcal{DP}_2[\![x = y\ z]\!] &= \{(y^\infty, x^0), (y^0, x^\infty), (y^\infty, x^\infty), \\
&\qquad (z^0, x^0), (z^\infty, x^0), (z^0, x^\infty), (z^\infty, x^\infty)\}
\end{aligned}
$$

Even without higher-order strictness analysis, though, a compiler may be able to detect that certain applications will always have unsatisfied arity (*i.e.*, Rule R7 rewrites). In that case, the top level of X completely ignores Z, and we have the following equations:

$$
\begin{aligned}
\mathcal{DC}_2[\![x = y\ z]\!] &= \{(y^0, x^0)\} \\
\mathcal{DP}_2[\![x = y\ z]\!] &= \{(y^\infty, x^0), (y^0, x^\infty), (y^\infty, x^\infty), \\
&\qquad (z^0, x^\infty), (z^\infty, x^\infty)\}
\end{aligned}
$$

Choosing vertex sets other than the two-point set and incorporating higher-order strictness analysis are topics for future research.

7.9 Appendix: Proof of the "Collapsing" Lemma

In this appendix we state formally and prove the "collapsing" lemmas shown in Figure 7.2. Actually, both are just special cases of a single theorem. In that theorem, we identify two vertices s and t, and show that if t is an artificial vertex then t can be collapsed onto s as long as all edges to and from s and t are turned into potential edges, although certain edges formerly incident upon both s and t from the same origin can remain certain.

The property we need to preserve in the collapsed graph is that of Theorem 6.22: that for every context, there is an acyclic subset of the collapsed full dependence graph, which is also a superset of the collapsed certain dependence graph, that gives the ordering relationships between the vertices that remain. Now it turns out that there may not be an acyclic subset of the collapsed graph that simultaneously gives the ordering relationships between all vertices. Instead, we show that for any individual path in an acyclic subset of the original graph, there is a path in some acyclic subset of the collapsed graph. This is adequate to preserve the correctness of the partitioning algorithms to be given in the next chapter, as they respect all acyclic subsets.

Theorem 7.7 *Let (V, D_C, D_F) be a function dependence graph with distinguished vertices $s, t \in V$. Let D_C be partitioned into seven subsets according to the endpoints of each edge: $D_C = VV_C \cup VS_C \cup VT_C \cup SV_C \cup TV_C \cup ST_C \cup TS_C$, where TV_C, for example, contains the edges $(t, v) \in D_C$ for $v \in (V - \{s, t\})$. Let D_F be similarly partitioned into seven subsets.*

Note that each C-subscripted set is a subset of the corresponding F-subscripted set. Now define the dependence graph $(\tilde{V}, \tilde{D}_C, \tilde{D}_F)$ where t is collapsed into s as follows:

$$
\begin{aligned}
\tilde{V} &= V - \{t\} \\
\tilde{D}_C &= VV_C \cup \{(v, s) \mid (v, s) \in VS_C \wedge (v, t) \in VT_C\} \\
\tilde{D}_F &= VV_F \cup VS_F \cup SV_F \\
&\quad \cup \{(v, s) \mid (v, t) \in VT_F\} \\
&\quad \cup \{(s, v) \mid (t, v) \in TV_F\}
\end{aligned}
$$

Then if $u \xrightarrow{D}^+ v$, where $u, v \in \tilde{V}$, $D_C \subseteq D \subseteq D_F$, and D is acyclic, then there exists an acyclic $\tilde{D}$, where $\tilde{D}_C \subseteq \tilde{D} \subseteq \tilde{D}_F$, such that $u \xrightarrow{\tilde{D}}^+ v$.

Proof. We proceed by cases, based on the vertices included along the path $u \xrightarrow{D}^+ v$. Remember, this path can pass *through* the vertex t, but cannot start or end at t.

The path does not go through s or t.
    The path is contained wholly in VV_F, and so is unaffected by the construction. $\tilde{D} = D$, and $\tilde{D}$ is therefore acyclic.

The path goes through s: $u \xrightarrow{D}^+ s \xrightarrow{D}^+ v$.
    The same path still exists, and $\tilde{D} = D$. If for some reason D included edges to or from t that do not have analogs to or from s, the corresponding edges to or from s can be eliminated from $\tilde{D}$, since they cannot contribute to the path $u \xrightarrow{D}^+ s \xrightarrow{D}^+ v$. Hence, $\tilde{D}$ is acyclic.

The path goes through t: $u \xrightarrow{D}^+ t \xrightarrow{D}^+ v$.
    The path will now go through s instead. A similar argument as for the last case prevents the introduction of cycles by eliminating any extraneous edges involving s.

The path goes through s then t: $u \xrightarrow{D}^+ s \xrightarrow{D}^+ t \xrightarrow{D}^+ v$.
    The corresponding path in the collapsed graph has a cycle from s to s, but that can simply be short-circuited, and the two s-edges involved in the cycle deleted from $\tilde{D}$ to make $\tilde{D}$ be acyclic.

The path goes through t then s: $u \xrightarrow{D}^+ t \xrightarrow{D}^+ s \xrightarrow{D}^+ v$.
    Analogous to the last case.

The path starts or ends with s.
    Either is simply a degenerate case of the case that goes through s. ∎

   The proof reveals the mathematical reason why the edges to and from s and t are turned into potential edges: in various cases we needed the freedom to remove them to preserve the acyclicness of the subgraph containing a given path.

8 Constraint Computation and Partitioning

Chapter 7 presented the formal basis for analyzing dependences in programs, culminating in the definition of the function dependence graph, which was shown to contain dependence information (and therefore ordering information) for every context in which a function can be called. In this chapter, we show how to use the function dependence graph to partition a program into threads. We will show that for every context in which a function can be invoked, there is an interleaving of the threads that respects the requirement relation of all live variables of the function in that context.

There may be many partitionings possible for a given function. A code generator may want the freedom to choose among the various partitionings, depending on the characteristics of the target machine. For example, large threads might be appropriate for a uniprocessor target, while smaller threads could expose more parallelism on a multiprocessor. For some targets, it may be necessary to choose threads so that once started, they run to completion without waiting for other threads, while other targets may not have this restriction.

To give maximal freedom to the code generator, it will not be satisfactory to merely produce one acceptable partitioning from a function. Instead, we will produce a set of partitioning constraints, so that the code generator may choose any partition that is consistent with the constraints. We will give efficient algorithms both for constructing the constraints, and for producing threads consistent with the constraints.

8.1 Threads, Partitioning, and Correctness

The formal description of a partitioning is as follows.

Definition 8.1 *A* partitioning *of a set V of identifiers is a set $\Theta = \{\theta_1, \ldots, \theta_n\}$, where each thread θ_i is an ordered sequence of vertices $v_{i,1} v_{i,2} \cdots v_{i,|\theta_i|}$, $v_{i,j} \in V$, and where each element of V appears in exactly one position in one $\theta_i \in \Theta$.*

Partitioning is a description of ordering decisions taken at compile time. Specifically, if identifiers $v_{i,1}, v_{i,2}, \ldots$ comprise a thread θ_i in a partitioning, then the corresponding object code will have a sequential thread consisting of the code to compute $v_{i,1}, v_{i,2}, \ldots$, in that order. In any execution of that object code, the computation of the values of $v_{i,1}, v_{i,2}, \ldots$ is constrained to take place in that order.

Constraining certain identifiers to execute in a particular order effectively introduces additional dependences between them. These are called the *imputed dependences* of the partitioning.

Definition 8.2 *The* imputed dependences *of a partitioning* Θ*, notation* D_Θ*, is the set*

$$D_\Theta = \bigcup_{1 \leq i \leq |\Theta|} \bigcup_{1 \leq j \leq |\theta_i| - 1} (v_{i,j}, v_{i,j+1})$$

Correctness is defined in the following definitions.

Definition 8.3 *An* interleaving *of the threads in* Θ *is a permutation of the union of all elements of threads in* Θ*,* $v_{t_1,i_1} v_{t_2,i_2} \cdots v_{t_n,i_n}$*, such that for all* $a < b \leq n$ *if* $t_a = t_b$ *then* $i_a < i_b$.

Definition 8.4 *A partitioning* Θ *is correct with respect to an acyclic dependence graph* D *if there is an interleaving of the threads that is consistent with the partial order expressed by* D.

Corollary 8.5 *A partitioning* Θ *is correct with respect to* D *if* $(D \cup D_\Theta)$ *is acyclic; any topological sort of* $(D \cup D_\Theta)$ *is an interleaving that is consistent with* D.

Definition 8.6 *If* (V, D_C, D_F) *is a dependence graph, the* admissible subsets *of* D_F *are the acyclic* D *such that* $D_C \subseteq D \subseteq D_F$.

Definition 8.7 *A partitioning* Θ *is correct with respect to a function dependence graph* (V, D_C, D_F) *if* Θ *is correct with respect to every admissible subset of* D_F.

Recall that according to Theorem 6.22, for every context in which the function could be invoked there is an admissible subset of D_F that is the dependence graph for the live variables in that context. So if a partitioning is correct with respect to the function dependence graph, it will be correct with respect to the dependence graph for each context. There is then an interleaving of the threads that is consistent with the dependence graph's partial order; by Theorem 6.13 it is also consistent with the requirement relation; by Theorem 6.2 this interleaving is therefore a valid reduction sequence.

8.2 Partitioning Using Constraint Graphs

In this section we show how to obtain a correct partitioning for any function dependence graph. To give freedom to a code generator in choosing among many possible partitionings, we first derive constraints from the function dependence graph. The constraints are in the form of two more graphs: the *separation graph*, which indicates when two subexpressions must be assigned to different sequential threads, and the *a priori ordering constraint*, which indicates the relative ordering between subexpressions when assigned to the same thread.

To motivate separation and ordering as constraints, Figure 8.1 shows a small function (similar to the one from Section 3.1.3) along with its dependence graphs (again, using the solid/dashed convention). The cycles arise because for negative values of x, a and aa must be evaluated before b and bb, while for positive values of x the reverse is true. As we discussed in Section 3.6, the code which computes aa and bb must be placed in separate threads, so that either relative ordering is possible at run time. On the other hand, a and aa

144

```
conditional_example x =
   {p = x > 0;
    a = if p then bb else 3;
    b = if p then 4 else aa;
    aa = a + 5;
    bb = b + 6;
    c = aa + bb;
    in
       c};
```

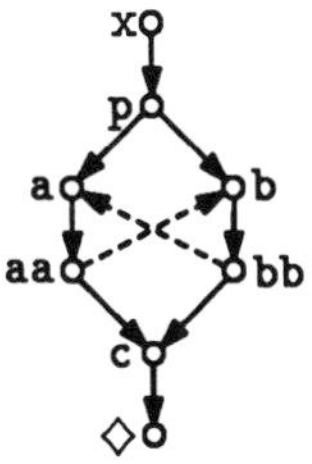

Figure 8.1: A Function with a Cyclic D_F

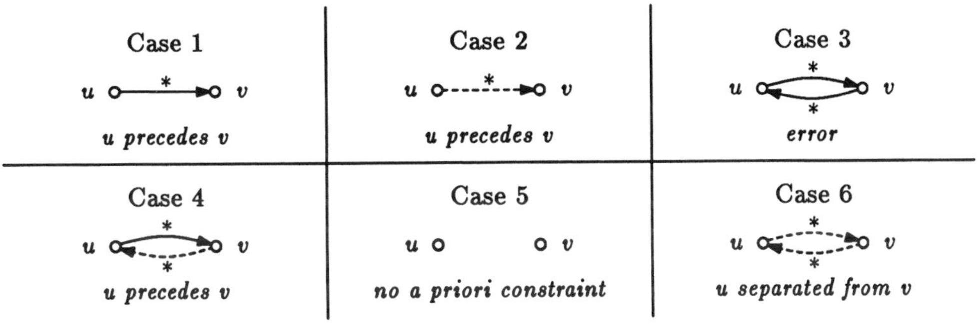

Case 1	Case 2	Case 3
$u \circ \xrightarrow{\quad * \quad} \bullet v$	$u \circ \dashrightarrow{\quad * \quad} \bullet v$	$u \circ \overset{*}{\underset{*}{\rightleftarrows}} \circ v$
u precedes v	*u precedes v*	*error*
Case 4	Case 5	Case 6
$u \circ \overset{*}{\underset{*}{\rightleftarrows}} \circ v$	$u \circ \qquad \circ v$	$u \circ \overset{*}{\underset{*}{\rightleftarrows}} \bullet v$
u precedes v	*no a priori constraint*	*u separated from v*

Figure 8.2: Partitioning Constraints Implied by Dependence Graphs

may be placed in the same thread, but if they are, a must precede aa. In general, cycles in $\vec{D}_F$ will result in separation constraints.

The constraints are obtained by considering paths in D_F and D_C. For every pair of subexpressions (vertices in V), there are six cases of dependence graph paths (plus three symmetric variations), as shown in Figure 8.2. In the figure, a solid line denotes a path in D_C, while a dashed line denotes a path in D_F that is not also in D_C (*i.e.*, a path in D_F that includes at least one edge not in D_C); interpreting these cases reveals how to construct the separation graph and the *a priori* ordering constraint. In case 1, u must precede v in every context, so u should precede v if assigned to the same thread. In case 2, u must precede v for *some* context, so again u should precede v when assigned to the same thread, so that the object code is properly ordered for that context. Case 3 implies that there are no contexts in which the dependence graph is acyclic, so that the function deadlocks no matter how it is invoked; if this case is detected, the compiler should signal an error and reject the function. In case 4 there is always a dependence from u to v, so while there is a path from v to u in D_F, no *admissible* subset of D_F will have this path; the interpretation is the same as for case 1. In case 5 there is simply no constraint at all, *a priori* (see the discussion below). Finally, in case 6, u must precede v in some context, but v must precede u in some other context. In this case u and v must be placed in separate threads

145

so that either ordering is possible at run time.

Mathematically, the constraints described in the above case analysis are expressed as follows:

$$S = \{\, \{u,v\} \mid (u,v),(v,u) \in (D_F^+ - D_C^+)\,\}$$
$$A = \{\, (u,v) \mid ((u,v) \in D_C^+ \wedge (v,u) \notin D_C^+) \vee$$
$$((u,v) \in D_F^+ \wedge (v,u) \notin D_F^+)\}$$

The *separation graph* $\vec{S} = (V,S)$ is an undirected graph with an edge between pairs of subexpressions that must be assigned to different threads. The *a priori ordering constraint*, $\vec{A} = (V,A)$ has a directed edge between u and v if u must precede v when assigned to the same thread.

To illustrate, here are the constraints inferred from the dependence graphs for the function in Figure 8.1 (the transitive edges in A have been omitted for clarity):

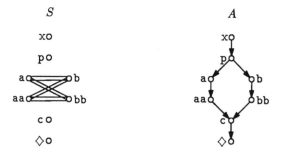

To partition this program into threads, we need only color the separation graph,[1] each color representing a thread. Each thread is then ordered according to the ordering constraint. For the example program, we see that at least two threads are needed, and that the a's must be in a different thread from the b's, as expected.

There is a small hitch in the procedure suggested above: if there is no edge between u and v either in S or in A, then there is no *a priori* constraint on their relative ordering if assigned to the same thread, but that does not mean that every such pair can be ordered independently. To illustrate what is meant, consider the following situation:

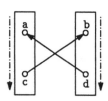

Here there are four subexpressions a, b, c, and d, with no separation constraints and two *a priori* ordering constraints, indicated by the solid arrows. They have been partitioned

---

[1] A *k-coloring* of an undirected graph assigns an integer i, $1 \le i \le k$, to each vertex such that adjacent vertices are assigned different integers.

into two threads as shown, where the flow of control in each thread runs from top to bottom. The thread orderings are independently consistent with the ordering constraint, *but the net result is incorrect*, as there is no interleaving of these two threads which satisfies the ordering constraints that exist between threads. The problem is that when subexpressions are assigned to the same thread, new dependence relations are effectively added by virtue of the sequential nature of a thread—these are the imputed dependences of the partitioning. This is why the ordering constraint is only an *a priori* ordering constraint, since assigning otherwise unconstrained subexpressions to the same thread propagates new ordering constraints through the graph.

The upshot is that the program is partitioned into threads by coloring the separation graph, but when the ordering within each thread is chosen care must be taken not to introduce any new cycles in the full dependence graph. Formally, given dependence graphs $\vec{D}_C$ and $\vec{D}_F$ and constraint graphs $\vec{S}$ and $\vec{A}$, a legal partitioning of V must satisfy the following conditions:

1. If there is an edge $(v_{i,k}, v_{j,l}) \in S$, then $v_{i,k}$ and $v_{j,l}$ are assigned to separate threads (*i.e.*, $i \neq j$).

2. If $(v_{i,k}, v_{j,l}) \in A$ and $v_{i,k}$ and $v_{j,l}$ are assigned to the same thread (*i.e.*, $i = j$), then $v_{i,k}$ precedes $v_{i,l}$ in the thread (*i.e.*, $k < l$); moreover,

3. Adding the imputed dependences D_Θ to D_F must introduce no new cycles into D_F; that is, $\mathrm{SCC}(D_F) = \mathrm{SCC}(D_F \cup D_\Theta)$, where $\mathrm{SCC}(E)$ denotes the strongly connected components of the graph (V, E).[2]

The following theorem establishes the correctness of partitions obtained in this way.

Theorem 8.8 *Let (V, D_C, D_F) be a function dependence graph, and S and A be the separation and ordering constraints obtained from that graph according to the definition above. Then any partitioning Θ satisfying the three conditions outlined above is correct with respect to the function dependence graph.*

Proof. We must show that for all admissible D, $(D \cup D_\Theta)$ is acyclic. Suppose $(D \cup D_\Theta)$ were cyclic; any cycle would have to be entirely within some strongly connected component of D_F, because of partitioning condition (3). Because D is acyclic, the cycle includes at least one segment entirely within D_Θ: $(u, v) \in D_\Theta^+$ but $(u, v) \notin D^+$, which by definition of D_Θ further implies that u and v were assigned to the same thread, with u preceding v. But since u and v are both members of some strongly connected component of D_F, either (a) $\{u, v\} \in S$, violating partitioning condition (1); or (b) $(u, v) \in A$ with $(u, v) \in D_C^+$, contradicting $(u, v) \notin D^+$; or (c) $(v, u) \in A$, violating partitioning condition (2). ∎

It is worth noting that the constraints derived in this section are not *minimal*, in the sense that there may exist a partitioning that is correct with respect to the function dependence graphs but nonetheless not consistent with the constraint graphs, according to the partitioning conditions outlined above. This is because a separation or ordering

---

[2]The strongly connected components of a graph (V, E) are the set of maximal subsets of V such that there is a path in E between every pair of vertices in a subset, in both directions.

constraint may have been introduced due to a path in D_F, but that path is not actually present in any *admissible* subset of D_F. In subsequent sections, we develop some algorithms that give better approximations. We note that the following question is NP-complete: is there an admissible D such that there is a path from u to v in D (the NP-completeness of this question is proved in Section 8.8). So it is unlikely that any practical procedure will be capable of finding every legal partitioning, or expressing minimal constraints upon partitioning.

8.3 Efficient Partitioning Algorithms

The constraint graphs were defined in the previous section in terms of transitive closures of the function dependence graphs. These definitions could be applied directly to compute the constraint graphs using transitive closure algorithms. Unfortunately, the best transitive closure algorithms are only as fast as the best matrix multiply algorithms, so the best constraint computation algorithm will have running time $O(|V|^3)$ (using Strassen's trick, this can be improved to $O(|V|^{\log_2 7})$, and similar tricks may reduce it further, but in any case never better than $O(|V|^2)$) [1].

We now describe a faster algorithm, based on the observation that all edges in S are contained in strongly connected components of $\vec{D}_F$.

Theorem 8.9 *Let S and A be the constraints obtained from the function dependence graph (V, D_C, D_F) as defined in Section 8.2. Then $\{u, v\} \in S$ if and only if u and v are in some strongly connected component of D_F, $(u, v) \notin D_C^+$, and $(v, u) \notin D_C^+$.*

Proof. (If) Since u and v are in some strongly connected component of D_F, $(u, v), (v, u) \in D_F^+$. $(u, v) \notin D_C^+$ and $(v, u) \notin D_C^+$ further implies that $(u, v), (v, u) \in D_F^+ - D_C^+$, therefore $\{u, v\} \in S$.

(Only if) $\{u, v\} \in S$ implies $(u, v), (v, u) \in D_F^+ - D_C^+$, and so in particular $(u, v), (v, u) \notin D_C^+$ and furthermore $(u, v), (v, u) \in D_F^+$ which means that u and v are in a strongly connected component. ∎

This suggests the following algorithm for computing S and A:

1. Find the strongly connected components of $\vec{D}_F$.

2. For each pair of distinct vertices u, v in a component, there is an edge $(u, v) \in A$ if $(u, v) \in D_C^+$, an edge $(v, u) \in A$ if $(v, u) \in D_C^+$, and $\{u, v\} \in S$ otherwise.

3. Form the reduced graph $\vec{D}'_F$ of $\vec{D}_F$ (the graph that has a vertex for each strongly connected component of D_F and an edge whenever D_F has an edge between vertices in two components). This graph is acyclic.

4. For each pair of vertex sets U, V in $\vec{D}'_F$ such that $U \xrightarrow{D'_F}+ V$, there is an edge in A from every vertex in U to every vertex in V.

Finding the strongly connected components of a graph has running time $O(V + E)$, where V is the number of vertices and E the number of edges, and finding transitive closures of

148

acyclic graphs has running time $O(V \cdot E)$ (using depth-first search). So the entire algorithm above has worst case running time $O(|V||D_F|)$.

Having found an efficient algorithm for computing S and A, we now turn to efficient algorithms for finding partitionings consistent with S and A, according to the three conditions given in Section 8.2. The first condition is equivalent to k-coloring the separation graph. The k-coloring problem is known to be NP-complete, but many efficient approximations are known [46, 76]. The second condition is just a topological sort of portions of A, but it has to be done in such a way to satisfy the third condition.

The efficient algorithm given above for computing constraint graphs suggests a procedure for ordering vertices so that the third partitioning condition is satisfied. Essentially, we will not compute A at all, but instead we will assign numbers to every vertex such that when two vertices are assigned to the same thread they should be ordered according to the numbers we assign. We compute these numbers at the same time the separation constraint S is constructed; afterwards, the code generator may divide the program into threads as it chooses (consistent with S), but must observe the assigned numbers when ordering each thread.

The algorithm is as follows. Two numbers are assigned to each vertex, called the *major* number and the *minor* number.

1. Find the strongly connected components of $\vec{D}_F$.

2. For each pair of distinct vertices u, v in a component, there is an edge $\{u, v\} \in S$ unless $(u, v) \in D_C^+$ or $(v, u) \in D_C^+$.

3. For each strongly connected component, perform a topological sort using the edges of D_C, assigning minor numbers to each vertex in the component. (That is, assign the minor number 1 to the first vertex in the topological ordering, the number 2 to the next, *etc.*)

4. Form the reduced graph $\vec{D}_F'$ of $\vec{D}_F$. This graph is acyclic.

5. Perform a topological sort on the reduced graph, assigning a major number to all the vertices of each component (all vertices in a given component receive the same major number).

When the program is partitioned into threads, each thread is ordered so that u precedes v only if u's major number is lower than v's, or if the major numbers are the same and u's minor number is lower than v's. This ordering is guaranteed not to introduce any additional cycles into D_F, no matter what partitioning is chosen (the proof is an exercise for the reader).

8.4 Improving the Constraint Graphs—Eliminating Inadmissible Edges

In Section 8.2 we remarked that the definitions of S and A given there are not minimal, in the sense that they may rule out some valid partitionings. In this section and the next, we present techniques that improve the quality of the constraint graphs.

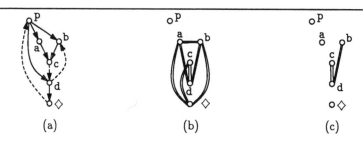

Figure 8.3: Example of Eliminating Inadmissible Edges

The most obvious improvement is to recognize that while determining whether a path exists in an acyclic D, there are certain *edges* which cannot be present in any D. Specifically, if there is a certain path $u \xrightarrow{D_C} {}^+ v$, then there is no admissible D, $D_C \subseteq D \subseteq D_F$ that includes (v, u); this is termed an *inadmissible edge*. All inadmissible edges can be eliminated from D_F before computing constraints. The most important way this pays off is in eliminating feedback edges to strict arguments of a function. An example is shown in Figure 8.3; (a) is a dependence graph obtained from the methods of Chapter 7, (b) is the separation graph computed from (a) without eliminating inadmissible edges, and (c) is the separation graph computed if the inadmissible edge $(\diamondsuit, p)$ is first eliminated from (a).

Because inadmissible edges cannot be present in any admissible subset of D_F, the correctness of eliminating them follows immediately. That is, a partitioning satisfying the three partitioning conditions, on constraint graphs computed with inadmissible edges eliminated, is correct with respect to the function dependence graphs.

Here is an algorithm for removing all inadmissible edges with $\Theta(|V|^2 + |V||D_C|)$ running time.

```
for u ∈ V do
    Reachable(u) ← ∅
    Mark(u) ← false
for u ∈ V do
    if ¬Mark(u) then
        DFS(u)
for u ∈ V do
    for v ∈ Reachable(u) do
        Remove (v, u) from D_F

procedure DFS(u) :
    Mark(u) ← true
    for each v such that (u, v) ∈ D_C do
        if ¬Mark(v) do
            DFS(v)
        Reachable(u) ← Reachable(u) ∪ Reachable(v)
```

This is just a depth-first search of D_C; depth-first search can be used in place of the usual transitive closure algorithm because D_C is acyclic.

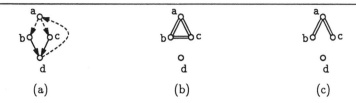

$$\text{(a)} \qquad\qquad \text{(b)} \qquad\qquad \text{(c)}$$

Figure 8.4: Example of Collapsing Strict Regions

8.5 Strict Regions

Figure 8.4 shows an example of another improvement that can be made to the approximate algorithm. Part (a) shows a function dependence graph, and (b) its separation graph as computed according to Section 8.2. The edge between b and c is extraneous, since there are no admissible subsets of D_F for which there is any dependence between b and c in either direction. There are no inadmissible *edges*, so the technique of Section 8.4 is of no help. We now describe the method of collapsing strict regions, which allows the approximate algorithm to produce the separation graph shown in (c).

Definition 8.10 *A* strict region *in a function dependence graph* (V, D_C, D_F) *is a subset* $V_S \subseteq V$ *with a distinguished exit vertex* $v_0 \in V_S$ *such that*

1. *$(D_F \mid V_S) = (D_C \mid V_S)$.*

2. *For all $u \in V_S - \{v_0\}$, $u \xrightarrow{D_C}{}^+ v_0$.*

3. *For any $u \in V_S - \{v_0\}$ there does not exist $v \in V - V_S$ such that $(u, v) \in D_F$.*

The first condition says that all arcs within the strict region are certain arcs (and also therefore that the strict region is acyclic). The second says that every vertex in the region has a strict path to the exit vertex. The third says that the only arcs leaving the strict region have the exit vertex v_0 as their origin (which is why it is called the exit vertex).

The maximal strict regions of a function dependence graph are disjoint; in the following discussion the set of all maximal strict regions in a function dependence graph is denoted $\mathcal{SR}$. Note that a single vertex satisfies the definition of a strict region, and so every vertex in V is part of some member of $\mathcal{SR}$.

Having identified strict regions, constraint graphs can be computed as before for pairs of vertices not in the same strict region. For two vertices u and v part of the same strict region, there is no separation constraint, and an *a priori* ordering constraint (u, v) only if $u \xrightarrow{D_C}{}^+ v$. Formally, the new definition of the constraints are:

$$\tilde{S} \;=\; S - \bigcup_{V_S \in \mathcal{SR}} (V_S \times V_S)$$

$$\tilde{A} \;=\; \left(A - \bigcup_{V_S \in \mathcal{SR}} (V_S \times V_S) \right) \cup \{ (u, v) \mid \exists V_S \in \mathcal{SR} \text{ s.t. } u, v \in V_S \wedge (u, v) \in D_C^+ \}$$

151

where S and A are as defined in Section 8.2. To obtain a correct partitioning from $\tilde{S}$ and $\tilde{A}$, the three partitioning conditions from Section 8.2 must be observed, plus one additional condition. All four conditions are enumerated below.

1. If $(v_{i,k}, v_{j,l}) \in \tilde{S}$, then $v_{i,k}$ and $v_{j,l}$ are assigned to separate threads $(i.e., i \neq j)$.

2. If $(v_{i,k}, v_{j,l}) \in \tilde{A}$ and $v_{i,k}$ and $v_{j,l}$ are assigned to the same thread $(i.e., i = j)$, then $v_{i,k}$ precedes $v_{i,l}$ in the thread $(i.e., k < l)$.

3. $\mathrm{SCC}(D_F) = \mathrm{SCC}(D_F \cup D_\Theta)$.

4. For all $V_S \in \mathcal{SR}$, $\mathrm{SCC}(D_F | V_S) = \mathrm{SCC}((D_F | V_S) \cup (D_\Theta | V_S))$.

Theorem 8.11 *Let (V, D_C, D_F) be a function dependence graph, and $\tilde{S}$ and $\tilde{A}$ be the separation and ordering constraints obtained from that graph according to the definition above. Then any partitioning Θ satisfying the four conditions outlined above is correct with respect to the function dependence graph.*

Proof. The proof is similar to the proof of Theorem 8.8, with an additional case at the end: (d) $u, v \in V_S$ for some $V_S \in \mathcal{SR}$. Then the cycle is entirely within V_S, violating partitioning condition (4), or the cycle is composed of subpaths of D and subpaths of D_Θ, where every edge in the D_Θ subpaths is within some strict region. But in that case, those subpaths of D would be part of cycle in D alone, since they would link strict regions in a cycle. ∎

The algorithm given at the end of Section 8.3 is easily extended to handle strict regions. In the extended algorithm, *three* numbers are assigned to each vertex: the major number, the minor number, and the subminor number.

1. Find the strict regions of (V, D_C, D_F).

2. For each strict region, perform a topological sort using the edges of D_C, assigning subminor numbers to each vertex in the region.

3. Form the reduced graph $\vec{D}'_F$ of $\vec{D}_F$ that has a vertex for every strict region, and an edge between two strict regions whenever there is an edge between a member of each of those regions in D_F. Form a similar reduced graph $\vec{D}'_C$ of $\vec{D}_C$.

4. Find the strongly connected components of $\vec{D}'_F$.

5. For each pair of strict regions U, V in a component, there is an edge $\{u, v\} \in \tilde{S}$ for all $u \in U$ and $v \in V$ unless $(U, V) \in D_C^{\prime +}$ or $(V, U) \in D_C^{\prime +}$.

6. For each strongly connected component, perform a topological sort using the edges of D_C, assigning minor numbers to each vertex in each strict region in the component.

7. Form the reduced graph $\vec{D}''_F$ of $\vec{D}'_F$ that has a vertex for each strongly connected component of D'_F. This graph is acyclic.

152

```
{...
    t1 = f1 a b;
    t2 = f2 t3 e;
    t3 = f3 c d;
    t4 = f4 f g;
    x  = f0 t1 t2 t4;
 ...}
```

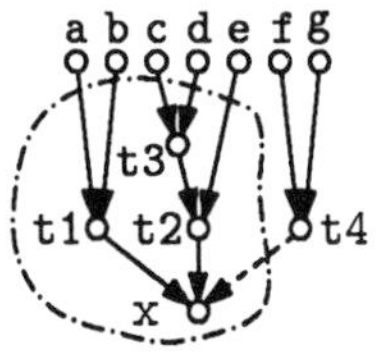

Figure 8.5: Program with a Strict Region

8. Perform a topological sort on D_F'', assigning a major number to all the vertices of each region in each component.

Now, after the function is divided into threads according to $\tilde{S}$, the vertices in each thread are ordered first by major number, then by minor number, and then by subminor number.

The term "strict regions" arises because they correspond to the sequential threads produced by existing lazy compilers that use strictness analysis. Consider the following program fragment (from the source language, not functional quads):

```
{...
    a = f0 (f1 a b) (f2 (f3 c d) e) (f4 f g);
 ...}
```

Now suppose that f1, f2, f3, and f4 are each strict in both arguments, and that f0 is strict in its first two arguments but not its third. Current lazy compilers which can infer this strictness information will insert forces and delays as follows:

```
{...
    x = delay (f0 (f1 a b) (f2 (f3 c d) e) (delay (f4 f g)));
 ...}
```

The compiled code for this fragment would place the calls to f1, f2, f3, and f0 all in the same thread, with the call to f4 in a separate thread.

Now consider what a compiler using the methods of this chapter would do with this program, given that it has access to the same strictness analyzer as the lazy compiler; Figure 8.5 shows the program after conversion to functional quads, and the dependence graph produced for it (to simplify the figure, it is assumed that all of the variables involved are scalar variables; the discussion remains the same even if the variables are non-scalar). Because f0 is not strict in its third argument, the dependence from t4 to x is potential, and the strictness of all other arguments involved is responsible for the other edges being certain. Now the vertices enclosed in the dot-and-dashed line form a strict region, and so with the strict region theorem we are guaranteed not to generate separation constraints between vertices in the region. The calls to f1, f2, f3, and f0 can therefore be assigned to the same thread, as in the lazy compiler.

153

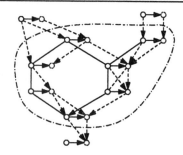

Figure 8.6: Example of a Strict Region in a Two-Point Dependence Graph

In general, detecting strict regions guarantees that we will never introduce a separation constraint between two subexpressions that would be assigned to the same thread by lazy compilers that rely on strictness analysis, no matter what constraint computation algorithm is used. Hence, threads generated from constraint graphs will be at least as large as those produced by lazy compiler technology.

There are two more strict region heuristics that warrant some discussion. The first is that an inverted version of the strict region theorem can be proved, where instead of a single exit vertex the region has a single *entry* vertex, with certain paths to every other vertex in the region. Through a similar proof, it can be shown that in these regions, too, there are no separation constraints and the only ordering constraints correspond to certain paths. The details are an exercise for the reader.[3]

The other point is that the strict region theorems can be extended to handle two-point and other multi-point dependence analysis. In the two point scheme, the definition of a strict region would be modified to allow for other vertices in the strict region which are not necessarily connected by certain paths to the exit vertex (see Figure 8.6). The definition of a two-point strict region is slightly more complex:

Definition 8.12 *A two-point strict region in a function dependence graph* (V, D_C, D_F) *is a subset* $V_S \subseteq V$ *partitioned into two subsubsets* $V_S = V_S^0 \cup V_S^\infty$, *where each subsubset has a distinguished exit vertex* $v^0 \in V_S^0$ *and* $v^\infty \in V_S^\infty$, *and which satisfies:*

1. *$(D_F \mid V_S^0) = (D_C \mid V_S^0)$.*

2. *For all $u \in V_S^0 - \{v^0\}$, $u \xrightarrow{D_C}+ v^0$.*

3. *$(v^0, v^\infty) \in D_C$.*

4. *For any $u \in V_S - \{v^0, v^\infty\}$ there does not exist $v \in V - V_S$ such that $(u, v) \in D_F$ or $(u, v) \in D_C$.*

---

[3]The earlier argument about strict regions can be viewed as an alternative justification for using strictness analysis to eliminate delays in a functional program. Mycroft [47] discusses two abstract interpretations of programs useful for eliminating delays, which he calls $E^\#$ and $E^\flat$. The first of these is what is generally termed strictness analysis, and so its use corresponds to strict regions as defined earlier. It appears that the use of $E^\flat$ as described by Mycroft has an analogous correspondence to inverted strict regions.

It can be shown that a correct partitioning can be obtained by including no separation constraints among the vertices in V_S^0, and ordering constraints among V_S^0 only when there is a path in D_C. The proof is an exercise for the reader.

8.6 Lazy Evaluation

Because lazy evaluation in functional quads is just a special case of the lenient rule for selecting a redex (Section 4.7), producing object code which mimics lazy evaluation is just a special case of lenient code generation. In lazy evaluation, a variable is not reduced to a value until it is known that its value is needed for the final result of the program. If a thread is executing, therefore, it should only initiate those threads which compute values known to be required for that thread's termination; a demand-driven implementation of tagged locations must be employed. Furthermore, if we force a thread because we need the value of some variable x, that thread must not compute anything not needed to compute the value of x, for there is no guarantee that those extra values will be required by the final answer. This implies a finer partitioning beyond what is required for lenient evaluation, so that each thread only computes a single value (perhaps along with other values always needed to compute that value). In other words, each thread should only compute the value of one tagged location, and its computation must certainly require the values of all untagged locations computed in the thread.

To achieve this extra partitioning, we need only appeal to the dependence graphs which we have already computed. If a variable is untagged in a thread, then the only dependence arcs leaving the corresponding vertex of the dependence graph will be to other vertices in the same thread. Conversely, the tagged location it computes will have some outgoing arcs to vertices in other threads. To satisfy the conditions for a lazy thread, we wish to find a region in the dependence graph such that there is only one vertex with outgoing arcs to vertices outside the region, and such that all arcs contained within the region are certain arcs. These are exactly the strict regions defined in Section 8.5, where it was shown that there are no separation constraints between the vertices of such a region. A correct partitioning for lazy code is produced, therefore, by finding maximal strict regions within the dependence graph. One simple algorithm simply finds a strict region for every vertex with more than one outgoing arc or with a single outgoing potential arc; vertices with a single outgoing certain arc are included in the same region as the vertex to which they point. This corresponds to the standard delay rule used in existing lazy compilers, as it has the effect of assigning to a separate thread the argument expressions to non-strict functions and each right hand side of a letrec block.[4] A more sophisticated algorithm could potentially find larger strict regions; see the discussion in Section 8.5.

Once the graph has been partitioned into strict regions, it is ordered and compiled as usual. Because these lazy threads store but a single tagged location, extra splitting for uniprocessor demand-driven scheduling (Section 5.5) is never required.

---

[4]Conditionals require special treatment in order to truly duplicate the standard delay rule. For instance, the algorithm described will always generate one or more separate threads for the arms of the conditional. The threads which compute the final value of each arm could be merged with the thread containing the left hand side of the conditional statement.

8.7 Feedback Dependences Revisited

In Section 7.5, it was shown that in compiling code for a function g which is called from other functions, there may be dependences imposed on g by the context in which calls to it appear. These feedback dependences take the form of potential edges from the $\Diamond$ vertex to each argument, and can be found in the dependence analysis rules given in Sections 7.6 and 7.7. Here is an example:

```
g x y =
    {a = x + 7;
     b = x + y;
     c = const <duple,a,b>;
     in
        c}
```

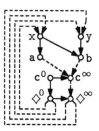

The dependence graph shown above is as produced by the two-point rules from Section 7.7, with ∞-vertices for scalar variables and all the vertices for the constant 7 omitted.

Now consider what happens if g is called from f as follows:

```
f x =
    {p = g x q;
     q = sel_duple_1 p;
     in
        q};
```

The first component of the tuple returned from g is fed back into g as the second argument. Were it not for the feedback edges in the dependence graph, the constraint graphs would have allowed b to be assigned to the same thread as a, with b appearing before a. Such code would be incorrect when g is called from f, because there is actually a dependence from a to b when called from this context. The feedback edges, though, result in a separation constraint between a and b, so that they are assigned to different threads. Note that assigning them to different threads is the best that can be done if all potential callers of g are not known, as there could be another function similar to f that results in a dependence from b to a.

The reader may be distressed to find that we must add potential dependence edges from the output to every input of a function, since doing so is likely to introduce many cycles into the graph, which will lead to many separation constraints and therefore tiny sequential threads. A mitigating factor is that in many cases the feedback edges will be inadmissible and therefore not affect code generation. Specifically, if a function is strict in an argument, then the feedback edges to that argument will all be inadmissible (see Section 8.4):

```
f x y =
    {z = x + y;
     in
        z}
```

Even so, that still leaves the vast majority of cases where feedback edges remain present, introducing cycles and inducing small threads. This is not a defect in our analysis technique, but simply the price of non-strictness. Recall that in all the examples of Section 3.1, the expressive power of non-strictness was gained through the use of some sort of cyclic dependence, either around a function call, a data constructor, or a conditional. This is no coincidence; non-strictness is useful *precisely* because arguments need not be completely evaluated before a call is made, but there is no reason to delay an argument unless that argument derives some information from a portion of the value produced by the call. Hence, the feedback edges are not an unwanted nuisance, but are responsible for all the benefit the programmer gains from using a non-strict language as opposed to a strict one.

Even though feedback edges are the price of non-strictness, we certainly do not want to charge the programmer any more than necessary. That is, a feedback edge should be eliminated whenever the compiler can show that there is no dependence from the output to that argument imposed by the caller, so that as few cycles are introduced into the dependence graph as possible. We have no results to present in this area, and simply point out that it is a research problem, perhaps the most important line of research to improve the quality of lenient compilation. There are two avenues that could be pursued. One is to analyze all callers of a function g and try to show that there are no contexts which introduce feedback dependences for some subset of g's arguments. This requires extensive interprocedural analysis, and is complicated considerably by the use of higher-order functions. On the other hand, if there are some situations which are provably feedback-free, two versions of g could be compiled, one which supports feedback and another which does not. The other avenue is to allow the programmer to tell the compiler that there are no feedback dependences for specific arguments, through the use of annotations. Both of these avenues should be explored to determine their feasibility and effectiveness.

8.8 Appendix: NP-completeness of Finding Admissible Paths in D_F

We commented that the following question is NP-complete: is there an admissible subset of D_F that has a path between two particular vertices? In this appendix we prove that fact.

We introduce the following graph problem, called *Constrained Connected Acyclic Subgraph*, which is equivalent to deciding whether there is an admissible subset of D_F with a path between two particular vertices. The definition of the problem is as follows:

Constrained Connected Acyclic Subgraph (CCAS)

INSTANCE: Directed graph $G = (V, E)$ with specified vertices $s, t \in V$ and partition of E into "solid" edges E_S and "dashed" edges E_D, $E_S \cap E_D = \emptyset$, $E_S \cup E_D = E$.

QUESTION: Is there a subset $E_D' \subseteq E_D$ such that the graph $G' = (V, E_S \cup E_D')$ is acyclic and there is a path in G' from s to t?

We will prove that CCAS is NP-complete by reducing an arbitrary instance of Exact

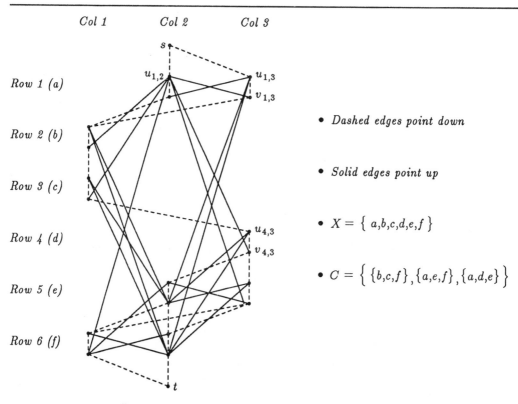

Col 1   Col 2   Col 3

Row 1 (a)

Row 2 (b)

Row 3 (c)

Row 4 (d)

Row 5 (e)

Row 6 (f)

- *Dashed edges point down*

- *Solid edges point up*

- $X = \{\, a,b,c,d,e,f \,\}$

- $C = \{\, \{b,c,f\}, \{a,e,f\}, \{a,d,e\} \,\}$

Figure 8.7: Construction Reducing X3C to CCAS

Cover by 3-Sets (X3C) to CCAS.[5] X3C is known to be NP-complete [23]; we reproduce below the definition given there:

Exact Cover by 3-Sets (X3C)

INSTANCE: Set X with $|X| = 3q$ and a collection C of 3-element subsets of X.

QUESTION: Does C contain an exact cover for X, *i.e.*, a subcollection $C' \subseteq C$ such that every element of X occurs in exactly one member of C'?

For a given instance of X3C, we construct an instance of CCAS in which the vertices V consist of a source s, a sink t, and a grid of pairs of vertices $u_{i,j}$ and $v_{i,j}$, in which each row of the grid corresponds to an element of X and in which each column corresponds to an element of C. (See Figure 8.7.)

Formally, let $N = |X|$ and $M = |C|$. Let ROW : $X \to \mathcal{N}$ be a bijection from X onto $[1, N]$ and COL : $C \to \mathcal{N}$ be a bijection from C onto $[1, M]$. Furthermore, let ROW^{-1} and COL^{-1} be the functional inverses of ROW and COL, respectively. V is then defined as:

$$V = \{s,t\} \cup \{\, u_{i,j}, v_{i,j} \mid 1 \le i \le N,\ 1 \le j \le M,\ \text{ROW}^{-1}(i) \in \text{COL}^{-1}(j) \,\}$$

---

[5]The author is indebted to Serge Plotkin, who after consultation with David Johnson suggested the construction used for this reduction.

The basic idea is to provide entirely dashed paths which start at s, pass through every row in sequence, and arrive at t. A particular path will therefore cover every row (and therefore every $x \in X$), using some subset of the columns (*i.e.*, some subset of C), and each such path induces a subgraph consisting of the edges on the path plus all the solid edges. We include solid back edges between pairs of columns that represent non-disjoint 3-sets, so that any path that does not correspond to an exact cover will have a back edge between two of its vertices. In this way, only those paths corresponding to exact covers will induce acyclic graphs.

The dashed edges are as follows:

$$E_D = \{(u_{i,j}, v_{i,j}) \mid u_{i,j}, v_{i,j} \in V\} \cup \{(v_{i,j}, u_{i+1,k}) \mid v_{i,j}, u_{i+1,k} \in V\}$$
$$\cup \{(s, u_{1,j}) \mid u_{1,j} \in V\} \cup \{(v_{N,j}, t) \mid v_{N,j} \in V\}$$

There is a dashed edge between each u and its corresponding v, and a dashed complete bipartite graph between the v's of one row and the u's of the next. In addition, there is an edge between s and every u of the first row, and between every v of the last row and t.

The solid edges are:

$$E_S = \bigcup_{\substack{c_1,c_2 \in C \\ c_1 \cap c_2 \neq \emptyset}} \{(v_{i,\text{COL}(c_1)}, u_{k,\text{COL}(c_2)}) \mid \text{ROW}^{-1}(i) \in c_1, \text{ROW}^{-1}(k) \in c_2, k \leq i\}$$

Since solid edges go only from v's to u's, there are no solid paths of length greater than one.

Lemma 8.13 *An instance of X3C has a solution if and only if the constructed instance of CCAS has a solution.*

Proof (Only If): Let C' be the solution to the instance of X3C; we construct a solution to the corresponding CCAS instance as follows. Since C' is an exact cover for X, there is a function f from X onto $[1, M]$ such that $f(x) = \text{COL}(c)$ where $x \in c$ and $c \in C'$. Let $x_1, x_2, \ldots, x_N$ be the elements of X such that $\text{ROW}(x_1) = 1$, $\text{ROW}(x_2) = 2$, *etc.* Then the following is a path in G composed entirely of dashed edges:

$$s, u_{1,f(x_1)}, v_{1,f(x_1)}, u_{2,f(x_2)}, v_{2,f(x_2)}, \ldots, u_{N,f(x_N)}, v_{N,f(x_N)}, t$$

Such a path exists by construction. Let E_D' consist of only those edges on the above path. It remains to show that $G' = (V, E_S \cup E_D')$ is acyclic. Since there are no solid paths of length greater than one, the graph is cyclic only if there is a solid edge between two vertices along the dashed path. But solid edges only occur between pairs of columns corresponding to non-disjoint members of C. Since C' is exact, it contains no such pair. The dashed path, therefore, does not pass through any pair of columns between which there is a solid edge, and so there can be no solid edge joining two vertices along the path. G' is therefore acyclic.

(If): A solution to CCAS is a set of dashed edges E_D' and a path from s to t. Given a solution, we first construct a canonical solution in which the path is composed entirely of dashed edges. By construction, an entirely dashed path must take the form:

$$s, u_{1,\text{COL}(c_1)}, v_{1,\text{COL}(c_1)}, u_{2,\text{COL}(c_2)}, v_{2,\text{COL}(c_2)}, \ldots, u_{N,\text{COL}(c_N)}, v_{N,\text{COL}(c_N)}, t$$

159

where $c_1, c_2, \ldots, c_N \in C$ and are not necessarily distinct. If a path from s to t contains solid edges, it must contain one or more segments of the form:

$$\ldots, v_{i,\text{COL}(c_a)}, u_{j,\text{COL}(c_b)}, \ldots, v_{i,\text{COL}(c_c)}, w, \ldots$$

where $j \leq i$, and w is either a u vertex or the final t. The solid edge is $(v_{i,\text{COL}(c_a)}, u_{j,\text{COL}(c_b)})$, and the segment preceding $v_{i,\text{COL}(c_c)}$ may also contain solid edges. Intuitively, a solid edge causes the path to jump back from a v vertex to a lower-numbered u vertex (or to a u in the same row). But if the path ultimately reaches t, it must pass through every row between this lower-numbered row and the last row, and in particular it must pass through row i again, although perhaps in a different column (*i.e.*, c_a and c_c are not necessarily the same). Now if this segment is part of a solution to CCAS, then it can be replaced by just:

$$\ldots, v_{i,\text{COL}(c_a)}, w, \ldots$$

thereby deleting the solid edge(s). There is guaranteed to be an edge in E_D between $v_{i,\text{COL}(c_a)}$ and w by construction; this edge may have to be added to E_D' if it was not already present. Adding this edge cannot introduce any new cycles since the two vertices involved were already connected by a path. By repeating this transformation, we arrive at a solution to the CCAS instance in which the path is entirely dashed.

Given an entirely dashed path, the solution to the X3C problem is:

$$C' = \{\, c \mid v_{i,\text{COL}(c)} \text{ is on the path} \,\}$$

Since the path passes through every row, the columns through which it passes must correspond to 3-sets which form a cover for X. Since the path passes through each row only once, the cover is exact. ∎

Theorem 8.14 *CCAS is NP-complete.*

Proof: A potential solution to an instance of CCAS is verified by checking for connectivity between s and t, and by checking for the acyclicness of G'. Since both tests can be performed in polynomial time, CCAS is in NP. An arbitrary instance of X3C can be converted to CCAS using the construction proved in Lemma 8.13. The conversion time is $O(M^2 N)$, being dominated by the construction of N bipartite subgraphs, each of size $O(M)$. Since X3C is known to be NP-complete [23], and since the conversion time is polynomial, CCAS is NP-complete. ∎

9 Conclusion

We have presented a method of compiling sequential code from non-strict functional languages in which non-strictness is treated separately from laziness. We take the view that the crux of producing sequential code is in taking ordering decisions at compile time, and in recognizing when those decisions must be made at run time. The first step infers relationships between the subexpressions of a program by analyzing data dependences. We then convert the data dependence information into constraints upon sequential code generation, where the constraints indicate not only relative ordering of subexpressions but also which subexpressions may not be ordered at compile time. From there, we are able to pursue a variety of code generation strategies, including producing lenient code and lazy code, for a variety of target implementations. The correctness of the compilation process is demonstrated through the syntactic theory of data dependence. A key component of that theory is the functional quads model of functional program execution, which has interesting properties in its own right.

We conclude by discussing the relationship of our work to other current research, and with some remarks about where our research leads.

9.1 Relationship to Other Work

To the best of our knowledge, this work represents the first attempt to consider non-strictness and laziness separately in the context of sequential code generation. There are, however, several research efforts which have some overlap with aspects of our work; we discuss these below.

9.1.1 Dataflow Languages and Compilers

The programming language Id [48], which arose out of dataflow work of Arvind *et al.* at MIT [4, 6], is one of the few (if not the only) examples of a functional language with non-strict, but non-lazy, semantics. We have drawn heavily from the work of this group, particularly in exploring the expressive power of non-strict non-lazy functional languages, and in compiler technology for dataflow architectures [67]. As we mentioned earlier, the operational semantics for Id given in [48] and [7] was the inspiration for functional quads, the theoretical foundation of our lenient compilation technique.

Compiling Id for dataflow architectures can be viewed as a special case of our work: in our terminology, dataflow is concurrent, eager, scheduling of object code where every subexpression is assigned to a separate thread. Since every thread is of size one, dataflow compilers need not be concerned with constraints upon partitioning, nor with ordering constraints, and so dataflow compilation is largely independent of the present work. On the other hand, to control the resource requirements of dataflow programs executing on parallel architectures it is often necessary to sequentialize portions of the code [5]. The kind of dependence analysis performed here then becomes useful in insuring that such transformations preserve the semantics of the program.

9.1.2 Sarkar and Hennessy

Sarkar and Hennessy describe a technique for partitioning dataflow code into "macro-dataflow" nodes, which are essentially sequential threads [56, 57]. Their source language is the intermediate form IF1 [59], a functional language with strict semantics. Because IF1 is strict, a total ordering on the subexpressions of the program can be found at compile time based on the syntactic structure (see Section 3.4). In other words, there are no separation constraints, and they are free to partition the program at will. They develop techniques which try to minimize the amount of inter-thread communication performed by the partitioned program.

9.1.3 Serial Combinators

Hudak's serial combinators [29] represent another method for partitioning functional programs into sequential threads. Like us, Hudak starts with a non-strict language, but unlike us, Hudak only considers lazy semantics. Essentially, he starts with the threads produced by a lazy compiler, and partitions them further so that the resulting threads have no internal parallelism. He performs some analysis to balance the thread scheduling overhead against the amount of computation performed in each thread; in this respect his work is similar to Sarkar and Hennessy's above.

9.1.4 Path Semantics

The *path semantics* developed by Bloss and Hudak [12] is an alternative approach for studying the order of subexpression evaluation in functional languages. Its goals are therefore very similar to the theory of data dependence we developed in Chapter 6, but their work has a very different structure. Whereas dependence graphs are a partial order on the subexpressions of a function, path semantics yields a set of total orderings, each element of the set corresponding to a possible sequence of subexpression evaluations that might occur at run time. Because their representation is a set of total orderings, they can preserve the correlation information that function dependence graphs do not: the set of paths computed for a function will simply not include total orderings that correspond to impossible combinations of potential dependences. Currently, path semantics has no special mechanisms for dealing with data structures.

Bloss and Hudak intend path semantics to be used in a variety of optimizations for lazy functional programs, particularly the elimination of redundant forces and unnecessary delays [13]. It would be interesting to see if path semantics can serve as an alternative basis for constructing constraint graphs. One potential difficulty here is that path semantics assumes lazy, not lenient, evaluation; perhaps this could be remedied by a different choice of axioms for primitive functions. Conversely, it would be interesting to see if function dependence graphs could serve as an alternative basis for the types of optimizations envisioned for path semantics.

9.2 Directions for Future Research

Throughout the book we have pointed out areas in which the theory or practice of lenient compilation could benefit from additional investigation. We summarize these areas here.

9.2.1 Extensions to the Formal Model

The main limitation of function dependence graphs is that they do not preserve information about *correlations* between potential dependences. In general, there will be many subsets of the potential dependences which are admissible but nevertheless cannot occur at run time. The most obvious example arises from conditionals: a conditional expression results in two potential dependence arcs, one from the output of each arm, but for no input to the program do both dependences occur simultaneously, nor for any input do neither occur.

It is not yet known whether the lack of correlation information will have a significant impact on the quality of code generated from our techniques; more experience is needed. It would also be worthwhile to see if the dependence model can be cleanly extended to include a notion of correlation. As we mentioned earlier, the path semantics of Bloss and Hudak [12] may have some relation to such a model.

9.2.2 Dependence Analysis

One of the chief strengths of our method is that the dependence graph framework is very general, in that it can exploit dependence information gained from a variety of analysis techniques. The ones we have explored in Chapter 7 are mainly simple syntactic methods, together with well-known strictness analysis techniques. Much more work is needed to investigate other ways of obtaining dependence information. We suspect that quite a bit of conventional imperative compiler technology can be harnessed, particularly subscript analysis [14] and other flow analysis techniques [2].

In Chapter 7 we have only scratched the surface in the area of dependence analysis for data structures. The multi-point approach seems very promising as it provides a unified framework in which different data types can be tracked with differing degrees of precision. Finding appropriate vertex sets for different types and developing methods for their analysis seems to be a very important area of research. We suspect that the multi-point model can also lead to a greater appreciation of the relationships between the multitude of strictness analyzers for non-flat domains that have recently proliferated [74, 35, 24].

9.2.3 Constraint Computation and Partitioning·

Computing constraints from requirement/dependence graphs is a problem whose solutions can likely be continually improved over time. More work is needed to progress beyond the simple-minded algorithms presented here.

The formulation of code generation in terms of constraint graphs is both a blessing and a curse. On the one hand, it provides maximal freedom to a compiler, as partitioning is constrained only by what is necessary to implement the semantics, and is not influenced by the structure of the analysis which revealed those constraints (contrast this with the G-machine compiler [37, 39], in which the generation of code is inextricably entwined with the

163

recursive descent through the source code). On the other hand, this freedom presents many more choices to the partitioning phase, which must deal with the interactions between the constraints, thread size, and inter-thread communication in choosing the best partitioning for a particular program. Investigating and evaluating heuristics to guide the partitioning phase presents a wide field for future effort. The work of Sarkar and Hennessy [57] may have some relevance.

9.2.4 Code Generation

The code generation techniques described in Chapter 5 are fairly straightforward, and do not attempt to take advantage of the many opportunities available for peephole optimization and the like. A lot of conventional compiler technology seems applicable here, particularly in the area of analyzing lifetimes to optimize the use of storage [44]. Most of the optimizations presented only considered program flow within a given thread. Flow analysis could be employed to analyze interactions between threads, exposing more opportunities for optimization [12]. All of these are fertile ground for further exploration.

9.2.5 I-Structures

I-structures are a non-functional language construct for array data structures which have significant advantages over purely functional arrays [7]. Although I-structures are not functional, I-structure languages can still be described by a confluent reduction system similar to functional quads (as we have mentioned, functional quads itself was actually inspired by a reduction system for I-structures), and so there is every reason to believe that the dependence graph framework developed in Chapter 6 can be extended to accommodate them.

On the other hand, dependence analysis of I-structure languages is likely to be considerably more difficult than for functional languages, because unrestricted use of I-structures leads to procedures which have side-effects. Strictness and its analysis are no longer valid criteria for deciding when the arguments to a procedure can have an effect on other computations in the caller; a different criterion that detects the relationship between argument computation and side-effects is needed (see also the footnote on page 17). With functional data structures, the computation which computes a given structure element is identifiable at the point of construction, but this is not so for I-structures. It is much more difficult, therefore, to decide the dependence relationships between various structure operations in a program. Finally, we note that because the writers of I-structure locations are not identifiable at the time of their construction, I-structure languages are *non-sequential*, and demand-driven evaluation is ruled out.

We should point out, however, that if a programming methodology is employed which restricts the non-functional uses of I-structures to the internals of a handful of functional abstractions, the remaining functional portions of a program can be analyzed exactly as if the language itself were functional. This is in fact the methodology advocated in [7].

164

9.3 Concluding Remarks

We believe the main contribution of our work is in providing a method of compiling functional languages which deals with non-strictness and laziness separately, so that the effects of non-strictness on object code can be isolated from the effects of laziness. This is valuable for two reasons. One is that it allows compilation which preserves non-strictness but not laziness, achieving more efficient code for programs which do not require the additional expressive power of lazy evaluation. The second is that it improves the understanding of how non-strictness and laziness are individually responsible for certain kinds of expressive power, and how they individually contribute to overhead in implementations. In particular, we have shown how a great deal of the overhead is a consequence of arguments to a function call depending on partial results from that call.

An important aspect of our work is that it tries to separate the aspects of object code quality that are traceable to a particular compilation algorithm and those that are inevitable consequences of the programming language semantics. This separation was accomplished by defining requirement graphs purely in terms of program behavior according to the operational semantics, and then showing that dependence graphs capture no more an no less than the ordering relationships expressed by requirement graphs. This allows any method for computing dependence information to be used, as long as it satisfies the necessity and sufficiency criteria. We also achieve separation between the algorithms used to obtain dependence information and the algorithms which convert this information into partitioning constraints, and between the various code generation options that are possible for non-strict object code. We do not claim to have provided the ultimate algorithms in any of these categories, only that their theoretical basis is sound, and that there do in fact exist algorithms which are practical and effective.

Finally, we believe that functional quads and its associated theory is an important step toward providing a common vantage point from which to understand a variety of functional language implementations, be they on sequential or parallel architectures, with lenient or lazy semantics, on von Neumann, dataflow, or reduction machines. Its main strength is that it exposes compilation and semantic issues such as sharing, order of evaluation, and the need to test whether an expression has become a value, while abstracting away from the details of how these are achieved in the implementation. Thus functional quads serves as a universal abstraction of functional language implementations, just as sequential quads serves as a universal abstraction of von Neumann architectures.

Bibliography

[1] A. V. Aho, J. E. Hopcroft, and J. D. Ullman. *The Design and Analysis of Computer Algorithms.* Addison-Wesley, Reading MA, 1974.

[2] A. V. Aho, R. Sethi, and J. D. Ullman. *Compilers: Principles, Techniques, and Tools.* Addison-Wesley, Reading MA, 1986.

[3] F. E. Allen. Control flow analysis. In *Proceedings of a Symposium on Compiler Optimization*, pages 1–19. Association for Computing Machinery, July 1970. (SIGPLAN Notices 5(7)).

[4] Arvind and D. E. Culler. Dataflow architectures. *Annual Reviews in Computer Science*, 1:225–253, 1986.

[5] Arvind and D. E. Culler. Managing resources in a parallel machine. In *Fifth Generation Computer Architectures 1986*, pages 103–121. Elsevier Science Publishers B.V., 1986.

[6] Arvind and R. S. Nikhil. Executing a program on the Massachusetts Institute of Technology tagged-token dataflow architecture. In *PARLE: Parallel Architectures and Languages Europe Volume II*, volume 259 of *Lecture Notes in Computer Science*, pages 1–29. Springer-Verlag, June 1987.

[7] Arvind, R. S. Nikhil, and K. K. Pingali. I-structures: Data structures for parallel computing. In *Graph Reduction*, volume 279 of *Lecture Notes in Computer Science*, pages 336–369. Springer-Verlag, October 1986.

[8] Arvind and R. E. Thomas. I-structures: An efficient data type for parallel machines. Technical Memo TM-178, Massachusetts Institute of Technology Laboratory for Computer Science, Cambridge MA, September 1980.

[9] L. Augustsson. A compiler for lazy ML. *ACM SIGPLAN Notices*, 19(6):218–227, June 1984. (Proceedings of the SIGPLAN 84 Symposium on Compiler Construction).

[10] H. P. Barendregt. *The Lambda Calculus*, volume 103 of *Studies in Logic and the Foundations of Mathematics*. Elsevier, Amsterdam, 1984. (Revised Edition).

[11] H. P. Barendregt, J. R. Kennaway, J. W. Klop, and M. R. Sleep. Needed reduction and spine strategies for the lambda calculus. Technical Report CS-R8621, Centrum voor Wiskunde en Informatica, Amsterdam, May 1986.

[12] A. Bloss and P. Hudak. Path semantics. In *Mathematical Foundations of Programming Language Semantics*, volume 298 of *Lecture Notes in Computer Science*, pages 476–489. Springer-Verlag, April 1988.

[13] A. Bloss, P. Hudak, and J. Young. Code optimizations for lazy evaluation. *Lisp and Symbolic Computation*, 1(2):147–164, September 1988.

[14] M. Burke and R. Cytron. Interprocedural dependence analysis and parallelization. *ACM SIGPLAN Notices*, 21(6):162–175, June 1986. (Proceedings of the SIGPLAN 86 Symposium on Compiler Construction).

[15] G. L. Burn, C. L. Hankin, and S. Abramsky. The theory of strictness analysis for higher order functions. In *Programs as Data Objects*, volume 217 of *Lecture Notes in Computer Science*, pages 42–62. Springer-Verlag, October 1985.

[16] F. W. Burton. Annotations to control parallelism and reduction order in the distributed evaluation of functional programs. *ACM Transactions on Programming Languages and Systems*, 6(2):159–174, April 1984.

[17] F. W. Burton. Functional programming for concurrent and distributed computing. *The Computer Journal*, 30(5):437–450, October 1987.

[18] C. Clack and S. L. Peyton-Jones. Strictness analysis—a practical approach. In *Functional Programming Languages and Computer Architecture*, volume 201 of *Lecture Notes in Computer Science*, pages 35–49. Springer-Verlag, September 1985.

[19] C. Clack and S. L. Peyton-Jones. The four-stroke reduction engine. In *Proceedings of the 1986 ACM Conference on Lisp and Functional Programming*, pages 220–232. Association for Computing Machinery, August 1986.

[20] P. Cousot and R. Cousot. Abstract interpretation: A unified lattice model for static analysis of programs by construction or approximation of fixpoints. In *Conference Record of the 4th ACM Symposium on the Principles of Programming Languages*, pages 238–252. Association for Computing Machinery, January 1977.

[21] J. Fairbairn and S. Wray. Tim: A simple, lazy abstract machine to execute supercombinators. In *Functional Programming Languages and Computer Architecture*, volume 274 of *Lecture Notes in Computer Science*, pages 34–45. Springer-Verlag, September 1987.

[22] D. P. Friedman and D. S. Wise. CONS should not evaulate its arguments. In *Third International Colloquium on Automata, Languages, and Programming*, pages 257–284, London, July 1976. Edinburgh University Press.

[23] M. R. Garey and D. S. Johnson. *Computers and Intractability: A Guide to the Theory of NP-Completeness*. W. H. Freeman, San Francisco, 1979.

[24] C. V. Hall and D. S. Wise. Compiling strictness into streams. In *Conference Record of the 14th ACM Symposium on the Principles of Programming Languages*, pages 132–143. Association for Computing Machinery, January 1987.

[25] S. K. Heller. *Efficient Lazy Structures in a Dataflow Machine*. PhD thesis, Massachusetts Institute of Technology, Cambridge MA, December 1988. (Expected).

[26] P. Henderson. *Functional Programming: Application and Implementation.* Prentice-Hall, Englewood Cliffs NJ, 1980.

[27] P. Hudak. A semantic model of reference counting and its abstraction (detailed summary). In *Proceedings of the 1986 ACM Conference on Lisp and Functional Programming*, pages 351–363. Assocation for Computing Machinery, August 1986.

[28] P. Hudak and A. Bloss. The aggregate update problem in functional programming systems. In *Conference Record of the 12th ACM Symposium on the Principles of Programming Languages*, pages 300–314. Association for Computing Machinery, January 1985.

[29] P. Hudak and B. Goldberg. Serial combinators: "optimal" grains of parallelism. In *Functional Programming Languages and Computer Architecture*, volume 201 of *Lecture Notes in Computer Science*, pages 382–399. Springer-Verlag, September 1985.

[30] P. Hudak and D. Kranz. A combinator-based compiler for a functional language. In *Conference Record of the 11th ACM Symposium on the Principles of Programming Languages*, pages 122–132. Association for Computing Machinery, January 1984.

[31] P. Hudak and L. Smith. Para-functional programming: A paradigm for programming multiprocessor systems. In *Conference Record of the 13th ACM Symposium on the Principles of Programming Languages*, pages 243–254. Association for Computing Machinery, January 1986.

[32] P. Hudak and J. Young. Higher-order strictness analysis in untyped lambda calculus. In *Conference Record of the 13th ACM Symposium on the Principles of Programming Languages*, pages 97–109. Association for Computing Machinery, January 1986.

[33] G. Huet. Confluent reductions: Abstract properties and applications to term rewriting systems. *Journal of the Association for Computing Machinery*, 27(4):797–821, October 1980.

[34] R. J. M. Hughes. Super-combinators: A new implementation method for applicative languages. In *Conference Record of the 1982 ACM Symposium on Lisp and Functional Programming*, pages 1–10. Association for Computing Machinery, August 1982.

[35] R. J. M. Hughes. Backwards analysis of functional programs. Research Report CSC/87/R3, University of Glasgow, March 1987.

[36] R. A. Iannucci. A dataflow/von Neumann hybrid architecture. Technical Report TR-418, Massachusetts Institute of Technology Laboratory for Computer Science, Cambridge MA, May 1988.

[37] T. Johnsson. Efficient compilation of lazy evaluation. *ACM SIGPLAN Notices*, 19(6):58–69, June 1984. (Proceedings of the SIGPLAN 84 Symposium on Compiler Construction).

[38] T. Johnsson. Lambda lifting. In *Functional Programming Languages and Computer Architecture*, volume 201 of *Lecture Notes in Computer Science*, pages 190–203. Springer-Verlag, September 1985.

[39] T. Johnsson. Target code generation from G-machine code. In *Graph Reduction*, volume 279 of *Lecture Notes in Computer Science*, pages 119–159. Springer-Verlag, October 1986.

[40] M. B. Josephs. Functional programming with side-effects. *Science of Computer Programming*, 7(3):279–296, November 1986.

[41] R. M. Keller, G. Lindstrom, and S. Patil. A loosely-coupled applicative multi-processing system. In *AFIPS-NCC Proceedings*, pages 613–622, June 1979.

[42] J. W. Klop. *Combinatory Reduction Systems*, volume 127 of *Mathematical Centre Tracts*. Mathematisch Centrum, Amsterdam, 1980.

[43] J. W. Klop. Term rewriting systems: A tutorial. Rapportnr IR-126, Vrise Universiteit, Amsterdam, 1987.

[44] D. Kranz, R. Kelsey, J. Rees, P. Hudak, J. Philbin, and N. Adams. ORBIT: An optimizing compiler for Scheme. *ACM SIGPLAN Notices*, 21(7):219–233, July 1986. (Proceedings of the SIGPLAN 86 Symposium on Compiler Construction).

[45] J.-J. Levy. An algebraic interpretation of the λ-β-K-calculus and a labelled λ-calculus. In λ-*Calculus and Computer Science Theory*, volume 37 of *Lecture Notes in Computer Science*. Springer-Verlag, March 1975.

[46] D. W. Matula, G. Marble, and J. D. Isaacson. Graph coloring algorithms. In R. C. Read, editor, *Graph Theory and Computing*, pages 109–122. Academic Press, New York, 1972.

[47] A. Mycroft. The theory and practice of transforming call-by-need into call-by-value. In *International Symposium on Programming*, volume 83 of *Lecture Notes in Computer Science*, pages 269–281. Springer-Verlag, April 1980.

[48] R. S. Nikhil, K. Pingali, and Arvind. Id nouveau. Computation Structures Group Memo 265, Massachusetts Institute of Technology Laboratory for Computer Science, Cambridge MA, July 1986.

[49] G. M. Papadopoulos. *Implementation of a General Purpose Dataflow Multiprocessor*. PhD thesis, Massachusetts Institute of Technology, Cambridge MA, August 1988.

[50] S. L. Peyton-Jones. The tag is dead—long live the packet. Message on Functional Programming mailing list, October 1987.

[51] S. L. Peyton-Jones, C. Clack, J. Salkild, and M. Hardie. GRIP—a high-performance architecture for parallel graph reduction. In *Functional Programming Languages and Computer Architecture*, volume 274 of *Lecture Notes in Computer Science*, pages 98–112. Springer-Verlag, September 1987.

[52] K. Pingali and Arvind. Efficient demand-driven evaluation. Part 1. *ACM Transactions on Programming Languages and Systems*, 7(2):311–333, April 1985.

[53] U. S. Reddy. Functional logic languages part I. In *Graph Reduction*, volume 279 of *Lecture Notes in Computer Science*, pages 402–425. Springer-Verlag, October 1986.

[54] J. Rees and W. Clinger. Revised[3] report on the algorithmic language scheme. Technical report, Massachusetts Institute of Technology Artificial Intelligence Laboratory, Cambride MA, 1986.

[55] H. Richards Jr. An overview of the Burroughs *norma*. In *Proceedings of the Workshop on Implementation of Functional Languages*, pages 429–438. University of Goteburg and Chalmers University of Technology, February 1985. (Technical Report PMG-R17).

[56] V. Sarkar and J. Hennessy. Compile-time partitioning and scheduling of parallel programs. *ACM SIGPLAN Notices*, 21(6):17–26, June 1986. (Proceedings of the SIGPLAN 86 Symposium on Compiler Construction).

[57] V. Sarkar and J. Hennessy. Partitioning parallel programs for macro-dataflow. In *Proceedings of the 1986 ACM Conference on Lisp and Functional Programming*, pages 202–211. Association for Computing Machinery, August 1986.

[58] M. Scheevel. NORMA: A graph reduction processor. In *Proceedings of the 1986 ACM Conference on Lisp and Functional Programming*, pages 212–219. Association for Computing Machinery, August 1986.

[59] S. K. Skedzielewski and J. R. W. Glauert. IF1: An intermediate form for applicative languages. Reference Manual M-170, Lawrence Livermore National Laboratory, Livermore CA, July 1985.

[60] S. K. Skedzielewski and M. L. Welcome. Data flow graph optimization in IF1. In *Functional Programming Languages and Computer Architectures*, volume 201 of *Lecture Notes in Computer Science*, pages 17–34. Springer-Verlag, September 1985.

[61] G. L. Steele. LAMBDA: The ultimate declarative. AI Memo 379, Massachusetts Institute of Technology Artificial Intelligence Laboratory, Cambridge MA, November 1976.

[62] G. L. Steele. RABBIT: A compiler for SCHEME. Technical Report AI-TR-474, Massachusetts Institute of Technology Artificial Intelligence Laboratory, Cambridge MA, May 1978.

[63] G. L. Steele and G. J. Sussman. LAMBDA: The ultimate imperative. AI Memo 353, Massachusetts Institute of Technology Artificial Intelligence Laboratory, Cambridge MA, March 1976.

[64] J. E. Stoy. *Denotational Semantics*. MIT Press, Cambridge MA, 1977.

[65] W. R. Stoye, T. J. W. Clarke, and A. C. Norman. Some practical methods for rapid combinator reduction. In *Conference Record of the 1984 ACM Symposium on LISP and Functional Programming*, pages 159–166. Association for Computing Machinery, 1984.

[66] K. R. Traub. An abstract parallel graph reduction machine. In *Proceedings of the 12th Annual International Symposium on Computer Architecture*, pages 333–341. IEEE, June 1985.

[67] K. R. Traub. A compiler for the MIT tagged-token dataflow architecture. Technical Report TR-370, Massachusetts Institute of Technology Laboratory for Computer Science, Cambridge MA, August 1986.

[68] K. R. Traub. Compilation as partitioning: A new approach to compiling non-strict functional languages. In *Functional Programming Languages and Computer Architecture*, pages 75–88. Association for Computing Machinery, September 1989.

[69] D. A. Turner. A new implementation techique for applicative languages. *Software— Practice and Experience*, 9:31–49, 1979.

[70] D. A. Turner. The semantic elegance of applicative languages. In *Proceedings of the 1981 Conference on Functional Programming Languages and Computer Architecture*, pages 85–92. Association for Computing Machinery, 1981.

[71] D. A. Turner. Miranda: A non-strict functional language with polymorphic types. In *Functional Programming Languages and Computer Architectures*, volume 201 of *Lecture Notes in Computer Science*, pages 1–16. Springer-Verlag, September 1985.

[72] J. Vuillemin. Correct and optimal implementations of recursion in a simple programming language. *Journal of Computer and System Sciences*, 9(3):332–354, December 1974.

[73] P. Wadler. Report on the programming language Haskell. (In Preparation), July 1988.

[74] P. Wadler and R. J. M. Hughes. Projections for strictness analysis. In *Functional Programming Languages and Computer Architecture*, volume 274 of *Lecture Notes in Computer Science*, pages 386–407. Springer-Verlag, September 1987.

[75] C. P. Wadsworth. *Semantics and Pragmatics of the Lambda-calculus*. PhD thesis, Oxford University, 1971.

[76] A. Wigderson. Improving the performance guarantee for approximate graph coloring. *Journal of the Association of Computing Machinery*, 30(4):729–735, October 1983.